Max Reinhardt

Portrait of Max Reinhardt circa 1905. Photograph by H. L. Held; courtesy of the Theaterwissenschaftliche Sammlung of the University of Cologne.

Max Reinhardt

From Bourgeois Theater to Metropolitan Culture

◆

Peter W. Marx

Translated from the German by Robert E. Goodwin

NORTHWESTERN UNIVERSITY PRESS
EVANSTON, ILLINOIS

To Miriam

Northwestern University Press
www.nupress.northwestern.edu

English translation copyright © 2024 by Northwestern University Press. Published 2024 by Northwestern University Press. Originally published in German under the title *Max Reinhardt: Vom bürgerlichen Theater zur metropolitanen Kultur,* copyright © 2006 Narr Francke Attempto Verlag GmbH + Co. KG. All rights reserved.

Printed in the United States of America

10 9 8 7 6 5 4 3 2 1

Library of Congress Cataloging-in-Publication Data

Names: Marx, Peter W., 1973– author. | Goodwin, Robert E. (Translator), translator.
Title: Max Reinhardt : from bourgeois theater to metropolitan culture / Peter W. Marx, translated from the German by Robert E Goodwin.
Other titles: Max Reinhardt. English
Description: Evanston, Illinois : Northwestern University Press, 2024. | Includes bibliographical references.
Identifiers: LCCN 2024012689 | ISBN 9780810138902 (paperback) | ISBN 9780810138919 (cloth) | ISBN 9780810138926 (ebook)
Subjects: LCSH: Reinhardt, Max, 1873–1943. | Theater—Germany—History.
Classification: LCC PN2658.R4 M26713 2024 | DDC 792.02/33092—dc23/eng/20240422
LC record available at https://lccn.loc.gov/2024012689

CONTENTS

Introduction   *vii*

Chapter 1
From Cabaret to the Deutsches Theater   *1*

Chapter 2
The Kammerspiele as Bourgeois Salon   *23*

Chapter 3
Circus Reinhardt: Giving Shape and Space to the Masses   *49*

Chapter 4
"Reinhardt Goes Global!": Tours, Guest Performances, Expansions   *85*

Chapter 5
Reinhardt and Film: A Missed Rendezvous?   *111*

Chapter 6
Reinhardt & Co.: The Economy of a Theater Concern   *129*

Chapter 7
Max Goldmann—Max Reinhardt: Between Participation and Exclusion   *149*

Conclusion
The Glorious Heyday and Obscure Demise of Reinhardtian Theater as a Historical Lesson   *167*

Notes   *177*

Works Cited   *195*

Index   *219*

INTRODUCTION

Wherever theater was thought of, his name was thought of too. His magic wand stretched over two continents, but the magical spell of his influence was cast further afield than that. Nobody would any more have thought in his case of talking about success and failure than they would have considered it a success on the part of the spring if its blossoms were to appear a few days earlier or later... Although he was not yet fifty, he was already a legend.
—Bruno Frank (1887–1945)

Esteemed? He is revered, admired, idolized. The word "genius" seems to have been coined expressly for literary critics to apply to Max Reinhardt.
—Paul Goldmann (1865–1935)

On the face of it, a book about Max Reinhardt would seem to require no special explanation. The mere name commands a respect that is even further enhanced by epithets like the "(great) magician," "professor," or "theatrarch." Nor does his significance for the history of the theater seem to require further justification; we need only recall statements like the first sentence of Heinz Herald's study of Reinhardt, which appeared as early as 1915: "Max Reinhardt has given new meaning to the concept of what a director [*Regisseur*] is."[1]

And in fact, a mere glance at some of his biographical milestones attests to his exceptional talent. Born Max Goldmann on September 9, 1873, in Baden bei Wien, he worked for a few years as a provincial actor before being hired by Otto Brahm in 1894 at the Deutsches Theater (German Theater) in Berlin. In 1901 came the opening night of Schall und Rauch (Sound and Smoke), the artists' cabaret that was cofounded by Reinhardt and where he officially directed his first play in 1902. In 1905 he scored a sensational success with his production of *A Midsummer Night's Dream* at the Neues Theater (New Theater), in which a revolving stage was first used for dramatic purposes rather than as a mere technical expedient. That same year he became the director of the Deutsches Theater. At this point we can use a few short captions to indicate the stages of his career:

1910: first arena production
1912: first guest performance in the United States

1919: inauguration of the Grosses Schauspielhaus (Big Playhouse), formerly the Zirkus Schumann, in Berlin

1920: inauguration of the Salzburg Theater Festival with Hugo von Hofmannsthal's *Everyman*

1924: *The Miracle* in New York, with 298 performances in one year

But the meteoric rise of his career was matched by its sudden demise. With the National Socialist "seizure of power" (*Machtergreifung*) in 1933, Max Reinhardt had to leave Germany and, after 1934, lived predominantly in the United States, where he died in 1943. During these years in exile he was never able to build on his earlier successes.

In light of all this, theater-historical scholarship attests with rare unanimity that Reinhardt must be considered one of the giants of modern theater history. Hardly any director in the German-speaking world—and the intoxication of superlatives might lead one to speak of Western theater as a whole—has so successfully established his and his work's importance over a comparable stretch of time while demonstrating such a range of forms and fundamental aesthetic approaches in the process.

And yet, on further examination the very self-evidence of the assertion must arouse suspicions. The myth of the artistic genius whose creativity and intuitive feel were the wellspring and motor force of his creations forecloses a more nuanced analysis. The adorative attitude in no way requires detailed familiarity with its object; on the contrary, it replaces such knowledge with universal—and ultimately vague—appreciation.

Such an approach cannot be adequate from a cultural studies perspective, which instead uses the apparent obviousness of such claims as a point of departure for revealing fissures, contradictions, and more complex interdependencies behind the self-evident facades. Thus, the aim of the following reflections is not to compose a hagiography—or a *chronique scandaleuse*, which is ultimately only hagiography under inverse auspices. We shall instead describe the specific form and the aesthetic principles of Max Reinhardt's theater, with the further idea of understanding to what extent it was the stage, actor, and reflex of its social and temporal context.

Methodological Considerations

> If the history of theater is to become true scholarship, it must acquire its own special methodology . . . The recent discussion of method by younger scholars in the history of literature, for instance, has on occasion very much irritated their older colleagues.[2]
>
> —Max Herrmann (1865–1942)

Introduction   ix

The methodological debate taking place in theater studies—specifically, its call for an independent methodological toolbox—has lost as little currency since its (co)founder Max Herrmann's admonition in 1914 as his observation that it "occasionally irritates" many contemporary colleagues.

And yet we must acknowledge that the situation has significantly changed: the challenge of coming to terms with various semiotic theories during the last forty years has brought about a distinct refinement of methodological consciousness.[3] Admittedly, the historiography of theater has participated in this development only in a qualified sense, since the focus of its discussion has been the study of contemporary theater. We can of course recognize features and approaches of a theatrical historiography that have been influenced by cultural studies, but we can hardly speak of an established model or a solid conceptual framework. Since there is no space here for a detailed and exhaustive discussion of these problems, the following discussion is intended only to highlight a few issues that will enable us to distinguish the outlines of such a historiography. Recently, we have seen an increased interest in theater history and its methodological requirements: Christopher B. Balme and Tracy C. Davis have presented a massive project in this respect with their six-volume set *A Cultural History of Theatre* (2017). As the two have pointed out, this project is meant to describe a new direction of theater historiography by focusing on theater with respect to all social and cultural circumstances. Yet, there is still a way to go.[4]

In the following, I will discuss some approaches from German theater history with a view to finding a useful approach to Max Reinhardt. The common basis of these approaches is the rejection in principle of a simplistic historicism which assumes that "history is made by great men." Instead, they focus in equal measure on theater as both aesthetic form and social institution in their manifold cultural interdependencies.

The point of departure for any kind of theater history is first and foremost the question as to the object, in other words, the question "What is theater?" In this connection, the theater studies scholar Rudolf Münz has concluded that it is ultimately illusory and untenable to imagine that theater can be conceptually defined by a set of constant and invariable characteristics. Münz has shown in his work on the "other theater" of the eighteenth century,[5] for example, that this concept—which underlies many attempts to write a "universal history" of the theater—is thoroughly problematic because it depends on the exclusion of all phenomena that do not fully coincide with the schema.[6]

With respect to the history of German theater, Münz found that the bourgeois theater of the eighteenth century—as formulated by authors like Johann Christoph Gottsched (1700–1766), Gotthold Ephraim Lessing (1729–1781), Johann Wolfgang von Goethe (1749–1832), and Friedrich Schiller (1759–1805)—became such a normative referential schema. The dominance of this theater in terms of both ethical implications ("moral institution") and semiotic structure (primacy of the literary text) has led to the marginalization and exclusion of other theatrical forms that in the social-historical perspective were arguably substantially more important and widespread. Gerda Baumbach has likewise pointed to this limitation with respect to comedy in Germany:

> German historiography of theater is clearly marked by an Enlightenment mentality ... [which] shows its influence up to the present in two ways. First, despite Modernism and Post-Modernism, the Enlightenment concept of theater and its terminology still tend to be adopted with only an apparent detachment from their normative implications. And second, the traditional selection of textual sources—due either to accident or, worse, prejudice—and the ways they are evaluated are still being passed on without critical examination.[7]

Thus, the narrowing of the historiographic outlook to this ideal does not simply take place within scholarly discourse, it also affects the selection of available sources. Even in many areas of popular theater in the twentieth century, for which there is a comparative abundance of attestations, conjectures on form and function are made only on the basis of such meager sources as police files. This form of "prior restraint" significantly determines the conditions of theater-historical work.

Andreas Kotte has described a possible way out of this dilemma:

> If we reject a narrow 18th-century concept of theater and recognize not the invention, but the institutionalization of theater as an achievement of Greek antiquity, some of the leading questions to be asked of theater historiography would be: How can situations and processes that lead to events represented on stage be structurally distinguished? ... We might suggest the following as a formula for such a historicizing approach: highlighted events shape society, and society shapes theater.[8]

If we follow this line of thought, we can immediately draw two conclusions. First, we need a comprehensive and consistent *historicization* and *localization* of theater. Such a historiography of theater—instead of seeking overarching ahistorical and supracultural constants—would be oriented toward an analysis of theater as part and product of a specific historical and cultural context. But, secondly, this perspective would not remain restricted to art theater in the narrower sense; it would apply to all other "prominent events" as well—folk practices, parades, openings of parliaments, and so on. This broadened understanding of the field of study would integrate the aesthetic and semiotic structures of theater into the background of societal forms of imagination and representation.[9]

Introduction *xi*

Hans-Peter Bayerdörfer has approached this subject from another angle in his essay "Probleme der Theatergeschichtsschreibung" (1990; "Problems of Theater Historiography"). Bayerdörfer sees the same constriction of scholarly perspective, but he ascribes it to a failure to draw sufficiently on existing archival materials. For example, whereas literary scholarship has access to a dense network of archives and research centers, and—even more importantly, in Bayerdörfer's view—possesses a clearly defined canon of textual sources, theater studies finds itself in a comparatively difficult situation. It isn't just the large number of people involved in the aesthetic product, but also the complexity of the way theater is organized that makes such definition hard to achieve. This is especially true because the sociocultural function of theater means that the audience always has to be taken into consideration. Thus Bayerdörfer remarks:

> The history of theater, since it is oriented to consumers and their behavior patterns as much as to productions and institutions, is always dealing with historical modes of consciousness, which are not simply derived from the epoch-making intellectual and religious systems of a given period, nor can they be considered a mere superstructure resting on basic social and material conditions. It thus concerns itself with conventional modes of thought, intuition, imagination, and feeling; with styles of communication, patterns of expression, implicit worldviews and world-images, all of which have their own historical development and their own historical law of inertia.[10]

On the basis of a thus broadened sense of the object of study, Bayerdörfer makes the case for a "history of mentalities" (*Mentalitätsgeschichte*) orientation according to the French model. "Mentality," in this context, means a complex of representations, values, and attitudes that are shared by the members of a given society without having to be explicitly thematized or discussed, and which have a decisive influence on their perceptions and actions. As a consequence of such an approach, Bayerdörfer writes:

> For individual cultural histories we may formulate it analogously: a turning-away from a one-sided bias toward creative individuality and the particular standard-setting work, and a turning-toward what Iffland and the last of his actors, Reinhardt and the last member of his audience, have in common.[11]

With this approach, he emphasizes that "the history of the outstanding achievements of thought and artistic design, the history of the cultural (and social) elite, is to be seen in the broad context of general culture and its guidelines."[12] Theater is here understood as a *social institution*, which is created not by the "artists" alone, but also by those social groups who attend its performances and thus open up the space necessary for it to function on the economic and intellectual level. No matter how ingenious the individual idea may have been or how extraordinary the conception of a particular production may appear even today, from the historiographic perspective it ultimately has to be understood in relation to the context in which the theatrical artwork functions—even, or perhaps even more so, when the work in question explicitly dissociates itself from that context.

This consideration means a change of scholarly perspective and leads to a reevaluation of the modus operandi. If we focus on the social character of theater, we also have to put its related ideas and terms to the test and analyze their implications. So, for example, the idea of the avant-garde, a concept that is crucially important for the historiography of twentieth-century theater,[13] is based on the idea of a comprehensive social and aesthetic rupture. The artists involved in it, characterized by the military epithet "vanguard," understood themselves (and historiography often follows them here) as part of something "new" that was radically different from already existing structures.

Yet if one applies the principle outlined by Bayerdörfer to this phenomenon, it becomes clear that the very idea of a rupture always requires the inscription of the "vanquished" society as a negative reference. Thus, instead of endorsing the ways the avant-garde describes itself, it is neccesary to describe the social and cultural conditions of the historical context in order to be at all able to recognize what function the "rhetoric of rupture" serves and what its basis is. The colorful, aggressive rhetoric of the avant-garde often conceals a silent consensus that shapes the presuppositions of this movement (or movements) at least as much as the innovative character of its ideas.

On one decisive point, however, Bayerdörfer agrees with the concept of theater history outlined by Münz (and others): the systematic broadening of the field of study means abandoning the idea of high culture or "serious" theater (*Höhenkammtheater*). The conventional notion that historiography acts as a kind of artistic referee that ultimately decides what should be remembered and what should subside into a more or less graceful oblivion now becomes obsolete. It is replaced by a historiographic principle that gains in complexity precisely because it considers all forms of theater (and "prominent events") without prejudice, and so becomes capable of describing their interactions.

The extent to which such a methodological point of departure can change the idea of the area of study can be illustrated by a quick glance at the history of film. In his study *Filmgeschichte und frühes Kino* (2002; *Film History and Early Cinema*), Thomas Elsaesser makes the case for replacing the history of film with the "history of cinema" (*Kinogeschichte*): "The shift from the history of film to the history of cinema involves . . . the palpable impulse to research historical audiences and the history of audiences as such."[14] The programmatic importance of this declaration becomes apparent only when we see how it relates to Elsaesser's definition of cinema as an institution:

Introduction

> The term ["cinema"] itself points to a whole series of clearly heterogeneous aspects: the social spaces and ideological discourses that were necessary to bring an audience together; the competition between production companies to secure access to and control over film technology; the changes in marketing . . . and—perhaps most importantly—the gradual standardization of a product which producers and audiences alike pigeonholed and recognized through the appearance of star actors or, stated more generally, through a stable horizon of expectations.[15]

Many of the points Elsaesser makes for replacing the history of film with the history of cinema have already been mentioned in our introductory discussion of the historiography of theater. In making his distinction, Elsaesser articulates a shift that cannot be characterized in the same way with respect to theater studies because of the specific conditions of theater, but this difference can nevertheless sharpen our awareness of methodological implications. In a nutshell, Elsaesser rejects a history of film that depends on artifacts alone and outlines a history of cinema that also takes the technical, social, economic, and cultural conditions of such artifacts into consideration.

It might seem at this point that theater scholars could sit back comfortably with a complacent smile on their faces, because in theater the conditions of production are so interwoven with the artifacts that it would seem impossible to separate them even by definition. But on closer inspection, the implicit rebuke of Elsaesser's far-reaching approach touches a sensitive spot for the historiography of theater, too, and challenges it to define its object of study more explicitly. And here we see the need for an opening up, not just in the sense of Bayerdörfer's history-of-mentality perspective, but also as a broadening in the area of subject matter in terms of the various factors to be taken into account. To be specific: a phenomenon like Reinhardt's theater especially requires a scholarly perspective that examines economic and organizational conditions rather than merely concentrating on the analysis of stage productions. Theater history in the sense of a comprehensive culture-historical study cannot be confined to a history of stage productions: it also requires an analysis of the relationship between particular stagings and theater as a site of production and reception.

But such a comprehensive perspective presents scholarly theater historiography with a crucial problem. Positing the relation between theater and society as the central question entails the further question of the value to be placed on the individual stage production. For if we do not want to reduce the history of theater to a purely social history, it will remain important to place the individual play, the concrete theatrical production, at the center of scholarly analysis.

On the other hand, we have to guard against the danger of overrating such productions. A simple numerical example relativizes the significance we might attach to individual productions as aesthetic events. Reinhardt's legendary 1905 production of *A Midsummer Night's Dream* had a total of 305 performances between January 1905 and June 1906. If we assume that the Neues Theater on the Schiffbauerdamm with its 890 seats was always sold out, then a total of 271,450 people saw the production. If we set this impressive number in relation to the estimated 2.4 million people who made up the population of Berlin in 1900, we see that 11.7 percent of all Berliners saw the performance. (This assumed audience figure would correspond to approximately 0.48 percent of the German population [56,367,200] at the time.) Should we nevertheless insist that the production was a representative key text of German society at the turn of the century?

Obviously, a cultural studies–oriented historiography of theater cannot rely on quantitative criteria. What we need instead is a methodological orientation that finds a way to mediate between the individual theatrical event, the individual stage production, and the social context. In this regard, Christopher B. Balme in his essay "Kulturanthropologie und Theaterhistoriographie" (1994; "Cultural Anthropology and Theater Historiography") has pointed to a possible enrichment of theater history by applying the anthropological concept of culture, especially as it has been worked out by Clifford Geertz.

In his central essay "Thick Description: Toward an Interpretive Theory of Culture" (1973), Geertz suggested an anthropological approach that places the individual cultural event at the center of interest, in what he called "thick description." According to Geertz, thick description is characterized by a microscopic approach:

> This is not to say that there are no large-scale anthropological interpretations of whole societies, civilizations, world events, and so on . . . It is merely to say that the anthropologist characteristically approaches such broader interpretations and more abstract analyses from the direction of exceedingly extended acquaintances with extremely small matters.[16]

This postulate of seeking the perspective of investigating "extremely small matters" sits well with theatrical study, and Balme has expressly praised Geertz in this connection: "Geertz's merit and that of the anthropologists indebted to his approach consists in the shifting of scientific interest from systems thinking to a micro-perspective on the society under investigation."[17] The avoidance of "systems thinking" keeps theater studies from marginalizing its proper object of study by regarding it as a bearer of "societal messages"—a development that ultimately converts the study of theater into a form of sociology and therefore makes it impossible to discuss the individual aesthetic product.

But how would thick description look in a concrete situation? Geertz describes it as follows:

> Rather than following a rising curve of cumulative findings, cultural analysis breaks up into a disconnected yet coherent sequence of bolder and bolder sorties. Studies do build on other studies, not in the sense that they take up where the others leave off, but in the sense that, better informed and better conceptualized, they plunge more deeply into the same things.[18]

The process of cultural analysis is less a matter of ferreting out new facts—although in theater studies especially there are always new sources to be explored—than of expanding our understanding in a sort of spiraling movement, a very conscious process of repeated analysis of "small matters" (individual stage productions, say) in order to arrange them in further contexts. In the course of this spiraling movement, we become better able to make statements about the society in question: "The aim is to draw large conclusions from small, but very densely textured facts; to support broad assertions about the role of culture in the construction of collective life by engaging them exactly with complex specifics."[19] In this way, we may succeed in establishing a connection between very precise analyses of individual stage productions, or other phenomena, and the broader contexts. Theater (in all of its aspects) is thus described as part of the broader network of social processes, as a place where a society can project itself onto a stage and reflect on itself, and as a forum for cultural disputes. The perspective opened up by Geertz's microscopy and its related discourses allows us to place the "small matters" at the center of discussion without having to puff them up or leave them individually disconnected.

Summing up the preceding discussion, we can say that a cultural studies model of theater historiography is distinguished by the following features:

- historicization of the concept of theater
- expansion of the area of study in the light of overarching issues
- avoidance of a fixation on "serious" theater
- opening up of the perspective to all levels of theater: not just a history of stage productions
- microscopic procedure in the sense of "thick description"

Such an approach will not merely contribute to a description of theater in its historical context, it will also situate the history of theater within the general history of culture.

Historical Context

Within the span of Max Reinhardt's own lifetime (1873–1943), we can single out several key turning points in the historical environment. First, on the political level, under the heading of the (new) nationalistic order, there were the following ones:

The founding of the German Reich (*Reichsgründung*) in 1871 restructured Germany's political sphere under Prussian hegemony by establishing the imperial dynasty of the house of Hohenzollern and excluding the Habsburg empire in accordance with the "lesser German solution."

The proclamation of the Weimar Republic in 1918 as a consequence of the First World War was another milestone of political history. With this step, Germany for the first time became a parliamentary democracy with a liberal constitution.

Finally, the National Socialist seizure of power (*Machtergreifung*) in 1933 put an end to this development by dissolving the new democratic structures and installing an authoritarian and murderous regime.

This process, however, had not only a political dimension, but a cultural component that cannot be underestimated. The historian Benedict Anderson describes the process of "becoming a nation" (*Nationwerdung*), which was by no means limited to Germany in the nineteenth century, in his study *Imagined Communities* (1983). The basic assumption in Anderson's argument is that the abstract concept of the nation-state could only be implemented in the actual lives (*Lebenswelt*) of its citizens through various mediation processes. The nation in this sense is not a quantifiable entity, but the product of the cultural imagination: "In an anthropological spirit, then, I propose the following definition of the nation: it is an imagined political community—and imagined as both inherently limited and sovereign."[20] Because this feeling of inhabiting an all-encompassing community, which is indispensable for the emergence of the idea of a nation, was not directly experienced (nor could it be), it required special efforts to develop images of these communities that were capable of producing a social effect.[21] Anderson ascribes a key role to the press (which became a dominant force in the nineteenth century) in this process, but we can just as well draw a parallel to the theater of the period, since it often enough took part in the national discourse.

The process of becoming a nation was accompanied by a political move to the Right. Up until 1871, nationalism and liberalism were mutually compatible concepts directed against authoritarian government, but after the *Reichsgründung* an enduring change took place:

> Once the political shift of 1878–79 occurred, "national" no longer meant advancing the emancipation of the middle and working classes, but preserving and defending the existing conditions against all who stood for more cosmopolitan attitudes, more freedom and equality. It was therefore part of the nationalist faith, as the right understood it, to sharply challenge those they saw as insufficiently nationalistic in this sense.[22]

This development of a conservative nationalism influenced further political developments once the German monarchy collapsed in 1918. The catchphrase "democracy without democrats" for the Weimar Republic is an attempt to describe this state of affairs—a lack of democratic attitudes and substance, which can also be seen to have contributed to the growing strength of National Socialism.

The political changes were accompanied by comprehensive and lasting social changes. The high reparations payments France was required to make after its defeat in the war of 1870–71 led to the economic boom of the so-called "founding years" (*Gründerjahre*), which made possible an industrialization in Germany comparable to what had already taken place in Great Britain and France in the first half of the nineteenth century.

This industrialization in turn changed Germany's demographic structure, contributing to urbanization on an unprecedented scale. Berlin's population rose from 170,000 in 1800 to over 2.4 million in 1900. But Berlin was only the tip of the iceberg. In Germany as a whole, the percentage of those who lived in cities (defined as places with over 5,000 inhabitants) rose from 12 percent in 1800 to 49 percent in 1910. The city not only became the critical habitat for nearly half the population of Germany, it also became the epitome of the modern era as well as its central object of reflection.[23]

These transformations, which radically altered both societal structures and the sphere of individual experience (*Lebenswelt*), were not merely passively reflected in cultural artifacts; the latter were a crucial part of the reshaping process, and here theater played a major role. Manfred Brauneck has pointed to the fact that the number of theaters in Germany more than doubled between 1870 and 1913–14, going from 200 to 463 stages.[24] Urban culture was very much a matter of theater culture, although the latter is not necessarily equivalent to our notion of high culture. To the contrary, theater was primarily a form of economically oriented entertainment: state subsidies maintained only court and municipal theaters, which represented less than half of all stages. With the introduction of freedom of trade (*Gewerbefreiheit*)—in 1869 in the North German Confederation and then in 1871 in the entire German Reich—it became easier to establish theaters, and theater collectively became an important branch of the economy.[25]

Even this rough outline allows us to see the extent to which theater at the end of the nineteenth century was bound up with the social, economic, and cultural dynamics that marked German society as a whole. This development intensified in the 1920s, partly because the liberal framework of the Weimar Republic opened up more opportunities for action and simplified many procedures, but also because the "birth" of film and the growing importance of cinemas fundamentally altered the fabric of entertainment culture.

In order to better appreciate the significance of theater in this society, we need to take another look at the social changes indicated above by the catchwords "industrialization" and "urbanization." If industrialization was leading to the emergence of the working class (the proletariat), urbanization was changing not just the character of urban culture, but the social classes that supported it. The position of the middle class (the "bourgeoisie") was becoming defined less and less by antagonism to the nobility and more and more by an anxious desire to set itself apart from the workers. Added to this was the factor of internal migration, which was filling the cities with large numbers of people who needed to be integrated into the social system.

The words "bourgeois" (*Bürger, bürgerlich*), "bourgeoisie" (*Bürgertum*), and "bourgeoisness" (*Bürgerlichkeit*), words often used to describe the middle class, are terms that, especially in the context of the avant-garde movement at the beginning of the twentieth century, took on negative connotations, evoking the caricature of the philistine.

On second glance, however, this pre-critical and often polemical usage proves to be problematic due to its lack of terminological precision. Recent investigations in this area have revealed how heterogeneous the phenomena grouped under the rubric "bourgeois" actually were. The idea of "bourgeoisness" suggests a historical continuity that cannot be substantiated on either social or ideological levels. On the contrary, the rapid growth of cities forces us to acknowledge a quantitative expansion of the bourgeoisie and the need to come up with a new definition for it. Put the other way around, the concept of "bourgeoisness" (alongside the nation) represented a central integrative idea; it offered a canon of behaviors and values that made it possible to include segments of the new urban social strata.

This integrative function, however, could only fulfill the idea of bourgeoisness because it was no longer defined, as it was in the eighteenth century, by "substantial" qualities like ownership or education, but rather defined by a specific lifestyle. In this regard, Jürgen Kocka defines bourgeoisness as preeminently a culture, an ensemble of values, behaviors, and so on.[26] Dieter Hein and Andreas Schulz add:

> The community of bourgeois subgroups is essentially based on a cultural praxis of everyday life which celebrates social solidarity overall. No one doubts that the bourgeoisie introduced norms and standards of behavior in the 19th century which—in the area of household decor, clothing, and manners, for example—were accepted irrespective of class and status.[27]

Bourgeoisness presented itself in the second half of the nineteenth century essentially as a performative praxis. In other words, anyone who actively participated in this culture could become bourgeois. Theater and other institutions of social life became points of crystallization for this identity, places where the opportunities but also the boundaries of this model identity were publicly enacted, demonstrated, and negotiated.

These were negotiated in and through the theater in two ways: first, on the level of theatrical productions and the ethical and aesthetic paradigms they presented; but secondly, through the existence of theaters in one or another of their specific forms. The bourgeois connection to the subsidized court theaters was never entirely severed because the latter were structurally fitted to the requirements of the court, which only partly coincided with those of the urban (neo-)bourgeoisie. The wave of new private theaters established as a result of the introduction of free trade in 1869 answered the growing need for a bourgeois theater in the narrower sense: it created a theater in which bourgois citizens were no longer the paying "guests" of the aristocracy, but which they factually supported on the cultural, organizational, and economic level.

This becomes especially clear in the case of three important Berlin theaters that were founded during the 1880s: the Deutsches Theater, opened in 1883 by Adolphe L'Arronge (1838–1908), as well as the Berliner Theater and the Lessingtheater, opened by Ludwig Barnay (1842–1924) and Oscar Blumenthal (1853–1917), respectively, in 1888.

Viewed in this light, this book's subtitle, *From Bourgeois Theater to Metropolitan Culture*, already describes the central perspective of the present work. Max Reinhardt's theater can be seen as a typical example of the bourgeois culture on which it pointedly relied and to which it aimed to display its goods and offer a social space. It developed in the context of the expanded understanding of bourgeoisness we have described above, but simultaneously outgrew it and became part of an international, *metropolitan culture*.[28]

For although the bourgeois culture of the late nineteenth century remained bound to the framework of the nation-state, around the turn of the century internationalist tendencies began to become more prevalent. The catchwords of this development were, first, the increased dissemination of film, which made it possible to replicate "cultural products" and present them in many different places; and second, the fact that theatrical tours were gaining in importance. Included under this heading are short-term engagements, such as Reinhardt was constantly undertaking with his theater, but also lengthy guest appearances. For the latter, independent ensembles were formed whose hallmark it was to be "on tour."[29]

Internationality became the defining trademark of this culture; a nationalistic frame of reference was not simply absent, it would have explicitly stood in the way of the success of such troupes. At its heart was a cultural exchange that no longer wished to offer the public the possibility of "national recognition," but instead created a repertoire that linked London, Paris, New York, and Berlin. The impact of this development transformed the nineteenth-century urban capital into a metropolis, a cultural center whose cosmos transcended the idea of national borders.

With this in mind, however, the picture on the cover of the German edition of this book (here, see page xxv) shows a utopia in a metaphorical as well as a literal sense. This design for a Reinhardt Theater in New York by Joseph Urban (1872–1933) is the imagistic sediment of the project to create a permanent performance space for Reinhardt in the United States and thereby create a lasting transatlantic theater axis. The building itself—the vision of an architect who, like Reinhardt, came from Vienna—embodies the utopia of such a liberal, transnational culture: aspiring to the heights and brightly lit, it stands out against the darkness of the city, offering a place for which people could strive.

The hopeful euphoria that radiates from this design gleaming with golden hues has an odd effect on a viewer of today—for this never-realized vision is juxtaposed with our knowledge of subsequent historical developments that not only found Reinhardt more homeless than anyone could have imagined just a few years earlier, but also saw National Socialism destroy all hopes of creating such a metropolitan culture and banish Berlin from the metropolitan community. Thus the dynamic indicated by my book's subtitle might in an extended sense describe the course of German history as reflected by the image of this theater.

Theater-Historical Context

The theater boom that started in 1869 completely changed the landscape of German theater, but it turned the Berlin theater scene upside down. The Königliches Schauspielhaus (Royal Playhouse), which up to that time had been its most important venue, became less significant than the private theaters almost immediately.

But despite or, more likely, precisely because of theater's sudden growth, it was a constant object of criticism. Max Martersteig (1853–1926) polemicized against these new openings in his seminal essay "Das deutsche Theater im neunzehnten Jahrhundert" (1904; "The German Theater in the Nineteenth Century"):

> The extension of free trade to theatrical enterprises of all kinds had hardly become law when speculation, which had obviously long been preparing for the occasion, rushed in to exploit the ready opportunities . . . In the music halls was introduced a species of drama that presented the deplorable scum of farces, operettas, and folk plays, kneaded together into dreadful monstrosities in which couplet-comedians and cabaret chanteuses shone as the dramatis personae.[30]

But Martersteig's pessimistic diagnosis is hardly an individual case. On the contrary, a tradition of critical lamentation arose in parallel with Berlin's rise to the most important German-speaking theater capital: Heinrich and Julius Hart, "Das 'Deutsche Theater' des Herrn L'Arronge" (1882; "The 'German Theater' of Mr. L'Arronge"); Conrad Alberti, *Ohne Schminke: Wahrheiten* über das moderne Theater (1887; *Without Make-up: Truths about the Modern Theater*); Maximilian Harden, *Berlin als Theaterhauptstadt* (1888; *Berlin as Theater Capital*); Paul Linsemann, *Die Theaterstadt Berlin* (1897; *Berlin as Theater City*); Karl Strecker, *Der Niedergang Berlins als Theaterstadt* (1911; *Berlin's Demise as a Theater City*); and finally what is probably the best known of these writings, *Das Theater der Reichshauptstadt* (1904; *The Theater of the Imperial Capital*) by Siegfried Jacobsohn.[31]

Common to all these laments—beyond all differences in the aesthetic preferences of each—was the obviously unfulfilled hope for a bourgeois theater with artistic claims and a convincing aesthetic expression of the problems of the time.

Such criticism becomes understandable only in the context of typical forms of production before the new development. Until late in the nineteenth century, the court theater system was essentially based on virtuosity: famous actors and actresses in glittering roles (Hamlet, Faust, Maria Stuart, Lady Macbeth) toured the country supported, as a rule, by a cast of pick-up actors previously unknown to them.[32]

A look at the scheduling statistics of the Royal Prussian Theaters (Berlin, Kassel, Hannover, Wiesbaden) is also eye-opening. Excluding Berlin, which because of its preeminent position was not quite in the same category, we find that the others offered an average of 300 performances per season (with a two-month holiday) and had a repertoire of approximately 85 plays. Most productions had between two and four performances. These rough figures alone, though they would naturally require further analysis, reveal that the performance practice of the time bears no comparison at all to what we find today, where a typical production in a state or municipal theater will have a four-to-six-week rehearsal period. These production standards, by contrast, probably only allowed for mere "blocking rehearsals." But such a huge repertoire not only affected the actors—it was only possible because most productions were played with standard stage sets.[33]

The legendary Meininger Hoftheater (Meiningen Court Theater) of Duke Georg II of Saxe-Meiningen (1826–1914) offered an aesthetic alternative that was a radical departure from this system. Georg II developed a kind of theater that was not only based on common rehearsals with the ensemble cast, but was especially intended to create an impact with its stage sets and costumes. Fully in the style of the emerging historicism of the time, these latter were no longer drawn from a (more or less arbitrary) catalog of stylized costumes, but rather claimed historical authenticity. We get a clear sense of the impression this variant practice made on audiences by reading theater critic Karl Frenzel's (1827–1914) description of Shakespeare's *Julius Caesar*:

> The picturesque costumes of the individual actors, the groups they form, the surging and ebbing, the noise, the cries: everything merges into a unity which, though a product of art, study, and arduous work,

yet appears in perfect freedom as unadulterated Nature . . . Here indeed is a cultivation ground and school of dramatic art, the which to witness is a pleasure that yields delight and stimulation in so many different aspects.[34]

Encouraged by such reactions—but also to cover the costs of such a lavish enterprise—the Meiningen troupe began going on extensive tours in 1874, which brought them to Berlin, Vienna, London, and Moscow, among other places.[35] Notwithstanding divergent views, the Meiningen style of presentation in a very short time set standards that the aesthetics of theater in the coming years could not afford to ignore.

This experience led to the opening of a great number of new theaters in the following years that owed much to the Meiningen aesthetic, while turning to contemporary literature much more than the earlier troupe did. The first of these was the Deutsches Theater, which was initially set up as an actors' association, but was very quickly taken over by Adolphe L'Arronge, who was also successful as a playwright.[36]

In the 1880s, inspired by stimuli coming out of France and Scandinavia, a new current formed within the bourgeoisie that showed a critical interest in the aesthetic treatment of themes connected with the consequences of modernization. The emerging literary movement of Naturalism promised to fill this gap, but modernization's "losers" as well as the problems caused by social change were not adequately reflected either on stage or in the public consciousness. To create a forum for this, in 1889 the Freie Bühne (Free Stage) was founded in the form of an "association theater" (*Vereinstheater*), and a journal of the same name was published in connection with it. The association's chief goal was to foster the theatrical breakthrough of naturalistic literature. To this purpose, members of the association made use of a special rule in the censorship regulations, according to which there were no constraints on private or closed performances. The association made its public debut with a performance of Ibsen's *Ghosts*.

The most important step in the staging of naturalistic drama took place when Otto Brahm (1856–1912), one of the founding fathers of the Freie Bühne, leased the Deutsches Theater from L'Arronge. Brahm's programmatic maxim was to finally achieve the breakthrough of Naturalism not only by staging the corresponding dramas, but by changing his actors' playing style as well. They no longer delivered their lines in the "high stage tone," but patterned themselves on the way people spoke in daily life and sometimes used dialect. This aesthetic fit the naturalistic dramas very well, but it presented a great discrepancy in the staging of classical texts, which Brahm had to include in the repertoire to make the public happy.

This was the time and place of Max Reinhardt's first appearance on the Berlin stage, yet, though his career began here, he describes this period with great ambivalence:

Brahm went so far with his Naturalism that he would say, as long as people in real life spoke no verse, he wanted none on the stage either . . . I was part of his theater for nine long years and very much his friend—he was really a worthy man . . . But I gradually came to suffer under the burden of performing every night . . . Also most of the naturalistic performances involved eating on stage, usually dumplings and sauerkraut, which was good, but you can also get sick of it after a while—in any case, I began to find the whole atmosphere excruciating and was outspokenly unhappy.[37]

When Reinhardt left Brahm in 1902 and eventually, in 1905, even became the director of the Deutsches Theater, which Brahm had to give up in 1904 under pressure from L'Arronge, many took this instance of "patricide" as a historical turning point for the theater. This was given especially clear expression by Siegfried Jacobsohn (1881–1926), who, in the foreword of his 1910 book on Reinhardt, describes him as the one who was needed to bring an uncompleted historical process to fulfillment:

> Thus this book builds on my first book and makes a historical connection. *The Theater of the Imperial Capital* describes how Berlin became Germany's first theater city. But it also explains why Berlin as late as 1904, despite the massive amount of work it did on its theater, had not yet come up with a version that could without presumption be called German Theater. That kind of theater, I said, would have to be a synthesis of what L'Arronge and Brahm had achieved, for each of them . . . had only directed half a theater. This new book, which quite deliberately begins with the year 1905, proclaims it as Reinhardt's glory to have created the desired synthesis.[38]

The theater boom, the controversy surrounding Naturalism, and the specific culture and entertainment requirements of the Berlin bourgeoisie at the turn of the century all set the stage for Max Reinhardt, whose appearance as director in both senses of the term (*Regisseur* and *Theaterdirektor*) was greeted by critics as a redemption.

The Structure of This Book

To depict Max Reinhardt's works exhaustively and with encyclopedic zeal would explode the framework of this book and at the same time fail to meet its goal. Instead, the following pages will describe the special character of Reinhardt's aesthetic at particular stages of its development, as well as the cultural position of his theater in the context of a society undergoing modernization and other forms of change.

Following Reinhardt's own programmatic agenda, our first step will be to describe the various theatrical formats he tested and made use of over the course of his career. Here it suffices to trace the arc from the "small form" of cabaret through the chamber plays to the monumental arena productions.

Secondly, we will take up the topic of the organization and cultural conditions of this latter type of theater. Taking *The Miracle* as our basis, we will illustrate the form and structure of metropolitan culture as Max Reinhardt conceived and practiced it, in order to then turn the discussion to its relation to film. A separate chapter will deal with the organization and economic structure of his theater.

Then, against the background of tensions between bourgeois art and metropolitan culture, we have to ask how far Max Reinhardt's theater can be regarded as a part of German-Jewish history. This will lead us finally to ask whether the bit of theatrical history we have traced may be taken as a "historical lesson."

Since the book is not an exhaustive account of Max Reinhardt and his accomplishments, its aim is not completeness, but rather "thick description" applied to a high cultural milieu. Thus Max Reinhardt and his theater are shown to be a mirror of their time, as well as an active part of its cultural negotiations.

Joseph Urban's design for a proposed Reinhardt Theater in New York, from the cover of the German edition of this book. Courtesy of the Joseph Urban Estate at Columbia University.

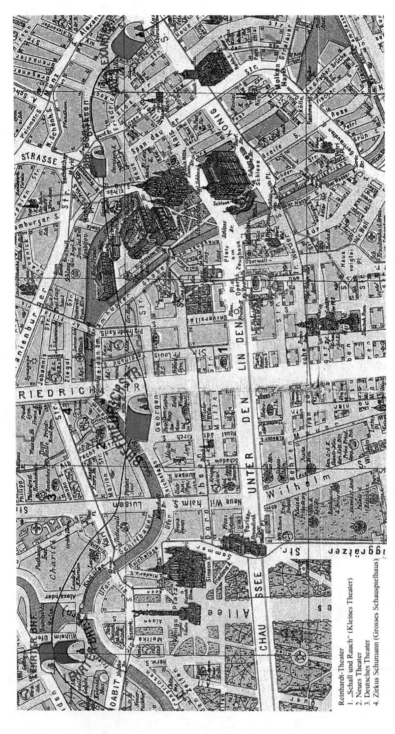

Reinhardt-Theater
1. „Schall und Rauch" (Kleines Theater)
2. Neues Theater
3. Deutsches Theater
4. Zirkus Schumann (Grosses Schauspielhaus)

Figure 1. Map of Berlin showing theater locations, 1905

Chapter 1

✦

From Cabaret to the Deutsches Theater

Theater: Spaces—Designs—Formats

It is thoroughly characteristic of Max Reinhardt's work that—in contrast to many other "theater reformers"—he left no comprehensive theoretical statement behind, but the fundamental features of his work can already be found outlined in a short text from 1901. Here he states his emphatic allegiance to a festive, opulent, life-affirming theater:

> What I have in mind is a theatre that will again give joy to people, that leads them out of the grey misery of everyday life, beyond themselves, into a sunny and pure atmosphere of beauty. I can feel that people are fed up with finding their own misery again in the theatre and that they are longing for brighter colors and a heightened sense of life.[1]

This sketch reflects both the constraints of Naturalism, with its maximally detailed reproduction of reality, and the conditions of life in modernized society ("the grey misery of everyday life"). But it points above all to Reinhardt's directorial style, which was fueled by a volatile use of all available theatrical resources. In contrast to other representatives of the historical avant-garde, Reinhardt refused to limit himself to a single form, propagating instead a programmatic eclecticism that viewed theater's polymorphism as a wealth of aesthetic possibilities.

Thus Reinhardt argues for a juxtaposition of stage forms, each serving its own specific purpose:

> We should really have two stages simultaneously, a big one for the classics and a smaller, more intimate one for the chamber art of modern writers ... And actually—don't laugh—one ought to have a third theatre as well. I am quite serious about that and I already see it in front of my eyes: a very large theatre for a great art of monumental effects, a festival theatre, detached from everyday life, a house of light and solemnity, in the spirit of the Greeks.[2]

From today's perspective, it is astonishing how Reinhardt kept working on the systematic development of this triad during the later course of his career. This idea of three juxtaposed spatial types will serve as our structural principle in the following pages.

Schall und Rauch: The Circuitous Route from *Brettl* to the Deutsches Theater

If we start tracing Reinhardt's career from the moment he left the ranks of Brahm's ensemble, the first phase has to be named after the cabaret Schall und Rauch (Sound and Smoke; the German phrase has the connotations of the English "smoke and mirrors"). This consisted of a small group of Brahm's actors who were tired of the programmatic Naturalism and started presenting "players' evenings" in addition to their regular activity, mostly for their theatrical colleagues. In 1901 this informal coalition became the cabaret ensemble Schall und Rauch, which by October of that same year had the wherewithal to move into its own playhouse at the prestigious address Unter den Linden 44.

This institutionalization gave Reinhardt the chance to dissolve his contract with Brahm—though only amid quarrels and a fine for breach of contract—by the end of 1902. It is worth noting that with this step the name Schall und Rauch disappears and the house that had opened only a year previously now becomes an "art theater" with the name Kleines Theater (Little Theater).

Although this episode seems to represent only a short phase of Reinhardt's theatrical praxis over many years, it was in this period that his contractual and artistic emancipation occurred. We can see that this undertaking was certainly no mere means to an end if we bear in mind that Reinhardt himself kept returning to the idea of cabaret theater—the final time in the 1920s, when a second Schall und Rauch arose under completely different auspices in the framework of the Grosses Schauspielhaus (Big Playhouse). But cabaret in its interplay with other forms had far-reaching significance aside from Reinhardt's own case. For example, Rudolph Bernauer (1880–1953) and Carl Meinhard (1875–1949)—who were to become two of Reinhardt's most significant competitors—began their career as the Böse Buben (Bad Boys).[3]

In order to describe these professional and artistic paths in more detail, in the following pages I will give a brief summary of the popular theatrical forms and contemporary discourses cabaret was able to draw on, and what position it occupied within Wilhelminian society. Then, in the light of these interrelationships, I will finally describe Schall und Rauch both as an element of Reinhardt's formal pluralism and as a cultural institution.

Cabaret (French and German), *Variété*, and *Tingeltangel*: Prehistories

Although we now take cabaret for granted as a basic component of theatrical culture and also see it, as satirical forum, as a part of political discourse, a historical study has to begin with the acknowledgment that cabaret in Germany is about 120 years old. To appreciate the significance of this "discovery," we should first describe the historical background of the term "cabaret" and the influences that might have determined its cultural position.

Interest in the evolving genre of the cabaret was based primarily on its position as a point of intersection between two social spheres and discourses. This intermediary position explains cabaret's rapid expansion, but even more its multifaceted developmental potential. Even though the scholarly literature constantly bemoans the short life of the cabaret ensembles, this supposed deficiency belies the specific dynamism that characterized the cultural sphere that cabaret functioned in.

Figure 2. View of the interior of Le Chat Noir

The roots of cabaret, as the name itself suggests, lie in France, more exactly in Paris. Here the legendary Chat Noir was founded on December 18, 1881, a café that had its own theatrical space containing a small stage.[4] This new form was characterized by a program consisting of various short, independent acts called "numbers" that were announced and linked together by a *conférencier* (host, master of ceremonies). Beyond this, it was the *conférencier*'s role to engage with the audience, and the distinctly coarse tone he used in doing so became cabaret's trademark.

The best known *conférencier*—and still an iconographic presence today because of Toulouse-Lautrec's poster—is certainly Aristide Bruant (1851–1925), who was also the occasional host of the cabaret Le Mirliton. While other *conférenciers* were known for their stinging irony, Bruant made use of very strong, sometimes vulgar language in his songs and commentaries.[5]

Although the Chat Noir is supposed to have developed spontaneously out of a meeting place for actors, it nevertheless drew on existing traditions and integrated familiar elements into its dramaturgy and modes of presentation. One of the biggest attractions of early cabaret was a shadow theater run by Henri Rivière (1864–1951). This theater consisted of a screen on which shadow silhouettes were projected (in some cases of well-known personalities of the period) and a chorus that accompanied the images with speech and music.[6] Rivière achieved such perfection in his stagings that they are widely regarded as foreshadowing the arrival of film as a screen art. From here we might draw a line to the German artist Lotte Reiniger (1899–1981), whose animated films of the 1920s continued the practice instigated by Rivière.

French cabaret explicitly regarded itself as an antibourgeois art form. The fact that it took place in the back rooms of cafés whose stages exuded the charm of the makeshift, rather than in large, glamorous theaters, had a programmatic character. The coarse tone and—in Bruant's songs especially—the critique of lower-class living conditions were constitutive elements in this staging of an antibourgeois gestus.

Yet we cannot speak here of an "autochthonous," "authentic" working-class or folk culture—quite the contrary, for the audience (and this corresponds to the later development in Germany) was made up predominantly of bourgeois and intellectuals. Cabaret gave them the chance to imagine a place outside bourgeois culture without requiring them to "really" abandon its sphere.

Despite its social-critical impetus, cabaret also adapted structures and formats of the commercial variety show (*Variété*, sometimes translated as "vaudeville"), which, as with the numbers format, it made part of its own fundamental structure.

Cabaret's effect on German intellectuals was very powerful once they encountered it, which occurred primarily in two ways. One was through the guest appearances in Germany of various cabaret ensembles and artists in 1898–99,[7] among them the chansonnière Yvette Guilbert (1867–1944).[8] The other was the 1899–1900 World Exposition in Paris, where many visitors came to know cabaret as part of the metropolitan way of life. It is hard to overestimate the impact of the Paris exhibitions on the forming of Western metropolitan culture: they were covered by all sorts of media and had a sustainable impact partly through the commodification of many cultural inventions and sensations, such as the cabaret.

We can name two relevant literary sources for this early reception, and especially for its interpretation and programmatic appraisal. The first is the 1890 novel *Forskrevet* (*Dedicated*) by the Danish writer Holger Drachmann (1846–1908), in which he outlines the idea of a "literary Variété." The other is the 1897 novel *Stilpe* by Otto Julius Bierbaum (1865–1910). Bierbaum's novel, which can be read as a parody of the traditional Bildungsroman, contains the defining formulation of the "supercabaret" (*Überbrettl*):

> We shall give birth to the *Übermensch* [superman] on the stage boards [*Brettl*]! We shall bowl this inane world over! We shall crown indecency as the one and only decency! We shall re-establish nakedness in all its beauty before the entire nation! We shall gleefully and lasciviously remake this infamous, morally ramshackle world into something hilariously and divinely impertinent![9]

This quotation from Bierbaum's roman à clef opens up two areas of discussion. The topos of the *Übermensch* refers to a reading of Nietzsche that emphatically postulates a cultural reorientation and "transvaluation of all values." Nietzsche's philosophy functioned as an instigator of numerous fin-de-siècle reform movements,[10] and in this context it signaled the radical rejection of an exhausted and by now merely epigonal culture. Ernst von Wolzogen made this reference to Nietzsche explicit in his Buntes Theater (Motley Theater) by prominently displaying the iconic Nietzsche bust by Max Kruse.[11]

The second central point of the Bierbaum passage—which we also find in many other authors of the early cabaret movement—is the programmatic elimination of taboos connected with sexuality. Even if many of the novel's relevant passages seem almost charmingly innocuous from our modern perspective, in the Wilhelminian context they constituted a radical provocation. The topos of nakedness is therefore to be taken as a sociopolitical statement.

Thus the "antibourgeois critique" of cabaret in Germany is best understood with reference to Nietzsche's philosophy on the one hand, and the thematization of corporeality and the removal of sexual taboos on the other.

But of course there is a strong connection between the two spheres. The critique of the bourgeoisie in the early cabaret movement should not be confused with the kind of social criticism we find in Naturalism; it is rather sociopolitical satire that targets the figure of the petit bourgeois (*Spießbürger*). The goal of the *Wandervogel* (bird of passage) movement for example—one of many life-reform or back-to-nature movements that existed during this period—was to overcome the bourgeois lifestyle, which it regarded as hostile to the body, overly confining, and antiquated,[12] but by and large, its members still came from this very same bourgeois milieu. We may correspondingly regard cabaret as a component of bourgeois self-criticism—and sometimes even self-hatred.[13]

In this light we can also appreciate the fascination felt for the variety show (*Variété*), which emphasized physical artistry, as opposed to conventional theater. We have only to think of the many different forms it took, one of which involved otherwise generally tabooed presentations of erotica (nude dancing, etc.), which relegated the variety show to the fringes of bourgeois culture. In this marginal position, however, a new evaluation of eroticism and sexuality, or more generally the expression of a new physicality, seemed possible.

Bierbaum—whose ironic tone in the quoted passage should not of course be left out of consideration—places cabaret in explicit opposition to the "pillars of society": "For all will come to us, to the music halls [*Tingeltangel*], who flee the theaters and museums with as much trepidation as they do the churches."[14] With the adoption of or allusion to forms belonging to the variety show, cabaret could expect to provoke the bourgeois understanding of morality in a way that corresponded to its own self-image.

The image constantly conjured up by Frank Wedekind (1864–1918), for example, of an overwhelmingly sensual femininity incapable of being bound by the conventions of the social order—most clearly embodied in his Lulu figure—corresponds completely to this fascination. (It almost goes without saying that such an image is a product of male desire, and that it seeks to shock the bourgeois moral sensibility, but by no means to disturb the basic patriarchal order so that women could achieve a better position in society.)

In this connection we should also mention the so-called *Tingeltangels* as a factor in the rise of cabaret. The origin of the term is unclear,[15] but it indicates a type of *Singspiel* hall where the female singers mingle with the guests as bar girls after the performances. A judicial decision of April 11, 1907, formulates it as follows:

> The *Tingel-Tangel* differs from the more elevated variety show in that its performances are meant to arouse the lower instincts, such as sexual lust . . . A person goes to the *Tingel-Tangel* to be aroused, to the variety show, to marvel at the more elevated and spectacular performances.[16]

Beyond this terminological distinction, which should be taken with a grain of salt, we can see that *Variétés* and *Tingeltangels*, as a collective fantasy of places of sexual libertinage, were a potent force behind cabaret's antibourgeois gestus. In this connection, Wolfgang Jansen has shown that the lure of an amoral lifestyle was a fixture of the antibourgeois self-image: "The German version of bohemian society, which included a large number of artists at the end of the nineteenth century, cultivated excessive drinking and mingling in prostitute circles on the literary as well as the personal level."[17]

But as much as variety shows and music halls were a fixture of the anti-bourgeois imagination, the cabaret movement itself aimed at an "artistic upgrading" of these entertainment forms. Symptomatic here is an essay that Ferdinand Avenarius published in a 1910 issue of the journal *Der Kunstwart* (*Art Custodian*): "But since the variety show, whether we like it or not, is in fact a force, we therefore have the duty and the obligation to ensure, according to our powers, that it be minimally bad, and, if possible, to make it good."[18] Jansen comments critically on such attitudes:

> Thus in the very decade in which the variety show had reached the pinnacle of its success, there arose a counter-movement, which sought to take over the dramaturgical principles of the "specialty" stage and build on its popularity, yet with the typically German mania for edification, largely denied the justification of the usual numbers.[19]

To round out the picture, there are still the many commercial entertainment theaters to be mentioned, whose repertoire was oriented to a broad public taste. The usual theatrical forms here, such as mini- and melodramas (both with musical accompaniment), do not clearly fit the variety show pattern, but are, again, echoed in the programs of early cabaret.

This was the context in which the first ensembles that, from today's perspective, we can classify as cabaret troupes formed in Germany around the turn of the century. On April 13, 1901, Die Elf Scharfrichter (Eleven Executioners) was founded in Munich, and scholarship recognizes this as the first German cabaret ensemble. It was not just their military costumes but the aggressively satirical tone of their performances that distinguished their productions. The most prominent member of the group, besides the already-mentioned Frank Wedekind, was Otto Falckenberg (1873–1947), the later director of the Münchner Kammerspiele (Munich Chamber Playhouse). The ensemble's satire too was directed more at the bourgeois sensibility than at political conditions. In what was one of the group's specialties, Wedekind accompanied his own songs on guitar, thus achieving the close combination of lyric and performance that Bruant too was known for.

Ernst von Wolzogen (1855–1943) is regarded as the "grandfather" of German cabaret, and was likewise the first to convert the idea of a literary variety show into a reality, with his Buntes Theater in Berlin in 1901. The mission of his new enterprise was decidedly didactic, a clear departure from Naturalism:

> The Naturalistic school has sought out the people in their work—let genuine writers seek them from now on in their satisfactions. Not the people in the sense of the rabble, for the literary tradesmen, who have nothing to do with art, do enough work for this element; but the people in the sense of the hundreds of thousands who have intellectual needs and are amenable to an ennobling of their taste.[20]

This "ennobling of . . . taste," as well as the elitist strain underlying such a formula, characterized the whole undertaking. In November 1901, Wolzogen opened his own theater—with no fewer than 800 seats—fitted out by the architect August Endell (1871–1925) in the full Jugendstil manner. A photograph of the interior gives a clear idea of the rich ornamentation, which critics singled out for positive comment.[21] But it also highlights the fact that Wolzogen's cabaret no longer sought the aura of a backroom theater; it was a return to the traditional theater space, with the stage clearly separated from the auditorium. The only feature reminiscent of the *Tingeltangels* and variety shows is the projecting forestage that allowed direct contact with the audience.

Figure 3. View of the Buntes Theater in Berlin

Since the Buntes Theater was always judged by its own high standards, initial euphoria soon gave way to disappointment. Although Wolzogen had announced that there would be some political numbers among other things, they were held within very narrow bounds. Typical, by contrast, was the comic song "The Merry Husband" ("Der lustige Ehemann," Bierbaum/

Strauss), which was enthusiastically received at the opening performance. The song, which satirically mimicked the self-absorbed world of the Biedermeier bourgeoisie, was sung by two actors in historical costume. The third stanza adequately conveys the song's intent:

> The world is out there somewhere,
> But it can go stand on its head!
> We really don't pay it much mind,
> And if by chance it weren't there,
> We'd still be doing just fine.[22]

The number was repeatedly incorporated into the subsequent programs, and though it certainly caricatured the false complacency of the Biedermeier period, at the same time it curiously perpetuated a nonpolitical strain of the bourgeois identity in that it had nothing to say about the real political conflicts of the period. The obvious historical remove, further underscored by the costumes, was a "protection" against the audience's carrying anything over into the present.

Opening night and the ensuing weeks brought the cabaret an unexpected and resounding success. Wolzogen went on to organize a tour for the summer months, leaving a core ensemble behind in Berlin under the direction of Hanns Heinz Ewers (1871–1943).

The guest performances seemed initially to ensure the Buntes Theater's financial prospects. But Wolzogen's very success became his nemesis. Within a very short time numerous new groups sprang up in imitation of his model and wooed a number of performers away from his ensemble. Between 1901 and 1905 alone, Berlin was the site of forty-two newly founded cabaret stages.[23]

The opening of the Buntes Theater came at a time when its chances of artistic and financial survival were decidedly iffy. Besides the economic problems, it turned out that the stiff competition made it almost impossible to keep the programs varied and up-to-date, so that, after the initial euphoria, attendance fell off relatively quickly. The Buntes Theater finally had to close in 1902 for financial reasons.

Karl Frenzel polemicized against the Berlin cabaret boom in a 1903 issue of the *Deutsche Rundschau (German Review)*:

> The number of its [Berlin's] theaters has grown alarmingly: the rollicking and frivolous invention of Ernst von Wolzogen known as the *Überbrettl* has in barely two years become as outmoded in its character as it has in the public's esteem. All those flimsily erected Thespian wagons with their declaiming poets and scantily clad muses have turned into standing theaters: the Kleines Theater, the Buntes Theater, and Trianon-Theater have become like the earlier theaters and make the same claims on writers, actors, and audience as those did.[24]

Just two prominent examples may serve to indicate the further course of this development. In 1904 Rudolf Nelson (1878–1960), primarily a composer of songs, cofounded the ensemble called Der Roland von Berlin (Roland of Berlin) with the actor Rudolf Schneider-Duncker. In contrast to Wolzogen's theater, their own, which was situated in a very exclusive neighborhood, offered with its approximately 150 seats a luxurious comfort that was also reflected in the admission price of 20 gold marks. Nelson managed to give expression to the new urban sense of life by being, among other things, one of the first musicians in Germany to play the new American popular music (ragtime). His theater remained successful for years, thanks not least to continued patronage from the court.

The second artist who absolutely has to be mentioned in this connection is Claire Waldoff (1884–1957).[25] She was probably the best-known female cabaret artist of her time, which can also be gleaned from the fact that she did not tie herself to a single ensemble but appeared in various theaters as a brand in her own right. Nelson was the major factor in launching her career, and in a very short time she became the uncontested personification of the "Berlin girl." Peter Jelavich describes her success as the expression of a collective longing for a figure to embody the urban, proletarian milieu—brought to life by the all-encompassing modernization of society:

> Although she invariably portrayed lower-class characters, she appealed to all social strata. Over time she came to perform in mass-cultural vaudevilles and revues as well as the most expensive cabarets . . . Her major function, though, was to establish a sense of community among Berliners of all social levels, to foster pride in their city and its modernity, and to sustain an image of assertiveness and self-confidence which all citizens could emulate.[26]

Cabaret—we can now conclude after this short review—established itself as an independent form in the context of a complex theatrical landscape by taking inspiration from different quarters and blending them into a single format. The dramaturgical principle of a sequence of numbers allowed it to juxtapose different kinds of performances without needing to harmonize their differences within a broader framework.

In the context of Wilhelminian society at the beginning of the twentieth century, cabaret signaled a broadening of the spectrum of bourgeois theatrical forms: the critique of the bourgeois lifestyle and its culture was not just the basic point of reference in this connection, it was to a large extent the very premise on which cabaret was built. The "popular" or "folk" element may occasionally figure in as gestus or represented content, but this was true only to the extent that bourgeois society allowed it to do so. This latitude is what resolved the apparent contradiction between Wolzogen's conservative and even elitist attitude and the establishment of a form of theater that made social-critical claims. In this perspective, the avowed intent of "ennobling" the variety show (or vaudeville) can be seen as the expression of a bourgeois "right of appropriation." This is especially clear in the case of Nelson, where cabaret fully turned into a "luxury item"—the representation of socially disadvantaged groups, in Claire Waldoff's acts, for example, takes the form of gestus. And here too the difference between cabaret and Naturalism becomes evident: the demand for political emancipation that we recognize in the latter, the idea of social engagement in general, was utterly foreign to early cabaret. Cabaret was part of an expanding domain of entertainment culture and had no wish to take part in political discourse.

Schall und Rauch

The scholarly literature typically regards Reinhardt's involvement with cabaret as a marginal aspect of his oeuvre. The most unambiguous statement of this attitude is the judgment of his son Gottfried (1911–1994), who writes about these beginnings:

> Max Reinhardt was anything but a cabaretist. Not only because he wasn't quite comfortable with this form of expression . . . but because he had no talent for it. Anyone today who reads the parodies published under his name, or listens to the recently released recordings, will find them dull, unless he is dazzled by the name.[27]

From today's perspective, the humor of the texts does in fact come across as somewhat labored and—since the things being parodied can only be identified through an exercise of philological acumen—primarily of historical interest. But despite such Lucullan objections, it is remarkable how Reinhardt and his colleagues adapted this new format to their own ends.

The cabaretistic undertaking originated in a small amateur circle that called itself Die Brille (Eyeglasses) and presented small parodies of familiar play styles. Most of the performers involved were employed at Brahm's Deutsches Theater and took part in this ensemble in addition to their regular duties. The group's formal emergence as Schall und Rauch came only in 1901. What occasioned the shift from a mostly private group that appeared before colleagues and friends was a benefit performance for the tubercular writer Christian Morgenstern (1871–1914), who remained employed at Schall und Rauch as an author in the years that followed.

Figure 4. The founders: Zickel, Kayssler, and Reinhardt

In July 1901 a joint-stock company, which involved Berthold Held (1868–1931) and Friedrich Kayssler (1874–1945), was set up to finance the cabaret.[28] In retrospect, we are surprised by the extent to which the enterprise in its early stages was already aiming beyond cabaret at the establishment of an art theater. Kayssler was openly speculating about it in a letter to Morgenstern.[29]

The already named were joined by Martin Zickel (1876–1932), who had been employed at the Deutsches Theater as a director (in today's sense, more of an assistant director) and had then cofounded the Sezessionsbühne (Secession Stage) with actor Paul Martin. It had been Zickel's goal to champion ambitious new dramas, especially those of Maurice Maeterlinck (1862–1949). He joined the Reinhardt circle after the financial failure of this undertaking.[30]

From Cabaret to the Deutsches Theater

Figure 5. Playbill for Schall und Rauch. Courtesy of the Theaterwissenschaftliche Sammlung of the University of Cologne.

The basic features of Schall und Rauch were already discernible in the opening night's program. The emphasis lay on theater parodies or small sketches from life on stage. Thus the number called "The Ten Just Men" ("Die zehn Gerechten") is a veiled parody of well-known theater critics who are shown in a short scene sitting next to one another at a premiere.

The seventh item on the program clearly had special importance, "*Don Carlos* at the Turn of the Century: A Tetralogy of Styles." Different styles of theatrical performance were parodied in four short sequences, but what is striking is the fact that the temporal spans of the respective "schools" become progressively shorter: "Old School (1800–1890), Naturalist School (1890–1900), Symbolist School (Sept. 1900–January 1901), Supercabaret School [*Überbrettlschule*] (January 18–31, 1901)."[31]

It is not just the broad scope of the number that shows its significance; it also allowed the players to define their own artistic interests through the representation of preexisting styles and isms. The parody can be understood as a metatheatrical commentary on the aesthetic conventions of its time. Reinhardt's early announcement (1901) of a diverse plurality of theatrical forms fulfills its promise here, though still in a satirical sense. If we have identified a programmatic eclecticism as a hallmark of Max Reinhardt's work, the cabaret provided the perfect framing for such an experimental approach.

Max Reinhardt—who can be taken as the central figure in setting the character of this undertaking—does not adopt the avant-garde gestus of establishing a style by rejecting all others, but shows instead that the strength of the new theater lies in a pluralism, a multiplicity of forms existing side by side. In Schall und Rauch this multiplicity appears in the garb of satire; in his later productions, by contrast, Reinhardt sets these diverse forms side by side on a thoroughly equal footing.

We can discern the theater's self-reflexivity in the way Schall und Rauch presents itself. The figure and gestus of the fool not only appear emblematically in Schall und Rauch's program booklets and other publications, they were dramatized in the prologues that were becoming a staple of the performances. Prologues provided the opportunity both to establish direct contact with the audience—and here we see a special adaptation of the *conférencier*'s colloquy that was typical of cabaret—and to give rein to ironic self-thematizations. Thus, for example, in the prologue that marked the opening of the new house, the wandering ghost of Schall und Rauch appeared on stage looking for a new home and finally presented the three fools with their fool's whip (which consisted of Wit, Sting, and Whimsy).[32]

In a similar instance, the situation of cabaret is thematized in a text attributed to Reinhardt himself called "The Descent to Hell of the 43rd Supercabaretist [*Überbrettlmensch*]." Various allegorical figures appear in a young theater director's dream and decisively determine his working conditions. In addition to the LLC partners, the Boring Manuscript and the Indecent Manuscript enter the scene, both trying to convince him to have themselves performed.

The latter figure—whom the embarrassed director characterizes as appearing in "corresponding form"—embodies the temptation factor and introduces a discussion on morality and censorship, which satirically thematizes the interplay between police censorship and, in this case, a mounting audience demand. In answer to the question "What's your attitude to morality?" it/she says:

> INDECENT MANUSCRIPT: In certain passages I'm even quite moral myself. Many others are of course completely free of it . . . I [*she blushes*] am no longer completely unperformed. [*Softly*] And I've also been reproduced already. But there are still many people who don't know me. So, my sweet little calf, won't you take me just the way I am? . . .
>
> DR. I.U.: [*starting to swoon*] Mama! Mama! . . . You're much too open, [*with another shy glance*] much—too—too—free. If you—I mean if madame would only deign to cover herself up a bit more . . . They're going to strike passage after passage, dear child; they'll ban your performance—
>
> INDECENT MANUSCRIPT: [*Laughing*] But, my sweet little rhinoceros, that's exactly what I want! Don't you know that it's precisely the forbidden fruits that taste the best? If I'm not going to be banned, you won't be able to use me at all. I'd have no meaning.[33]

The competition between the two manuscripts ends with the entry of other manuscripts and reaches its climax with the desperate outcry of the Volume of Poetry:

> Doctor, sir, please help me. I'm the mother of nineteen poems that are crying out for royalties. I'll soon be appearing in a new edition. I'll fill the house for you![34]

The scene, which goes on with the appearance of several more figures, including the audience and a theatrical agent, ends with the appearance of the Devil, who takes the theater director's burial measurements. Then he offers the director a deal: to become the most successful theater manager of all time, he has only to surrender his brain. When the director objects that he couldn't in that case fulfill his "sacred duty," the Devil replies:

> Just keep your shirt on! Who'd be upset by a trifle like that? You won't even notice it's missing. No one does. So then, just one more thing in confidence, a professional secret. I can tell you that I have the brains of most of the theater directors in my bag, and of many other successful gentlemen too. I can show you their testimonials.[35]

Apart from the humorous quality of the text, the scene is especially interesting for its structure. The parodistic framework of the Descent to Hell—a well-known topos of literature and the stage—not only makes it possible to abandon the prevailing realistic conventions, but also breaks with the primacy of the literary text by integrating pantomime and dance elements into the scene. The sometimes very detailed stage directions show that the skit was intended to have an opulent visual impact in addition to its verbal wit.

We should likewise take what Reinhardt writes to Berthold Held on August 4, 1901, concerning the furnishing of the new house, in the same sense:

> When you set up the stage, focus your attention on making it possible to change scenes in the blink of an eye, to have . . . the maximum leeway for ensemble scenes, and to shift scenes in the dark with an open curtain. The lighting should be rich in possibilities, lots of colors, and spotlights. The lighting has to replace scenery, which we are going to do without completely for the time being.[36]

Reinhardt's concept of Schall und Rauch shows us that the self-reflexivity of such theater parodies enabled him to define his theatrical interests, allowing him as a director in both senses of the word (*Regisseur*, *Direktor*) to establish a stage aesthetic that transcended the dominance of the word (and the prevailing attitudes of various schools or isms).

Thus it seems entirely consistent that the numbers format increasingly gave way to larger units. Comic songs and other short insertions had a mere side role in Schall und Rauch's programs. One-acters and excerpts from longer texts were an ever stronger component—a development that supports the thesis that Schall und Rauch was really a transitional phenomenon in Reinhardt's work—although such an interpretation risks losing sight of a basic condition of such experiments. It was precisely the open form of cabaret, which was only now becoming established, that made it possible for Reinhardt to use Schall und Rauch as a framework for testing various aesthetic approaches and developing his own point of view.

Apart from these experiments, Schall und Rauch's best-known creation, one that established its own tradition, was the introduction of the two characters Serenissimus and Kindermann.[37] Serenissimus was the prototype of the doddering, yet still authoritarian aristocrat, an unmistakable allusion to Wilhelm II and the ossified monarchical system. Kindermann functioned as his adjutant, whose basic role was to explain the things that were going on in the theater. Their first appearance, in May 1901, was in the context of a parody of Gerhart Hauptmann's *The Weavers*, but in the course of time they became one of Schall und Rauch's signature features.

Figure 6. Victor Arnold as Serenissimus. Unknown photographer. Courtesy of the Theaterwissenschaftliche Sammlung of the University of Cologne.

The two figures were not just political satire, which up to this point had played only a minor role in Schall und Rauch; they created a new level of performance that brought the audience into close contact with the stage: they became—comparable to Waldorf and Statler in the *Muppet Show*—intermediaries between stage and audience. Thus it was no rare occurrence for Serenissimus to step on stage to express his sovereign appreciation of the actors when he was pleased with a scene. He remarked, for instance, in connection with a version of *The Weavers* that had been especially watered down for him:

> Ser: Yes, well what I still wanted to say—uh—who was the play's author?—I've forgotten, uh . . .
>
> Kind: Hauptmann [the name means *captain* in English] is the author, Your Majesty.

> Ser: Ah, you don't say? Tell me, is the man still active?
>
> Kind: He is still quite robust, as far as I'm aware.
>
> Ser: Might well have become a major, such a man, don't you think? That—uh—other—uh—patriotic author, he *is* in fact a major, isn't he, Kindermann?
>
> Kind: Indeed he is, Your Majesty.
>
> Ser: Well, you might jog my memory when you get a chance, it'll set the matter in motion. Someone who can do something so fine—uh—should also—uh—*be* something fine! I'm right, don't you think—uh?[38]

Kayssler's "reworking" of *The Weavers* inverts the play's original social-critical content. Where the characters in the original text act out of dire necessity, in Kayssler's version they eat cake and oranges, and all conflicts are resolved at the conclusion by their singing the German anthem together. The show got especially high marks because Wilhelm II had canceled his loge seats at the Deutsches Theater when they staged Hauptmann's unadulterated play;[39] Serenissimus's appearance on stage thus parodies the Kaiser's attitude (which expressed itself in a continued disdain for Hauptmann) and resolves it in a satirical reconciliation.

Criticism of the Hohenzollern court was not confined to censorship guidelines; it also targeted the high-handed aesthetic of self-adulation that Wilhelm II preferred. The "unofficial court poet" Joseph von Lauff (1855–1933), the retired artillery officer alluded to in the just-cited passage, was most eager to provide such adulatory service.

Christian Morgenstern parodied this kind of genealogical drama in his small sketch "Der Laufgraf" (the name refers to a notorious 1897 play by Lauff called *Der Burggraf* [*The Burgrave*]). A character called Wulle Wulle, formerly vilified for seditious activity, returns, "ingenuous to the point of tears," as the stage direction indicates, and confesses:

> By God I'm no commander, your excellency. But here is my breast, here are my arms [*he bares both*], and in this I think as all others think—and several of them think just as I do.[40]

But despite these political and satirical references, we cannot call Schall und Rauch political cabaret in the narrower sense. Its satire was less daring and risky than it might seem. Peter Sprengel surmises that Serenissimus and Kindermann were reluctantly tolerated because no one wanted to admit that the inane and senile figure of Serenissimus could possibly resemble the Kaiser.[41] Peter Jelavich points to yet another consideration:

> In fact, monarchical institutions might even have benefited from the safety-valve effect of the Serenissimus scenes . . . Although the Serenissimus scenes were no compliment to princely houses, the general good-naturedness of the character and his endearing foolishness were a much safer option, for all parties concerned, than bitter accusations of incompetence . . . The Serenissimus scenes, like the satires on Lauff or Waldersee in the Motley Theater, proved that Berlin audiences of the Wilhelmine era enjoyed political parody, as long as it was performed in a good-natured, nonaggressive spirit.[42]

This reciprocal relationship of satire and social (and political) tolerance provided the leeway for Serenissimus and Kindermann to become a Schall und Rauch trademark. And it is proof of the vitality and flexibility of the cabaret and theater scene of the period that the two characters were not tied to specific actors or even to a specific theater. In the course of time Serenissimus and Kindermann appear on various other cabaret stages, with the proviso that Schall und Rauch be credited as their original source in the advertising.[43]

For Reinhardt and his colleagues, in contrast to Wolzogen, it was less a matter of establishing a new performance genre or "ennobling" the variety show than of simply making use of an opportunity to try out new forms. It is therefore symptomatic that Schall und Rauch renamed itself the Kleines Theater (Little Theater) as early as 1902, and that the company had almost completely abandoned the idea of cabaret.

For Reinhardt, however, it was only a temporary departure, for in 1919 he opened a new Schall und Rauch. This second incarnation, resident in the catacombs of the Grosses Schauspielhaus (Big Playhouse), took on a more pointedly political character under the influence of such authors as Kurt Tucholsky (1890–1935) and Walter Mehring (1896–1981). On the whole, it had a stronger orientation than Reinhardt's first cabaret to popular models: comic songs, set to music mostly by Friedrich Hollaender (1896–1976), and short numbers had a much bigger role, and one-acters and minidramas were gone. One of the best-known performers was Paul Graetz (1890–1937), who embodied (in this, something of a male counterpart to Claire Waldoff) a Berlin character speaking a typical vernacular. This kind of local connection was likewise associated with a stronger political perspective on the "average people." Reinhardt himself, however, took almost no part as a performer in this project.

The Place of Schall und Rauch: Its Meaning in Context (*Sitz im Leben*)

To speak about Schall und Rauch's cultural position, it is necessary first to bear its concrete spatial conditions in mind. After the success of the first shows in the "artists' house," Schall und Rauch opened its own theater bearing the name of its address: Unter den Linden 44.

The space was laid out by Peter Behrens (1868–1940) according to Kayssler's and Reinhardt's ideas. Behrens, a member of the Darmstadt artists' colony Mathildenhöhe,[44] was a guarantee of sophisticated interior design that did not simply reproduce existing examples.

Figure 7. Interior view of the Schall und Rauch.

And in fact Behrens succeeded in turning the former ballroom of the Hotel Arnim into an elegant space that was original in its design.[45] With its four hundred seats it was only half as big as Wolzogen's Buntes Theater, but its interior furnishings followed its example in its almost programmatic elegance. The aesthetics of the space, the avoidance of boxes or galleries, the allusions to Greek temple architecture, and the symbolic decoration of the walls—where small clouds of smoke were set next to various masks as a reference to the ensemble's name[46]—impressed visitors long after the first performance. One review called the room "the first artistic theater salon in Berlin."[47] This impression, in which the comparatively small and intimate size of the room certainly played a part, signaled Schall und Rauch's basic intent: the preciousness and luxuriousness of the ornamentation presented the greatest possible contrast to the *Tingeltangels* and variety shows; the orientation was rather to haut-bourgeois salon culture and its representational forms.

Matching this exquisite interior was the theater's eminently attractive location—Unter den Linden was one of Berlin's central traffic axes. The theater was situated therefore in the immediate neighborhood of the ministries and the palace of the imperial family, but also close to "official" educational and artistic institutions like the university, the Royal Playhouse (on

Gendarmenmarkt), and the Academy. Its location on this prestigious boulevard, with its proximity to busy Friedrichstrasse, clearly shows the extent to which Schall und Rauch was conceived of as a place of elegant, urbane evening entertainment that confidently placed itself at the heart of Berlin society.

On the other hand, it corresponded in type to the "façade theater," as Marvin Carlson has described this phenomenon in *Places of Performance* (1989):[48] in contrast to monumental theaters like the Royal Playhouse or the Royal Opera, it was integrated into the architectural context of the street, with only a nameplate betraying its function. It altogether lacked a lavish external design showing the kind of nuanced iconographic scheme that had become characteristic of the freestanding monumental theaters.

But whereas Carlson—with his eye on Paris—notes that many theaters established themselves in a "liminal zone" of public space, this was not true of Schall und Rauch. Quite the opposite: the remodeling of the former ceremonial rooms situated the theater at the center of the aspiring metropolis. The building type here does not signify any "concealment" of the theater or its marginalization. It is rather an expression of a rapid urbanization: theater "conquers" urban territory by bringing new use and meaning to existing spaces. In this respect, Schall und Rauch stands in a reciprocal relationship with urban growth, since such a form of entertainment is only possible in an urban context.

The location and the interior and exterior design of Schall und Rauch reflect a process of "colonizing" the city under new auspices. The newly generated urban space—repeatedly invoked by slogans like "Berlin is becoming a metropolis!" or "Berlin is becoming a cosmopolis!"—required a form of representation that made change a palpable experience for the individual. At the turn of the century the cabaret filled precisely this role. Thus we can only agree with Peter Jelavich's formulation: that cabaret had several fathers, but only the metropolis could be regarded as its "incubating and nurturing mother,"[49] although we might add that this nurturing mother could be properly reflected only in the eyes of her ward.

The upscale supercabaret concept as evinced by Wolzogen and Nelson took further form in the wave of revues that began around 1903. The revues not only adopted the variety show's numbers format, but decked it out in opulent trappings. The trailblazers of these developments were the so-called Annual Revues (*Jahresrevuen*) that took place regularly from 1903 in the Metropole Theater.[50] Here the self-dramatization of the urban lifestyle was no longer confined to the exclusive atmosphere of the salon, but was expanding into an early form of a mass medium.

In the course of 1903, the name Schall und Rauch was gradually replaced by the name Kleines Theater. This was not merely a labeling change, but the last stage of a programmatic shift, for in the final analysis the interest of those involved in Schall und Rauch was always focused on the development of an artistic theater. Thus, Reinhardt had already announced in a letter to the playwright Arthur Schnitzler (1862–1931) in August 1902 that he was now "launching a purely artistic undertaking."[51]

The shift, which had already been announced in the course of the various programs, was also an expression of a repertoire crisis. Intense competition from similar companies made it hard to keep up with the constant demand for novelties. Likewise, the limited size of a house with fewer than 400 seats forbade the extensive use of guest artists, since it would have been impossible to recover the costs.

The artistic breakthrough of the new plan of action came finally with the staging of Maxim Gorky's *The Lower Depths*, which Richard Vallentin (1874–1908) procured for Schall und Rauch in 1903. This production, which was performed over 500 times between 1903 and 1905, not only ensured the economic viability of the Kleines Theater, but also allowed Reinhardt to assume direction of the Neues Theater (New Theater) on Schiffbauerdamm. As a result, he now had two stages available for different formats.

The departure from cabaret was not seamless. Several elements remained active for a while; evidence shows that individual appearances of Serenissimus lasted into 1904, for example. But ultimately the shift that had loomed at the beginning of Reinhardt's whole enterprise—namely the quest for a new theater aesthetic—was the decisive step.

The detour through cabaret was necessary for Reinhardt and his colleagues because this new form gave them the necessary leeway for experimentation; but it also provided a framework for smaller dramatic and theatrical forms that had to find their place once the larger dramatic forms had become problematic. Cabaret not only offered aesthetic freedom in the area of satire, it could also ensure that the results were socially acceptable. It constituted a breathing space where repertoire could be performed that had little chance of seeing the light of day under the previously existing theatrical conditions.[52]

But in terms of Max Reinhardt's career, Schall und Rauch is also paradigmatic in a further sense. His "theater that will again give joy to people"[53] was not situated in the sheltered environment of subventioned art, but was deliberately introduced in the sphere of commercial or entertainment theater. The antagonism between "serious art" and the commercial "culture industry" that we are so fond of citing today appears to have had only limited validity in this instance. If anything, the dynamics of a polymorphous and closely interconnected theater culture were a virtual precondition for the development of this new theatrical model.

For cabaret as a genre the evidence is more ambiguous. It could only develop as an independent art form, marking itself off and holding its own against other art forms, when political circumstances had liberalized to such an extent that it could turn into a "real" forum of societal debate.

Chapter 2

✦

The Kammerspiele as Bourgeois Salon

On the Way to the German Theater:
"At Reinhardt's the Forest Turns at Seven-Thirty . . ."

And then came *A Midsummer Night's Dream*. And one saw a forest of genuine trees. One saw the ground covered with genuine green moss. One saw the moon, which shone with such artful perfection that the real moon could not have withstood the competition for a single night if the dear Lord, stirred by modern feeling, had entrusted Max Reinhardt with the illumination of the heavens.
—Paul Goldmann (1865–1935)

It truly was the dream of a summer night, with the forest revealing its lovely, teasing mysteries, a dream vision one could give full credence to, when Shakespeare's *Midsummer Night's Dream* crossed the stage of the New Theater.
—Ernst Heilborn (1867–1940)

The success of Gorky's *Lower Depths* in the Kleines Theater had the effect of relieving the theater company's biggest financial concerns on the one hand, but it simultaneously created a new problem on the other. In order to maximally capitalize on the success of the production, it had to be played as often as possible. But this meant that the hall was constantly in use. Thus, the success hindered the establishment of a broad repertoire, which was the only guaranteee of the company's survival in the long run. The acquisition of a second playhouse—expansion as flight forward—not only provided new aesthetic possibilities, it was also a matter of yielding to necessity.

In February 1903 Reinhardt acquired the Neues Theater on Schiffbauerdamm. Only a few yards from the Kleines Theater, it had opened in 1892 at an important traffic hub close to Friedrichstrasse and across from the train station of the same name. With its approximately 800 seats it could accommodate twice as many patrons as the Kleines Theater.[1]

Although the first productions there met with a uniformly positive reception, the major success the company so urgently needed eluded them for the time being. Inspired by the large space, Reinhardt turned to the classical repertoire with plays like Lessing's *Minna von Barhelm* and Shakespeare's *The Merry Wives of Windsor*.

The breakthrough, which ensured Reinhardt's personal future as a director as well as the economic future of his own theater company, came on January 31, 1905, with the premiere of Shakespeare's *A Midsummer Night's Dream*. Eduard von Winterstein (1871–1961) estimates that this production, which was repeatedly revived in altered form during the following years, had approximately 5,000–6,000 performances.[2]

Figure 8. Set model by Ernst Stern for Reinhardt's 1913 production of *A Midsummer Night's Dream*—also using the revolving stage. Courtesy of the Theaterwissenschaftliche Sammlung of the University of Cologne.

The audience was as overwhelmed by the opulence of the scenic design as by the direction of the actors and extras. Reinhardt used every means at his disposal to create the impression of a supernatural fairy world.

> Every creative effect the modern visual arts can wring from the mystery of a forest was employed in this production. Likewise everything

the stage has to offer in terms of scenic resources. Extravagant richness, but subordinated to the imperative of harmonic color.[3]

Another critic commented:

The scenography surpassed everything we have previously seen in Berlin. The elf-haunted forest, which of course consisted of artificial trees and a convincing imitation of a mossy green forest floor, presented images of captivating beauty. The wedding procession too, which was led by torchbearers into an amphitheater of white marble benches, was a masterpiece of staging.[4]

And finally, the effusive praise of Friedrich Düsel: "*A Midsummer Night's Dream* is one of the most beautiful things the German stage has ever seen."[5]

The key element in the mise-en-scène was the three-dimensional rendering of the forest, which created a mysterious, almost mythical space. This was a clear departure from the tradition of painted forest backdrops.[6] Winterstein, one of Reinhardt's actors, describes the scenography in his memoirs:

It was a genuine forest the audience saw when the curtain rose. Indeed, to make the illusion complete, great clouds of forest scent were sprayed onto the stage and soon spread through the whole auditorium. The fairies—no longer dressed in the obligatory bast skirts, but slim, half-naked girls covered only with green veils—holding hands and winding their way up, down, around, and through the trees to the sonorities of the Mendelssohn Scherzo—what an intoxicating spectacle this was! Bulbs bobbing and dangling from invisible strings created the illusion of fireflies, and a spotlight cast the reflection of moonlight on the foliage. In the background, part of the stage floor, perhaps 4 square meters in size, had been replaced by thick panes of glass that were lit from below, and the light struck the fairies dancing on the surface of this small lake in the likewise artificially simulated mists.[7]

But the biggest sensation was the installment of a revolving stage,[8] its first use in Berlin, and not just as a way of expediting the change of scenery, but as a dramatic resource that reinforced the whole atmosphere of the production.

For a split second it seems like a high-spirited coup de main when the whole forest construction with its foliage and pond, with Bottom, Titania, and her fairies, begins to turn before our eyes with the aid of a soundlessly functioning revolving stage. But why shouldn't the millwheel going round in dear Bottom's foolish head and the end of his dream be suggested by such radical symbolism?[9]

Even Paul Goldmann's polemic makes us feel the sensational effect of this presentation:

> At a prearranged moment the trees, the moss floor, and the pond start to rotate. The whole stage moves in a circle. Only the auditorium remains stationary; but Max Reinhardt's technicians will surely find a way to make this rotate too, thus enabling the audience, in an unprecedentedly modern blend of aesthetic delights, to combine the dramatic sensations with those of riding a carousel.[10]

Indeed, not only did Reinhardt's staging create the strikingly realistic illusion of a forest that was strengthened by all the senses, but he simultaneously emphasized the dreamlike quality of this scenic imagery by having the stage rotate before the audience's eyes. The fairy-world scenery did not just present a dreamlike tableau; the revolving of the stage made something dreamlike of the audience's own perception. The forest that danced before their eyes transformed the spectators into dreamers themselves.[11]

Figure 9. Dancing fairies in Reinhardt's *A Midsummer Night's Dream* (Berlin, 1905). Photographer unknown. Courtesy of the Theaterwissenschaftliche Sammlung of the University of Cologne.

The terms of conventional theater criticism were inadequate for grasping such a stage aesthetic, as a glance at the reviews readily indicates. Typical of this lack of comprehension is the constantly repeated lament that the quality

The Kammerspiele as Bourgeois Salon

of the actors—measured by their ability to speak the verses in a declamatory tone—was not up to par.[12]

An exception in this regard was Gertrud Eysoldt's (1870–1955) interpretation of Puck, which polarized criticism and had the most lasting effect in its defiance of the prevailing conventions:

> The strongest clash of opinions will be over Gertrud Eysoldt's Puck, so new, bold, and independent was her performance. This actor emphasizes, far more than anyone previously, the elemental, the earthy, rough, and ungainly quality of this elfin creature. She gives more of a troll than a playful pixie, and in so doing certainly comes closer to the Shakespearean conception than the others whose . . . decorous smiles contrast with the wanton neighing that the primitive nature and the task of this forest sprite demand.[13]

Figure 10. Gertrud Eysoldt as Puck. Photograph by Hans Ludwig Böhm. Courtesy of the Theaterwissenschaftliche Sammlung of the University of Cologne.

Gertrud Prellwitz also made this distinction in her appreciative review:

> This is no prankish little elf dancing before us in a ballet costume, but a cavorting faun, ugly, malicious, and good-natured at once, who takes coarse delight in practical jokes and confusion and is completely ruthless in the way he inflicts the direst pains on his comically bewildered victims, to the accompaniment of a jubilant "ho-ho-ho-ho."[14]

This "elemental" interpretation of Puck was not just a matter of costume, which no longer broadcast a "cherubic cuteness"; his "shagginess" and earthiness reminded people of a "Böcklinesque troll."[15] Maximilian Harden emphatically defended this reading of the role:

> For Puck is neither a wise Prospero's well-brought-up servant nor a perfumed, silk-dressed page loitering in palace chambers. No, this Robin Goodfellow is a sturdy bloke and the more sophisticated fairy-folk find him an awkward companion. He has a thousand pranks in his roguish brain: he gleefully pinches the nodding gossip awake from her beery nap, coaxes the tired traveler into a thicket, and rolls in raptures on the moss-cushioned ground when he successfully lures the stallion from an oat-filled manger by neighing like a mare in heat.[16]

With this interpretation of Puck, the play becomes a fanciful lesson on sensuality, sexuality, and their (supposed) civilized repression.

> In our laughter we understood the immutable philosophy of eros and were ready to number Puck among the sages of the world. For with the neighing that forces the stallion to choose between oats and mare he teaches us, in animal simile, to suspect what we shortly thereafter see in the higher realm of our volition: how fundamentally foolish it is in this world of instincts to proudly insist on the conscious awareness of homo sapiens.[17]

The critics who rejected Eysoldt's interpretation did so not just because it broke with tradition and disappointed their expectations; the spectrum of Eysoldt's past roles (Salome, Electra, Lulu)[18] cast an even longer shadow over its reception:[19] "The role of Puck was entrusted to the specialist in the female figures of Hofmannsthal and Wedekind, and she made a perverse street brat out of the sweetest elf that ever glided across the stage."[20] And in another review we read: "Strangely too, they had Puck played by Frau Eysoldt, the actress of perverse female roles, who made the elf into an ugly forest troll lacking all poetry, though his clownish pranks found favor with the audience."[21]

But what exercised the critics more even than Eysoldt's Puck was the question of whether the "creative mood of the performance,"[22] which was essentially generated by its scenography, suppressed the "spirit of the poetry" with mere extraneities. Theodor Müller-Fürer polemicized against the staging:

> Now that the manufacture of theater decorations has made use of every aid that capital, technology, and art can provide and become a respectable branch of industry in its own right, one can demand that it construct a lifelike forest on the stage: a group of trees with convincing branches and leaves; a mossy forest floor; small, gleaming woodland ponds reflecting the moon; reeds on their shores; fireflies in the trees and grasses. The foliage must rustle in the wind, the branch on which the faun plays his reed-pipe must crackle as he jumps down from it, and the very scent of the forest—though mixed with the odor of rubber from the tubes that dispense the steamy mists—must pour into the auditorium. All this Hugo Baruch & Co. can deliver to order in a reasonable period of time.[23]

Goldmann too resisted the opulence of the scenography:

> So there were all sorts of things to see in this staging of *Midsummer Night's Dream*, except for *Midsummer Night's Dream*. Instead of Shakespeare's poetry, genuine trees appeared on stage; instead of the poet it was the pretentious director who pushed himself to the fore; instead of the *Midsummer Night's Dream* of William Shakespeare, it was the *Midsummer Night's Dream* of Max Reinhardt that was performed.[24]

This criticism foreshadowed one of the symptomatic controversies of twentieth-century theater: the role and agency of the director. Although Reinhardt appears as rather tame in comparison with the later representatives of *Regietheater* (director's theater), the arguments remained more or less the same—fighting for the primacy of drama over performance. But just as interesting as Reinhardt's critics are his defenders: Ernst Heilborn, for example, compares his production with the stage conventions of Elizabethan theater, where the audience for the most part had to create the scenery in their imaginations.

Heilborn's conclusion is noteworthy because it ranks Reinhardt's theater praxis highly in its early twentieth-century context:

> But we are far from being an ideal audience; as overburdened inhabitants of a large urban capital, we lack imagination, and our actors speak verse as if they were reading from picture postcards. Shakespeare's staged poems have remained the same in the centuries since their creation, but the audience has changed, and changed completely. I therefore think it is appropriate for a director to hand us the glasses

we can no longer see without, appropriate to indulge our sense of color in order to open up a dreamworld in which people of the 16th century were at home without such stimulation, appropriate to consciously assist our poor, abused powers of imagination.[25]

If we accept Heilborn's analysis, Reinhardt's opulent theater created a space in which fantasy, the "dream of a summer night," could find its place in the context of a radically modernizing metropolis. His theater—and here we see that the scope of its resources clearly surpassed the possibilities of the Kleines Theater—opened up a collective realm of the imagination that was, by intent, no longer subordinated to the primacy of literature, but rather offered an aesthetic-theatrical experience sui generis.

In this sense, Reinhardt's staging of *A Midsummer Night's Dream* also defined in outline his whole theatrical project: it is no accident that he devotes himself chiefly to classical texts; on the contrary, he deliberately subjects them to a rereading, investing them with images and forms that, though not necessarily in their actual appearance, but in their conditions and possibilities, correspond to a modernizing way of life (*Lebenswelt*).

Ghosts (1906): Genealogy of a Performance

> Whoever fails to jubilate here falsifies the impression that has been made on him, if he has any feeling for art at all. I at least have never and nowhere felt a like impression in myself or observed the like in an audience . . . Criticism that measures the achieved by the achievable has nothing even to measure. It can only seek to trace the secret of this powerful impression.
> —Jacobsohn 1910b, 29

When Adolphe L'Arronge decided in 1905 to relinquish the direction of the Deutsches Theater to Max Reinhardt—and even to sell it to him in the medium term—he set the condition that Reinhardt had to give up all other theaters and devote himself to the Deutsches Theater alone.[26]

Reinhardt accepted, although only with the proviso that he be allowed to add a second venue. For this the architect William Müller (1874–1913) rebuilt the dance hall Emberg's Salon into the Kammerspiele (Chamber Playhouse) of the Deutsches Theater, which Reinhardt inaugurated at the beginning of his second season on November 8, 1906, with his production of Ibsen's *Ghosts*.

This production can be regarded as Reinhardt's theater-aesthetic manifesto as well as an attempt to define the cultural position of his theaters. By deciding on Ibsen's *Ghosts*, Reinhardt placed his work at the now-expanded Deutsches Theater in the genealogical line of this play's productions in Berlin since the 1880s. Beyond this, the success of Reinhardt's version marked a new stage in the development of bourgeois theater, one that can only be understood when viewed in its historical context.

The Norwegian dramatist Henrik Ibsen (1828–1906) is securely placed among the most important dramatists of the late nineteenth century. His best-known dramas, like *A Doll's House* (1879) and *Ghosts* (1881), form a canon of critical self-reflection on bourgeois society. Ibsen, who was a model for many German-speaking writers of the Naturalist movement, marked a turning point within bourgeois literature. Whereas the bourgeoisie's (still limited) social ascent and the changes it was slowly bringing about in the social structure (which would come to full bloom only after the French Revolution and not until the Weimar period in Germany) gave rise to a positive image of itself and its characteristic ethos in the literature of the eighteenth century, Ibsen's texts focus predominantly on the inner compulsions and aporias of bourgeois society.

The plot of *Ghosts* is quickly summarized. The drama takes place in the country house of the Alving family, where Captain Alving's widow is staying in order to dedicate an orphanage that she has endowed in her husband's name ten years after his death. Also there are her son Oswald, Pastor Manders, the carpenter Engstrand, and the latter's daughter Regina. In the course of the dialogue, it comes out that Helena Alving had once sought refuge from her alcoholic husband with Pastor Manders, a friend of her youth, who sent her back to her husband with an appeal to bourgeois morality. At that same time the husband had an affair, which produced a little girl—Regina—but this was hushed up when Engstrand (in return for money) accepted her as his own daughter. Mrs. Alving sees the endowment of the orphanage as a way of freeing herself from the shadow of her marriage.

Oswald, who has returned from Paris, tells of a different attitude to life, one centered not on the idea of fulfillment of duty, but on the opposite values of confidence and joie de vivre. In the second act, Mrs. Alving discovers that her son suffers from a disease that can be traced to her husband's debaucheries, which she has always sought to conceal. In addition, Oswald's desired marriage with Regina, which he sees as a positive prospect for his life, is impossible on the grounds of incest. At the end of the play the orphanage is burnt down, all the characters except Mrs. Alving and Oswald depart, and Oswald's disease breaks out in full—the drama ends in his death agony. The rising sun, symbol of a new beginning, remains an unreachable goal.

Ghosts is sometimes compared to *A Doll's House*. Certainly the parallels are pronounced, but so are the differences. Human relationships, especially marriage, seem to be plagued by lies and secrets. The discrepancy between appearance and inner disposition is inscribed in the characters themselves. Whereas Nora of *A Doll's House* diligently tries to fulfill the clichéd image her husband has of her (corporeally symbolized by the tarantella dance), Mrs. Alving would like to lend permanence to the public image of her husband, which is ultimately based on her personal renunciation, through the founding of the orphanage.

The dynamic of Ibsen's plays arises less from the inner motivations of the characters than from the eruption of their inner contradictions and those of the relationships in which they live. Here we note a distinct difference between *A Doll's House* and *Ghosts*. When Nora leaves her husband and family at the end of that play, we see it as an act of emancipation. *Ghosts* demonstrates the inverse variation: Manders thwarted Mrs. Alving's attempt to break out and sent her back to the hopelessness of her marriage. The rising sun at the end of the play is at odds with the dying characters—dying understood either as a physical reality or as an expression of the aporia of their situation.

One of the special characteristics of Ibsen's plays is that they show characters who occupy clearly defined social roles. Thus it is no accident that women are the central figures of the two dramas we are comparing. Ibsen thematizes the marginal position of women in the bourgeois social order of the late nineteenth century in order to dramatize the muddled state of social conditions. Precisely those figures who are primarily objects, if not victims, of the societal logic allow us to see its destructive mechanisms. Dieter Kafitz interprets each act's conclusion in keeping with this logic:

> The progress of Mrs. Alving's awareness, which gives the drama its dynamic tension, is sharply reflected in the symbolism of each act's conclusion: the noises coming from the side room at the end of the first act symbolize the "ghosts" of the past reaching into the present; the orphanage fire illuminating the window at the end of the second act signals the dissolution of the bonds of convention and simultaneously foreshadows the sunrise at the end of the final act, which may appear cynical if taken with reference to the outbreak of Oswald's disease, but, with regard to the main character, signals her final breakthrough to clarity of recognition.[27]

But it is also important to note here a decisive shift in drama as a genre. The play's structure is based not on a successive, progressive logic that is directed at a definite conclusion, but rather on dialogue and plot lines that culminate in the unveiling of the characters' past. The past is what determines the characters' lives. The clearest example of this is surely Oswald, whose physical and social existence is defined not just by his own, but much more by his father's past.

The title *Ghosts* (a more literal translation would be *Revenants*, German *Wiedergänger*) reveals a special programmatic dimension in this context. The fundamental issue of the text is an unredeemed past that determines the characters' present to such an extent that they have no other ways of acting. This lack of alternatives takes on a social-critical dimension in the context of the play, since the alternative of dissolving the marriage with Alving was thwarted by Manders. The latter's self-interpretation of his attitude as a great moral achievement is so undercut by the catastrophe of the characters' lives that the very system of such morality is called into question.

But for all his criticism of such hopelessness, it is nevertheless clear that Ibsen remained bound to the structures of bourgeois society:

> Though a sharp critic of bourgeois society, Ibsen nevertheless derives his value criteria from liberal-bourgeois enlightenment thought. He rejects any social upheaval that would set the collective in the place of the failing individual, and places his hopes in a "revolution of the human spirit" based on individualism.[28]

Thus it is hardly surprising that the play's utopian potential is in keeping with bourgeois values: "The positive kernel that springs from the husk of his social-critical dramas is the free spirit he fails to find in the social reality of his time."[29] Any improvement of the situation is only thinkable as an improvement of bourgeois conditions whose fundamental character (and historical dominance) remains ultimately untouched. Any "hereafter" to bourgeois society appears unthinkable.

This frame of reference establishes a new, unspoken version of the Aristotelian "estates clause" (which maintains a strict separation between the "better" personages and more serious concerns of tragedy and the "worse" personages and more trivial concerns of comedy). Ibsen's characters come by and large from the upper levels of the bourgeoisie, and social problems such as those created by industrialization—which play an important role in the works of German Naturalist authors—surface only peripherally in these texts.

The fact that the play's performance genealogy began in 1882 with its debut in Chicago is not simply the result of a liberal theater politics in the United States; it also exemplifies a long and intensive engagement with Ibsen in American literature. But it would be a whole other subject (out of place here, unfortunately) to study the development of a critical bourgeois intellectual culture in the United States that was oriented to the European models of the late nineteenth and early twentieth centuries.

The play's genealogy of performances in the German-speaking world began in 1886 with a production in Augsburg—another performance of the play by the Meiningen Ensemble that same year in Berlin was banned by the police. On January 9, 1887, there was a private performance at the Residenztheater.[30] This production triggered a sustained discussion of Ibsen's dramatic works that was still very much current in 1889 when the association called Freie Bühne (Free Stage)[31] began its operations with another production of *Ghosts*.

The programmatic intent behind the choice of this play, which had become synonymous with social-critical literature, is unmistakable and was correspondingly remarked on by most of the reviewers. Thus, for example, Isidor Landau, who was more than skeptical about the drama in the first place, wrote: "The choice of *Ghosts* could not fail to be interpreted programmatically, could only be a way of saying that the new production intended to connect with an older attempt with the same orientation."³² Landau expressly connects his description of the evening's success with the discourse that arose around the earlier staging of the text: "The earlier, serious objections to the overly crass drama of inherited disease condensed into a loud hissing this time too. But the real signature of the day remains its glowing success."³³

It is typical of the discourse surrounding Naturalist drama in the broadest sense that Landau denies the theme's "suitability for art":

> The drama of inherited softening of the brain can seize, arrest, and torture its audience, but it cannot achieve a single aesthetic purpose! . . . If Ibsen becomes the model, it may very well be our experience that people without his wealth of ideas, without his creative power, will be regarded as great writers if they bring cholera or delirium tremens to the stage.³⁴

This prejudice influenced the public's attitude in the years ahead—an attitude that seemed more appropriate to the anatomical than to the bourgeois theater. One contemporary caricature makes this appraisal especially pointed: in the cartoon, Liberated Woman and Heredity (which has lapsed into drunkenness and degeneration) serve as freestanding sculptures over the pediment of the Naturalist theater. But the bourgeois patron—if he does not immediately vomit—flees holding his nose.

Figure 11. Caricature of the Freie Bühne by an unknown artist. Published in the *Kladderadatsch* 43, no. 17, 1890.

With respect to Reinhardt's production of 1906, however, the genealogy takes on special meaning when we bear in mind that, though the inaugural production of *Ghosts* at the Freie Bühne in 1889 had been officially directed by Hans Meery, it was Otto Brahm who provided the decisive interpretation of the play. But Brahm, who would later put on *Ghosts* at the Deutsches Theater, with Reinhardt as actor, was fired because L'Arronge had no confidence in the sustained success of his programmatic Naturalism. Reinhardt had been accused by many as being responsible for L'Arronge's unexpected decision, and his taking on of *Ghosts* was considered to be a continued form of patricide.

Reinhardt's production responded to this genealogy: just as a production of *Ghosts* marked the beginning of Brahm's Berlin theater career, so Reinhardt staged the same play at the beginning of his activity at the Deutsches Theater, which had now become as large as he wanted with the opening of a second theater, the Kammerspiele (Chamber Playhouse).

At first glance, it seems ironic that Reinhardt would choose the centerpiece of the very aesthetic movement that had thwarted Brahm's success at the Deutsches Theater, but on second glance, the irony of the choice reveals the production's significance. Deliberately choosing to take on the "ghosts" of theater history allowed Reinhardt, who was widely celebrated as their vanquisher, to introduce the contours of his own theatrical concept.

At the heart of the production of *Ghosts* stood Reinhardt's collaboration with the painter Edvard Munch (1863–1944), who designed the set.[35] Contrary to his usual practice, Reinhardt did not require Munch to come up with precise designs, but merely asked for sketches as a "stimulus to the mise-en-scène."[36]

This already suggests the first break with tradition. Reinhardt was no longer aiming at the ideal of the most authentically realistic representation possible; for him realistic concerns were subordinate to the total visual impression. A letter to Munch in which he relates his interpretation of the play directly to the latter's sketches indicates this strategy:

> I firmly believe that with your help we can so attune characters and scenery to each other, and so set them off from each other, that we will illuminate still hidden depths of this sublime work and do an altogether respectable piece of work. Till now the German stage has put the spotlight on a more or less successful clinical study of insanity and left everything else in the shadows. The reverse is the right approach in my judgment.[37]

This passage shows how much of an effort Reinhardt was making to develop a new, independent approach to Ibsen's drama, and that in doing so he gave full consideration to its performance and interpretation history. He was not trying for a strictly realistic "study of insanity." It is typical of Reinhardt that he chose what many would have regarded as the circuitous route of spatial and scenographic matters to bring the hidden nuances of the text to light.

Another passage from the same letter emphasizes the extent to which space in this instance was always understood as the characters' inner space:

> To the rear perhaps two stairs lead to the raised conservatory, whose rear wall consists completely of floor-to-ceiling glass windows affording a view of the landscape. This landscape visible from the rear windows is the soul of the space, so to speak; it changes accordingly and substantially influences the mood within.[38]

He then goes on to explain the landscape images in the individual acts. Thus, concerning the "soul of the space" in the third act, he writes: "At the very end, full, cold, desolate sunlight from the rear, so that the piece ends with a grand finale like a symphony."[39]

Reinhardt structures theater's many different sign systems from the very beginning as an aesthetic whole. The theatrical space is less the characters' *Lebenswelt* than the objective correlative of their inner state. Munch for his part supported this vision by making the figures in his sketches partially blend into one another, or by making the border between them and their external environment fluid.

The theater scholar Carl Niessen relates this stage design to the drafts of the Meiningen Ensemble:

> It would be interesting to compare this complete rejection of Meiningen-like tangibilities with the sketch Duke Georg II made when Ibsen answered with the description of a Norwegian landscape . . . As Munch saw it, the stage design should be no more than a psychic suggestion, a thickening of tragic fog.[40]

Heinz Herald, in his study of Reinhardt, used the term "atmosphere" in an attempt to express this detailed working out of the theatrical space that weaves literary text, light, scenography, mood, and actors' bodies into a unified texture.

> This is why the the metaphor of a play's atmosphere is so felicitous. It conveys the impression that the play's "air" is the first thing the director comes up with in a stage production; everything else slowly grows out of this, takes on concrete shapes: but it never denies its origin, the fundamental mood from which it all arises . . . We have the feeling that a person entering from another world—from our street, for example—would suffocate; that the people in the play gradually develop other lungs to make them capable of breathing this air, which likewise gradually transforms them into completely different beings.[41]

The reviews constantly emphasize—as with Reinhardt's other productions—the significance of this atmosphere as a structuring principle and fundamental compositional element. In terms of a semiotic analysis, we would speak of a close meshing of different sign systems that depend less on an external principle like realistic imitation than on a system of internal correspondences and oppositions.

Thus, for instance, we can describe Reinhardt's sophisticated color system as an important vehicle of such structural elements. The correspondences between costumes and elements of stage design—or, as he suggested in the letter to Munch, the agreement between background landscape, lighting, objects on stage, and dramaturgical baseline—fuse together into an overall structure.

Erika Fischer-Lichte, who goes into a detailed discussion of the concept of atmosphere in Reinhardt's aesthetic, explains:

> Atmosphere belongs neither to the objects or persons who seem to radiate it, nor to those who enter the space and sense it physically. In a theater space, atmosphere is usually the first element to seize the spectator and open him to a particular experience of that very space.[42]

This concept informs Reinhardt's rereading of Ibsen's text. With the creation of a general atmosphere that owes much of its inspiration to Munch's sketches, the play loses its "documentary" character and Oswald's disease becomes more of a metaphor. Thus Reinhardt makes a shift that reverses the direction of the turn Ibsen himself had made: if the author uses the title as a metaphor for the cross-generational disease,[43] Reinhardt explicitly refers to the uncanniness that resonates in the metaphor and allows it to become visible on stage.

This aestheticization, however, blunts the play's social-critical point: societal relationships are pushed into the background by being embedded in such a dominant aesthetic context. The criticism of social problems takes a back seat to a new interiority. Siegfried Jacobsohn emphasizes this change in the understanding of the drama:

> Brahm remained bleak out of pure objectivity . . . The drama of rebellion had long been overtaken by the drama of resignation . . . *Ghosts*' tendentiousness has reformed our ethics; it has passed over into our flesh and blood; we have utterly exhausted it; it has done its duty; it can go. Ibsen's humanity remains perpetually young. To have brought it to light in all its purity is the progress, the deed, and the unspeakable beauty of this production. This new vision of *Ghosts* has so utterly brought Reinhardt's genius to artistic life that next to it his most worthy achievements become slighter.[44]

Even if we bracket Jacobsohn's enthusiasm, it is still striking how completely the perception has changed. Where Isidor Landau still feared that Ibsen's example might drive the idea of beauty from the stage, Jacobsohn now celebrates Reinhardt's production as a victory of "unspeakable beauty." This is also how we should understand the fact that Heinrich Stümcke concludes his review with a reference to the play's controversial performance history: "It is oddly touching to remember that twenty years ago the performance of *Ghosts* was a venture made as difficult as possible by police officials."[45] Reinhardt's production seems to have broken through the scandal of the text. Its thoroughgoing aestheticism, the subordination of all elements to the dominant principle of atmosphere, which derives from the visual and painterly rather than the linguistic domain, made possible a reception of the text that resisted immediate reference to social and temporal conditions.

With this in mind, we may reread Herald's above-quoted characterization of atmosphere in a new light, for it makes two assertions. On the one hand, he refers to the inner harmony the atmosphere produces, but on the other—and the image of suffocation speaks clearly here—the atmosphere seems to mark the theatrical space off from the audience's daily world. Reinhardt utilizes this possibility in his staging of *Ghosts* to develop a new interpretation of the text, one that shifts it from a sociopolitical to an aesthetic discourse.

With this production, Reinhardt did not simply take a counter-approach to the play's previous production genealogy; he rather placed himself in a complex interdependent relationship to it in a way the audience could easily recognize. The production is related to Brahm's work in several places,[46] and even Reinhardt's casting had a number of oblique theater-historical references.

Reinhardt himself played the carpenter Engstrand in his own production, the same role he had played in 1900 under Brahm. But an even clearer reference to the play's performance genealogy appears in the casting of Agnes Sorma (1865–1927) as Mrs. Alving[47]—she had played Regina in the 1889 production at the Freie Bühne. Sorma by herself virtually embodied the genealogical continuity of the Deutsches Theater. She had begun under L'Arronge, was then engaged there for a long time under Brahm, and was now continuing her work under the "new" landlord in a new set of roles.[48] Here is Jacobsohn again:

> Everything fades: Bertens is a Cinderella, Dumont a mob orator, Butze a housekeeper, Hennings a salonière, Bleibtreu a heroine. Here first we have the full tragedy. What a mistake it is to take Mrs. Alving as so much of an intellectual that she could have written the revolutionary tracts herself, whereas they have only made her aware of what was lying muffled within her. She does have both brain and spirit. But her brain sits in her heart, and her spirit in her instinct. Magnificent how effortlessly and exhaustively Sorma gets that right.[49]

Jacobsohn attributes an evolutionary logic to the performance genealogy—something we find in other critics too to some extent—when he adds in another passage that a Regina as Sorma played the role in Brahm's production would have been disastrous here.[50] This perspective, which sees in Reinhardt a fulfillment—rather than a mere continuation—of the theater reform project initiated by Brahm, is also shared by Heinrich Stümcke:

> If the performance of *Ghosts* in the Residenztheater on that memorable 9th of January, 1887, stands as a milestone, the present one can be considered a capstone, for all the conditions necessary to show precisely this work of the great Norwegian to full effect seem to have been completely fulfilled in this production.[51]

This analysis gives voice to the same evolutionary logic Reinhardt's champions used when they vaunted him as the "vanquisher" or "fulfiller" of a theater history that had hitherto remained merely fragmentary. But the complex intertwining of genealogical threads makes it obvious that even the innovations of his aesthetic can only be recognized in a dialectical relationship with its predecesors.

Kammerspiele (1): Questions of Space

Yet Max Reinhardt's production of *Ghosts* was not just his "response" to the ghosts of Berlin's theater history. Above all it marked the beginning of his new activity at the Deutsches Theater with both of its components: the big house and the new Kammerspiele. Only when he had both stages at his disposal did he have the opportunity to implement his program of a differentiated theatrical and spatial aesthetic.

The basic features of the rebuilding[52] were already foreshadowed by the new home of Schall und Rauch, later the Kleines Theater. Reinhardt attached the greatest importance to plush decor and an appealing, intimate setting. With 346 seats (as of 1906), the Kammerspiele's new theater space was even smaller than the Kleines Theater, which had 366.

The elegant furnishings of the Kammerspiele were also singled out for praise by the reviewers. Thus in the *Norddeutsche Allgemeine Zeitung* we read:

> The architect William Müller . . . has subjected the ramshackle building to a fairy-tale transformation. From a ballroom for those who were not always of the best society has arisen a theater interior which in its cohesion and genteel simplicity seems to offer the best guarantee of an aura that will continue to bind both stage and audience. The red seats (the comfort of which might be somewhat dangerous for the

phlegmatic spectator), the auburn mahogany wainscoting covering the walls, a neutral ceiling whose sole decorative feature is a crystal crown—all this makes a ceremonious, if somewhat stiff impression.[53]

Looking at a cross-section of the building, we are struck by the fact that besides the actual theatrical spaces, there is a set of adjacent rooms intended for social occasions. One of the latter was fitted out by Munch with the so-called Frieze of Life (also called the Reinhardt frieze). According to legend at least, the frieze owed its existence to the attempt to win Munch over to do the scenery for *Ghosts*. Munch was not interested in designing the set unless the commission included the creation of an exclusive, modern decor for the entire building on the highest artistic level.

The rear of the foyer opened into a small elliptical room whose wainscoting echoed the decor of the auditorium. In the middle of the room stood the Ibsen bust by Max Kruse (1854–1942)—a remarkable commentary, considering that his Nietzsche bust stood in Wolzogen's Buntes Theater. But a glance at the repertoire shows clearly that this was less of a programmatic statement than a gesture: "Nor would the Kammerspiele become an Ibsen stage, despite the opening performance and the bust."[54]

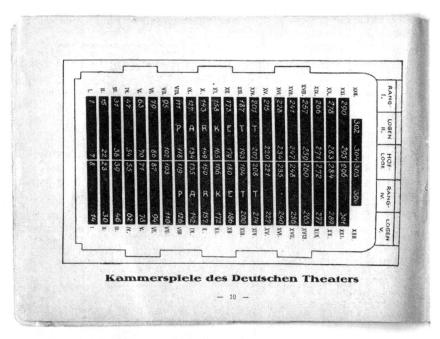

Figure 12. Seating plan of the Kammerspiele.

The Kammerspiele as Bourgeois Salon

Just as with Schall und Rauch, the interior furnishings recalled conventional theater spaces only in their basic spatial layout, not in their actual design, as Maximilian Harden explains: "Hardly anything here recalls theater style. No stucco, no galleries, no bright footlights. A room that holds three hundred people; the stage right in front of them, at hardly a remove ... It's practically a salon."[55] Harden's reference to a salon—the epitome of bourgeois culture—seems more than casual. The interior furnishings and the new name for the theater rather support the connection. Reinhardt's pricing policy, designed to preserve exclusivity, belongs in the same category. Entry to the first performance cost 20 marks, and formal attire was also required. And even though he had to lower the prices considerably as early as 1907, the Kammerspiele still remained relatively expensive in comparison with the Deutsches Theater. In 1906 the most expensive ticket for the Deutsches Theater cost 8 marks 20, while the first rows in the Kammerspiele cost 15 marks. In other words, even after the drop in price, this theater offered a comparatively costly and exclusive enjoyment.

Figure 13. One of the luxurious foyers of the Kammerspiele. Photographer unknown. Courtesy of the Theaterwissenschaftliche Sammlung of the University of Cologne.

Alfred Kerr was critical of this:

> I can't decide whether by requiring formal attire Reinhardt was pursuing a secondary aim that after all is not indissolubly connected to art . . . All Berliners, who may know nothing otherwise, are enchanted by the imposed "must do" and never ask to what extent the twenty marks amount to a speculation on what Ibsen sometimes calls the appeal of the repellent.[56]

The exclusivity of the Kammerspiele did in fact generate the "secondary aim" of giving this public space the veneer of a private salon, as the actress Tilla Durieux (1880–1971) reports in her memoir:

> The evening was celebrated with great pomp and circumstance; the red velvet seats supported bejeweled ladies in full evening dress and men in coat and tails. It was like a gathering in a private house. The Berlin cognoscenti all knew each other and missed no opportunity to look around and be seen.[57]

This impression of a private salon may—despite Kerr's insinuation—be regarded as a central element, perhaps not of the art, but of the cultural function of this theater. The tradition of salon culture for which Berlin was so renowned at the beginning of the nineteenth century could not be maintained under the pressure of an urbanization that was restructuring the social environment. Too many participants, too much change, prevented the kind of exchange that required a fluid transition between the bourgeois public and the private sphere.[58]

Reinhardt responded to this loss by deliberately placing his theater in this half-public sphere, and thereby providing a stage for bourgeois self-presentation whose habitus pointedly evoked the elegant style of the high bourgeois way of life. Of course, this concept also altered the way theater was experienced, as Maximilian Harden explains: "Unless you sit too far back you can see the quivering of nostrils and cheek muscles. You sometimes have the uncomfortable feeling of committing an indiscretion."[59] Harry Graf Kessler (1868–1937) confirms this impression in his diary when he reports that the actors were profoundly irritated by the reserve of the audience's reactions:

> The audience completely silent again, no applause. The actors are in despair over it; but the truth is, people feel like they're in a salon, not a bad atmosphere for introducing touchy subjects or something very new without scandal. People know their neighbors and so are reluctant to be demonstrative.[60]

This proximity was architecturally buttressed by a small set of stairs that connected the auditorium to the stage. Reinhardt had already developed this idea in 1901 for the layout of Schall und Rauch, as he explains in a letter to Berthold Held: "As I see it, it is *absolutely* necessary to have a set of stairs from the stage to the audience. We can use this to good advantage and it enhances the intimacy. Maybe a few steps on either side, which you can make allowance for in the sketch."[61]

Figure 14. Facade of the Kammerspiele. Photographer unknown. Courtesy of the Theaterwissenschaftliche Sammlung of the University of Cologne.

But here the difference between Schall und Rauch and the Kammerspiele becomes especially clear again. From its very start cabaret thrived on the permeability of the boundary between audience and stage, even if Schall und Rauch used it only sparingly. One thing that remained, at least theoretically, of the old smoke- and pub-theater tradition was the idea of a common taproom where the assigned roles of player and spectator were only provisional. In the Kammerspiele, however, the two were clearly separated. No suspension of the boundary was ever contemplated: it would have gone against the whole aesthetic program. Marianne Streisand has dealt with this phenomenon in her study *Intimität* (2001; *Intimacy*) and come to the following conclusion:

> But in fact the symbolic stairs between players and spectators in the Kammerspiele were more of a paradox. An ideal and real communion of all participants in the aesthetic experience was clearly intended. But the whole architectural configuration of the interior was functionally targeted at nothing less than shutting the audience out as much as possible during the performance, assigning it an "absent present" role . . . The stairs did not signify that the audience was to use them to participate actively in the events on stage.[62]

But this paradox poses the question of how the boundary line was drawn. One possible answer lies in the already cited passage from Heinz Herald:

> We have the feeling that a person entering from another world—from our street, for example—would suffocate. That the people in the play gradually develop other lungs to make them capable of breathing this air, which likewise gradually transforms them into completely different beings.[63]

The concept of "atmosphere" explains the special relationship between actors and audience in the Kammerspiele. Reinhardt could risk the stairs because his aesthetic principles already drew the boundary line. His understanding of art permitted the option of spatial proximity because the aesthetic barriers of a serene and completely self-contained artworld made crossing them unthinkable. Seen from this perspective, the stairs are an *ex negativo* reminder: the theoretical possibility of overcoming the separation in such a simple way makes one all the more conscious of what keeps the two spheres apart. They are a visual symbol of the fact that aesthetic composition has transformed the stage into an "other world" to which the spectator can never have access.

Yet as special as Reinhardt's concept of the Kammerspiele was, in order to understand it historically, we need to recall that it was by no means a unique experiment. On the contrary, the idea of a salon theater was very much in vogue at the turn of the century.

The first attempt at a chamber theater came as early as 1895 with Max Halbe (1865–1944), among others, as the driving force. The play was Strindberg's tragicomedy *Creditors*, which was performed in the salon of the poet Juliane Déry (1864–1899) before some forty guests. Contrasting with Reinhardt's concept, these experiments represented a conscious retreat from the public to the private sphere. In the preserved photographs, we can barely distinguish the players from the audience. The second production is more interesting from the theater-historical perspective: the first ever performance of Georg Büchner's *Leonce and Lena*, which took place in a private park, also in 1895. After these two attempts, however, the experiments petered out.

More influential, and repeatedly cited as a point of reference in the critical and scholarly literature, was the idea of an "intimate theater" outlined by August Strindberg (1849–1912) in his afterword to *Miss Julie*; and in 1907 he in fact cofounded the Intima Teatern (Intimate Theater) in Stockholm with the stage director August Falck (1882–1938).[64]

The spread of this idea under various auspices raises the question of the aesthetic and dramaturgical implications of this form of theater.

Kammerspiele (2): The Function of a New Form of Text

In the context of the various reform and avant-garde currents at the beginning of the twentieth century, Reinhardt's Kammerspiele and the "intimate theater" movement were certainly both a sign of crisis and a search for a way out of it. Not the least of its inspirations was a dramatic form that became very significant at the end of the nineteenth century, namely the one-act play. Besides Strindberg, one of the principal representatives of this genre was Arthur Schnitzler (1862–1931). This kind of text developed, parallel to the genesis of various short prose forms, out of a need to find an alternative to drama in its traditional form.

This crisis, as described by Peter Szondi in his *Theorie des modernen Dramas* (1959; *Theory of Modern Drama*),[65] was the result of a change in the self-understanding and very concept of the bourgeois identity. Naturalism had focused on the way the individual is determined by the social environment, but now literature thematized—we see this exemplified in the works of Strindberg and Schnitzler—the individual's internal, psychological state. It is hardly an accident that this development ran parallel to the rise of psychoanalysis as practiced by Sigmund Freud (1856–1939), but also to the growing importance of psychology generally.[66]

The one-acter—the small, "intimate" form of dramatic composition—can thus be understood as a process of internalization. Michaela L. Perlmann says, with respect to Schnitzler and Strindberg:

> August Strindberg's rejection of the full-evening play did not merely signal the end of the well-made piece centering on intrigue; more significant was the fact that dramatic action generally was yielding the stage to the portrayal of psychological developments, states of consciousness, and state-of-affairs descriptions of social conditions which up to this point were reserved for the epic form.[67]

This interiority, however, demanded a new theatrical framework. Or, to put it differently, if conflicts were being shifted to the inner world of the household or of the characters themselves, then it was only appropriate that theatrical productions would move from large public theaters into smaller spaces. The experiment of Halbe and the Intimate Theater in Munich was a logical extension of this development in that it situated the play's fictional setting in the setting to which it refers, namely the bourgeois salon.

This shift was applied to the level of theatrical aesthetics. The smaller spatial conditions ultimately required a different style of representation. The grand gestures and lavish costumes of the big stage were out of place here. The removal of conflict to the interpersonal sphere corresponded to the quest for a new theater aesthetic.

Figure 15. Performance of Ibsen's *Ghosts* (Vienna, 1905). Photographer unknown. Courtesy of the Theaterwissenschaftliche Sammlung of the University of Cologne.

Reinhardt's actors carried this out to a special degree, sometimes to the chagrin of the critics, who felt compelled to point out their deficits compared to the conventional acting style. Thus the following polemic of Paul Oskar Höcker, directed at the Oswald of Alexander Moissi (1879–1935):

> Mr. Moissi [Oswald in *Ghosts*], that man of interesting catarrhs, is still lisping and gurgling, his prose and disconnected speech so inaudible that he can hardly be understood eight rows back. But he speaks all the more forcefully with his hands. Talent he has, without question. But, for the time being, he's a dilettante who can neither walk, talk, nor stand still on the stage. Even in life, nonchalance can be something fine and charming. But we have to have the feeling that

the man has the forms under control. We can't always be thinking he completely lacks a good upbringing.[68]

Read without regard to Höcker's polemical intent, the passage shows an acting style that no longer complies with the requirements of the big stage, but is rather attuned to a space where, as Maximilian Harden remarked, the audience can see "the quivering of nostrils and cheek muscles."

But the short dramatic forms also opened up new perspectives on the dramaturgical level. In contrast to full-evening plays, which make use of a conflict-based structure dynamically oriented toward a final resolution, the one-acter has more the character of a sketch and can be self-contained without having to resolve the characters' conflicts. The characters' "destiny," however, no longer seems dynamic; on the contrary, it can also be characterized by stasis.

In light of the then-prevailing aesthetic and cultural conventions, the short dramatic forms were further significant in a way that hardly matters today, but at the turn of the century certainly attracted much attention. In a cultural environment where the full-evening play was the norm, the one-acter necessarily came across as a programmatic refusal. Its very form, regardless of any thematic implications, attested to a subversive strategy or at least an attitude of resistance to traditional theatrical forms.

Putting all these considerations together, we can see how deliberately Max Reinhardt with his Kammerspiele wrote himself into the, at that time, still recent history of the Berlin theater, but also how much he sought to redefine the cultural position of his theater with this new format. But this very attempt to establish the Kammerspiele as an exclusive theatrical salon ultimately met with great difficulties. With approximately 350 seats, which were very expensive for the time, it was impossible to offer any program for an extended run and still hope to cover the house's costs. This was a dilemma that many cabaret theaters had already faced. Reinhardt could hardly avoid a price reform aimed at making the Kammerspiele affordable to a larger public.

When we compare Schall und Rauch with the Kammerspiele, it becomes clear that Reinhardt systematically sought a cultural positioning that was oriented toward the bourgeois *Lebenswelt* of his intended audience. To be sure, the reviewers did not greet this evocation without reservations. Thus Friedrich Düsel wrote in the *Deutsche Zeitung*:

> And so I couldn't help worrying that in the belly of this Trojan horse the diverting pomposity and coquettishness of society would be smuggled into the aesthetic domain of the theater, and that the programmatic need to be constantly offering something very special, very exquisite, to

the happy three hundred who could subscribe to such evenings would be seduced into a preference for the over-refined and over-seasoned.[69]

Düsel's reservations, which he incidentally did not regard as confirmed, refer to the topos, then typical, of the parvenus whom he suspected were behind the exclusiveness of this theater. Aside from Düsel's personal judgment, this line of argument is especially interesting inasmuch as it reflects the social changes that had occurred and highlights the extent to which bourgeois culture at the beginning of the twentieth century had become a culture of performative lifestyle and was no longer based on alienable "possessions of the spirit." Yet part of Reinhardt's success was clearly based on the fact that he provided a place and a stage for bourgeois self-presentation.

Chapter 3

✦

Circus Reinhardt: Giving Shape and Space to the Masses

The crowd's afoot! What casts the spell at the former circus ring?
They're playing of old Sophocles good Oedipus the King.
Who wakes the old boy from his sleep of many centuries?
Who brings his teeming populace on stage for all to see?

And whose bright voice is calling out:
"My heart is but a theater house!"?
Who needs the entire audience
To mass before his podium?
It's Max, dear Max, the regisseur,
There's no one else so tough or pure.
Mere Schumann Street is quite too small,
But Schumann Circus seats them all.

Who stands the people on their heads with his experiments?
Who buys the Lunapark entire with all its ornaments?
Who builds a courtly temple theater there in Temple Court?
Who fascinates the populace like General Bonaparte?

Who will one circus soon outgrow,
For only two will do, you know . . .
Who creeps about by bush and stone?
I think it's our Napoleon!
I think it's Max the regisseur.
He fills the seats you can be sure.
A piece of fruit dropped by the door
Would have no room to touch the floor!

—Otto Reutter (1870–1931), "Max der Regisseur" (1911)

The Deutsches Theater, but even more its Kammerspiele, represented a successful attempt to adapt bourgeois culture and its lifestyle to the conditions of a modernizing metropolis. On the basis of an aesthetic program that regarded the stage as less of a "moral institution" than a place of delight and sensuous pleasure, Max Reinhardt created a venue for bourgeois self-dramatization (*Selbstinszenierung*) where a programmatic rereading of canonical texts did not need to be appreciated via the circuitous route of bourgeois-intellectual expertise, but made a direct appeal to the audience through its sensuousness.[1]

Yet if we think back to the programmatic sketch of 1901, we notice that part of the Reinhardtian system still remained unfulfilled: the festival or arena theater. Reinhardt began to experiment with this format, which was intended for several thousand spectators and so was diametrically opposed to the spatial ideal of bourgeois theater, in the 1910s with his productions of *Oedipus the King* (Sophocles/Hofmannsthal 1910), *Everyman* (Hofmannsthal 1911), and *The Miracle* (Vollmoeller 1911). The culmination of this development was the opening of the Grosses Schauspielhaus (Big Playhouse) in Berlin in 1919 and the founding of the Salzburg Festival in 1920, where the staging of *Everyman* in the Domplatz was to become a fixed trademark.[2]

With these projects Reinhardt reached beyond the repertoire of bourgeois culture and imagined theater as a celebration or festive ritual—not just as an extension of, but also as the antithesis to the tradition of bourgeois theater: "The concept of festival theater ... postulated that the apron separating the actors from the audience be eliminated and that all present be understood as participants and co-actors in a play."[3] These projects, which the critics attacked with a special vehemence, were not only a continuation of his concept of theater in an aesthetic sense, but also more importantly a complex nexus of different discourses and cultural practices that all centered on the phenomenon of the masses. Besides explanatory models from the sphere of sociology, psychology, and the philosophy of culture, the circus and revue formats of popular culture also made a contribution here.

The Masses as Object of Reflection

The quantitative growth of cities and the economic changes underlying this development led to a crisis in traditional models of society, which crystallized especially around the phenomena of the "masses" and the "metropolis." Both of these terms occupied a prominent place in the discourse of modernization in the late nineteenth and early twentieth centuries, and no other pair of terms evoked such hopes and fears.

The crisis produced not only a series of explanatory and interpretive models, but also, in a certain sense, sociology itself as an academic discipline. Ferdinand Tönnies (1885–1936) was the key figure: his seminal work

Gemeinschaft und Gesellschaft (1887; *Community and Society*) laid down a categorical distinction that permanently influenced the discourse of modernization. In his attempt to determine conceptually the different ways human beings have lived together, he came up with a model of antagonistic social forms in which many of his contemporaries thought they recognized themselves.

On one side was the concept of *Gemeinschaft* (community), which is based on and strongly resembles the family:

> The Gemeinschaft by blood, denoting unity of being, is developed and differentiated into Gemeinschaft of locality, which is based on a common habitat. A further differentiation leads to Gemeinschaft of mind, which implies only co-operation and co-ordinated action for a common goal.[4]

Opposed to this is *Gesellschaft* (society), which is an

> aggregate of human beings . . . [who] live and dwell together peacefully. However, in the Gemeinschaft they remain essentially united in spite of all separating factors, whereas in the Gesellschaft they are essentially separated in spite of all uniting factors . . . Here everybody is by himself and isolated, and there exists a condition of tension against all others.[5]

Whereas *Gemeinschaft* is a matter of living together in a spirit of common interest and inner psychological agreement, peace in *Gesellschaft* is only (laboriously) achieved and secured through rules and laws.

> Gesellschaft as a totality to which a system of conventional rules applies is limitless; it constantly breaks through its chance and real boundaries. In Gesellschaft every person strives for that which is to his own advantage and he affirms the actions of others only in so far as and as long as they can further his interest. Before and outside of convention . . . the relation of all to all may therefore be conceived as potential hostility or latent war. Against this condition, all agreements of the will stand out as so many treaties and peace pacts.[6]

It is no accident that Tönnies's formulation recalls Thomas Hobbes's (1588–1679) description in *Leviathan* (1651) of humanity's pre-civilized state. This is the *bellum omnium contra omnes*, the "war of all against all," which is eliminated only by the development of a political state. Tönnies describes society, localized in the (large) city, as the truce of this Hobbesian war.

Georg Simmel (1858–1918) takes up this notion of a mere truce in his essay "Die Großstädte und das Geistesleben" (1903; "The Metropolis and

Mental Life") when he characterizes modern life as marked a priori by an antagonism between the individual and society:

> The deepest problems of modern life stem from the claim of the individual to preserve the autonomy and individuality of his existence in the face of overwhelming social forces, of historical heritage, of external culture, and of the technique of life. The fight with nature which primitive man has to wage for his *bodily* existence attains in this modern form its latest transformation.[7]

The central site of this antagonism is the metropolis, the living environment that produces a specific state of mind—Simmel speaks in this context of "intellectuality" and an "intensification of nervous stimulation."[8]

In terms of the Hobbesian truce, the metropolis figures as a site of permanent strain on the individual's senses, of lasting alienation. Simmel speaks here of the "ravishments of metropolitan life,"[9] a metaphor that makes the relationship between the individual and the metropolis blatantly clear. The superficial calm of great cities turns out to be a deceptive fiction disguising the actual tensions.

The metropolis as "historical site of the masses"[10] is a threat to the individual on one hand, but on the other—and here Simmel's reflections clearly transcend the familiar topoi of cultural pessimism—it offers a special opportunity, for it creates a dialectical nexus between quantitative growth, society's claim on the individual, and the individual's own freedom:

> To the extent to which the group grows—numerically, spatially, in significance and in content of life—to the same degree the group's direct, inner unity loosens, and the rigidity of the original demarcation against others is softened through mutual relations and connections. At the same time, the individual gains freedom of movement, far beyond the first jealous delimitation. The individual also gains a specific individuality to which the division of labor in the enlarged group gives both occasion and necessity.[11]

The historical and cultural significance of the metropolis is defined by its broadened scope of action, for its frame of reference extends beyond traditional horizons. "The sphere of life of the small town is, in the main, self-contained and autarchic. For it is the decisive nature of the metropolis that its inner life overflows by waves into a far-flung national or international area."[12] Such a broadening goes beyond the antagonism between community and society described by Tönnies. Simmel is able to see the dynamic quality of modernization, even if his view of it—we can almost speak here of a nostalgic attitude—still tends to stress ambivalence, as Gisela Müller sums it up: "Through the modernization of society the individual gains a whole new freedom, which however can increase not his sense of well-being, but rather only his 'discontent with modernity,' as it was later called in connection with Simmel."[13] Simmel's line of argument, which is as philosophical as it is sociological in its perspective, seeks to situate and understand modernization under the rubrics of cultural, economic, and social factors. The metropolis and the masses ultimately remain unknown quantities whose character can only be recognized indirectly by their effects on the individual.

While Tönnies's and Simmel's arguments still center on the individual (as opposed to society), it is the individual's opposite, the mass population, that is the key social phenomenon of the period, and one that is equally ubiquitous and enigmatic. Theoreticians of all sorts—from the political Left and Right, from scientific and scholarly circles—have tackled it. Most famous and influential was the French psychologist Gustave Le Bon (1841-1931) in his book *La Psychologie des foules* (1895; *The Crowd: A Study of the Popular Mind*), which became a cornerstone of mass psychology generally.

Le Bon's argument is based on the conviction that the masses cannot be described simply by using quantitive criteria, but are rather to be understood as a group with certain common characteristics. He sets up a law for the psychological unity of crowds[14] that states that the crowd develops a "collective mind" with the following characteristics:

> We see, then, that the disappearance of the conscious personality, the predominance of the unconscious personality, the turning by means of suggestion and contagion of feelings and ideas in an identical direction, the tendency to immediately transform the suggested ideas into acts; these, we see, are the principal characteristics of the individual forming part of the crowd. He is no longer himself, but has become an automaton who has ceased to be guided by his will.[15]

Le Bon describes the individual's absorption into the crowd as a lapse, as a descent from an individual to a "creature of drives" and a "barbarian."[16] This descent corresponds to his determination that the crowd is distinguished by mediocrity, in the sense of the lowest common denominator.[17] Thus Le Bon ascribes to the crowd a susceptibility to authoritarian direction and irrational action.

This theory of the masses—a clear reaction to the modernization processes of the late nineteenth century—is of interest, aside from its dubious scientific tenability, because it attempts to describe a specific social dynamic. The ideal of bourgeois enlightenment is so thoroughly inscribed into these reflections that the crowd (especially in its effects on the individual) can only represent a loss or fall. The enlightenment ideal also stands in clear opposition to Le Bon's thesis that the crowd requires a strong leader personality because on its own it lacks ethical perception. In view of the totalitarian regimes of the twentieth century, we can hardly read these reflections without sustained discomfort.

As a historical phenomenon, however, mass psychology shows the extent to which the "massification" that was evident in the world of daily experience represented an epistemological break: the very notion of bourgeois identity and individuality was scarcely compatible with evolving living conditions. More than a melancholy symptom of loss, the thematization of the masses demonstrated the need to find a figure of thought that would make it possible to still imagine a common social life at all—an attempt that in its context almost unavoidably presumes the failure of modernization.

What becomes clear from this is that we only find a positive, or at least a more subtle, concept of the masses in authors who on political grounds want to make precisely those strata of the population that have been written off as the masses the subject of action. Thus, the self-confessed Social Democrat Theodor Geiger (1891–1952) ascribes a culture-critical function to the masses in his study *Die Masse und ihre Aktion* (1926; *The Masses and Their Action*): "As a social form of life . . . [the masses] signify protest against mechanization, i.e., the enslavement of man through social objectification. If we understand community and society in Tönnies's sense, then the masses are the protest against society that derives from the spirit of community."[18] Of course, Geiger too understands the masses as a "phenomenon of decline,"[19] because they indicate the disintegration of an existing (national) community. But as a revolutionary force, Geiger thinks, the masses can co-effect an actual healing of these conditions—a healing, to be sure, that can only take place beyond or after the end of bourgeois society.

> In protest against the established order and the objectification of social life, the masses bring about in themselves a sudden reversion to a disposition of pure natural will [*zu rein wesenwilliger Haltung*]. Despite the contradictions inherent in the conditions of social life from which the masses arise, and despite the contradictions of human beings themselves in the age of mechanization, when the masses act, there takes place a homogenization—a momentary harmonic dissolution—of heterogeneous individuals . . . Despite its destructive intentionality, the emotionality of the masses has positive value to the extent that it realizes the community of natural will [*wesenwilllige Gemeinschaft*] in protest against an age that is characterized by the decline of community.[20]

The tension between a diagnosis of loss, such as we find in Le Bon, Simmel, and Tönnies, and a visionary topos like Geiger's can be seen as symptomatic of the struggle for an adequate interpretation of modernization and its consequences. But the multitude, as well as the argumentative and rhetorical intensity, of such theories testifies to the urgency of the questions that prompted them. It was an urgency, however, that was not to be dispelled by resort to theoretical abstractions: it broke new ground in its search for adequate representation as well.

The Masses as Aesthetic Object

To borrow Benedict Anderson's terminology,[21] social figures of thought require "imagination" if they are to become a lasting part of a society's *Lebenswelt*. They need a solid place in the "common pictorial ground and fund of images within a cultural tradition,"[22] because only in and through such images can they be experienced by the individual and become concepts that guide knowledge and action.

Related to this, Peter Fritzsche, in his study *Reading Berlin 1900* (1996), has pointed to the constitutive significance of the print media in creating an urban habitat that he designates the "word city."[23]

> However, the constitution of this public space was as much the work of fiction as the function of commerce. The cosmopolitan did not simply set out to see the diversity of the city. The metropolitan encounters were always guided by the layout of the word city as well as the design of the built city.[24]

Fritzsche's argument that the city's public space was decisively influenced by its portrayal in the booming newspaper sector can be supplemented by remembering that there was also a "stage city" as well as a "word city": the theater had developed into a veritable mass medium since 1869. Max Epstein in 1914 calculated that there were 100,000 seats available every night in Berlin's theaters.[25] Half of these belonged to "variety shows, music halls, and cinemas," and 30,000 were offered by "regular" theaters. The ratio increased in the 1920s, when the revue gained special status as an independent art form.

> In 1926 the Berlin revues were drawing 11,000 visitors every day. This of course did not signal any sudden upheaval of behavior in a city of four million. But [when it is] measured by the hysterical reaction of a major part of the Weimar press to phenomena of modernization, we might be justified in seeing the new attraction as a sign that the public was undergoing a change of attitude.[26]

The variety and abundance of theater forms in Berlin offered an especially rich arena for imagining and staging not just modernity, but the masses themselves. Behind the exclusivity of the Kammerspiele as an adaptation of the bourgeois salon, we can discern the mirror image of a counterproject with the hitherto "invisible" masses at its center. In these diverse forms of popular culture, the masses both enter the limelight of the stage and sit as spectators in the auditorium: the urban masses encounter themselves.

Here the fringe areas of bourgeois culture played a decisive role, as we see negatively portrayed, for example, in Max Martersteig's philippic:

> In the circus, acrobatics, dressage, and clowning are made to serve a more ambitious vision. Forms of exhibition that derive from parades, pantomimes, and dance performances find a home there, forms whose flamboyance often overshadows what is typically found on metropolitan opera stages and satisfies sensual needs to a questionable degree.[27]

Martersteig's repudiation of the circus was rooted in the fact that its new forms of presentation[28] went beyond the previous norm and so crossed the "boundary" to theater.

Karl Frenzel had already sharply criticized this transgression in 1891: "The pantomimes and the circus encroach ever more recklessly on the stage, and the chorus of extras keeps pushing the spectators further into the background."[29] The transgression had to do both with the lavishness of the presentations and with the fact that such "variant forms" occupied an ever-larger space in the purely quantitative sense. While conventional theaters were rarely able to seat more than 1,000 people, the so-called "specialty theaters" had from 1,600 to 3,000 seats at their disposal,[30] and the circus buildings even had space for 2,500 to 3,500 spectators on average.[31] The art forms on display there did not typically correspond to the cultured offerings of the bourgeois stage, but they appealed to a broad spectrum of the public, crossing all social boundaries. The cultural effect of theater (with all its variant forms) extended far beyond the spectators who were actually present at a performance, stretching well into what Peter Fritzsche describes as the "word city." As the preferred object of press coverage, the theater became a firm fixture of the "collective imaginary."[32]

The revue, which had been taking hold since the beginning of the century, now became the epitomic form of popular theater. It was linked to the concept of the masses in a double sense: first because of the great number of its performers and the extravagance of its scenography, and second because of the size of the audience it wanted to reach.

The signature feature of the revues was the so-called girl troupes, large dance ensembles that cultivated a specific kind of stage aesthetic centering equally on the bodies and the movements of the female dancers. The very organization of these troupes indicates a permanent cultural shift compared with conventional theatrical troupes, for they were literally "global players": the Tiller Girls, for example, were based in London, the Ziegfeld Girls in New York. The names of the troupes were so much of a brand that it was possible and even usual for different ensembles of the respective troupes to make guest appearances in different countries simultaneously. What was decisive for their success was not the unique characteristics of the performers but their mass synchronization. This circumstance quickly made the girl troupes an object of cultural-philosophical reflection.

Best known in this connection is the interpretation of Siegfried Kracauer (1889–1966), who saw in the girls a mirroring or reflection of the capitalist production process. According to Kracauer, the girls formed a "mass ornament," a self-sufficient geometrical structure in which the individual dancer still counts, but only as part of a more comprehensive whole:

> The bearer of the ornaments is the *mass* and not the people [*Volk*]. For whenever the people form figures, the latter do not hover in midair but arise out of community . . . The patterns seen in the stadiums and cabarets betray no such origins. They are composed of elements that are mere building blocks and nothing more. The construction of the edifice depends on the size of the stones and their number. It is the mass that is employed here.[33]

Just as the ornament is its own end, so the capitalist production process is its own end in the sense that its rationale lies not in a structure of need, but in the profit-seeking of a producer. Similarly, Kracauer argues, the mass ornament, as seen for example in the girl troupes, does not answer a need, but simply serves the mass imagination (as conditioned by capitalism). Kracauer trenchantly formulates the connection: "The hands in the factory correspond to the legs of the Tiller Girls . . . The mass ornament is the aesthetic reflection of the rationality to which the prevailing economic system aspires."[34]

Kracauer's argument can be summarized in two points. First, he assigns a higher valuation to the assumed superficiality of the revue by describing it as a crystallization of the connection between society and the economy.[35] But secondly, he also shows that this connection is a pure mirroring rather than the object of critical reflection: the mass ornament opens up no kind of emancipatory horizon, as is traditionally expected from art. According to Kracauer, who takes an obviously deprecatory position in this connection, the mass ornament is a central component of the mass imagination. But it exhausts itself in this function; it is not part of an overriding, far-reaching cultural or social-critical process.

In the context of bourgeois culture in a state of crisis, the mass imagination—the mass becoming image—seems significant, quite apart from its (missing) critical potential, to the extent that the phenomenon becomes at all visible and therefore culturally negotiable. Although the traditional view is that the mass ornament serves only to document the devaluation of the individual, it has a decisive role, Kracauer argues, in developing a figure of thought.

Fritz Giese (1890–1935), who examined the girl troupes in light of the need to come to terms with the metropolis, offers an entirely different reading, though one very similar in its basic assumptions and point of view. His central thesis is that the metropolis is marked by its own peculiar rhythm, which finds expression in the girl troupes' dances. Giese's discussion of the girl phenomenon is linked to a geographical contrast between America (the United States) and Europe, the former being synonymous with a modern society. Giese sees the girl troupes, which he analyzes in light of other (reform) movements in dance, like those of Rudolf von Laban and Émile Jaques-Dalcroze, as embodying a new image of women that has already assimilated the experience of the metropolis and modern life.

The girl troupes' "lack of artistic expression," which they seek to make up for through an athleticism that entails especially frequent training, is not a deficiency in Giese's view, but the expression of an "American essence" (*amerikanisches Wesen*) that is better suited to the demands of the modern world than to European ideals. For the latter, modernity—embodied in the metropolis—represents primarily an experience of loss. Giese summarizes his position as follows:

> The girls teach us the value of general uniformity, the idea of a heightened average vis-à-vis an overemphasized eccentricity which perhaps makes the individual more individual than he can really tolerate. They teach us an appreciation of women that is more than just an unusual spectacle, but rather represents indubitable progress toward a genuine humanity. We recognize their distance from the predatory attitude of men; we see their higher appraisal by their male friends; we become aware of a relationship between the sexes that aims at an amicable eros between equals instead of mere sex.[36]

Although from today's perspective this grappling for a non-sexualized interpretation of the "girls" seems rather labored, it is still noteworthy that Giese uses a familiar topos of cultural criticism by describing America and Europe as antagonistic poles of cultural development.

This figure of thought demonstrates that popular forms of entertainment could assume such a central role in cultural reflection because, among other things, they transcended the context of national culture and thus permanently extended the collective store of images.

This transcendence of a national framework was by no means confined to the field of theater. Quite the contrary: theater should even be regarded as a latecomer in this respect, for it must have been very difficult for an art form that was still so concentrated on the primacy of language to cross such a boundary.

More influential in the forming of a world-image (in the literal sense) were the world expositions that had been held at irregular intervals since their institution in London in 1851.[37] Such expositions, which were far more than a trade fair for industry professionals, offered a broad panorama of artistic exhibits in addition to displays of products, and allowed countries to stage their national self-images. As a consequence they attracted masses of visitors. The Paris Exposition of 1889, for example, was attended by 25 million people.[38]

The broad diversity in visitors' backgrounds offered exhibitors a tremendous opportunity to display their technological expertise, though the cultural function of such displays went well beyond the demonstration of technical possibilities. For instance, the Krupp Company in 1851 displayed a block of steel weighing two tons—an unheard-of achievement at that time. The exhibit's already considerable effect on contemporaries was further enhanced by the fact that the block damaged every vehicle that had transported it and ultimately broke through the floor of its installation at the exhibition. These accidents, if they were such, demonstrated the utter novelty of this in-itself unspectacular object.[39] Alfons Paquet (1881–1944), in his study titled *Das Austellungsproblem in der Volkswirtschaft* (1908; *The Problem of Exhibition in the National Economy*),[40] draws attention to the fact that sensational displays were a constitutive part of such exhibitions:

> The fact that the undertaking has such a limited heyday temporally speaking means that to a certain extent things are calculated for the power of their effect, their attractiveness to the greatest number of visitors; there is an almost tropical ornateness, an intoxication; in a word the installations have a festive character.[41]

The extent to which the world expositions were, and still are, actually anchored in the collective imaginary is made clear by the example of the Eiffel Tower—the classic emblem of Paris in our understanding—which was likewise the product of a world exposition.

In 1892 Hans Delbrück (1848–1929) wrote two noteworthy essays in which he made the case for a world exposition in Germany, which, however, never came about. Delbrück notes that such an exposition could "give expression to" what was revolutionary in technological developments and their effects on daily life and "make [it] immediately known."[42] The distinction he made between "mediated seeing and seeing for oneself"[43] clearly indicates the fundamental theatricality of world expositions, whose effect could only be communicated to a public that was directly present. According to Delbrück, expositions brought the signs and credentials of the time to immediate view:

> The great mass of people may only be indulging their curiosity—but that isn't so entirely useless, since these people otherwise live lives of complete apathy. Only a few people have a real drive to learn, but for these few it will bear fruit a thousandfold . . . For a world exposition has a formative effect on the entire population, enriches their views, educates their taste, and teaches them to compare the achievements of individual countries with one another.[44]

In their concentrated form, world expositions served the important function of giving countries the chance to present themselves on the world stage:

> Coming as they did with the growing military and economic power of modern nation-states, the consolidation of large colonial empires, the mass migration of populations, and the rapid rise of industrialization, world's fairs offer for analysis a virtual phantasmagoria of "imagined communities" and "invented traditions."[45]

World expositions offered an independent interpretation of the masses: here mass and modernization were understood not as loss, but as a copiousness that could be managed through technological progress.

Whereas world expositions defined the concept of the masses on the global—or, in the terminology of the time, cosmopolitan—level, without ever renouncing the framework of the nation-state, there arose beginning in 1871 a new theatrical genre that sought to define the masses in their specific quality by finding a point of reference beyond modernization and social dynamics. The national *Festspiel* (festival, pageant) arose as a genre that focused on the masses as an ethnically homogeneous people (*Volk*). Scenic memory or "re-imagination" was supposed to attest to the persistence of the masses through all historical currents of change. The very concept of *Festspiel*, of course, goes back to Richard Wagner (1813–1883) and the foundation of the Bayreuth festival in 1876. Wagner had conceived this festival as a secular pilgrimage to celebrate and propagate national identity. With it, he programmatically shied away from major towns but deliberately withdrew to the Franconian forest.

Thus, for example, Felix Dahn (1834–1912), in his *Festspiel zur Feier des neunzigsten Geburtstags des Feldmarschalls Grafen Helmuth Moltke* (1890; *Pageant to Celebrate the Ninetieth Birthday of Field Marshal Graf Helmuth Moltke*), presented an ancestral lineage that stretched from the Germanic chieftain Arminius, who had defeated the Romans in the Battle of the Teutoburg Forest in 9 BCE, to Friedrich Barbarossa and down to "numerous German warriors, soldiers, and commanders from antiquity to 1815."[46] The pageant ended with the entrance of "Woodland Germany," who glorified the jubilarian with an encomium to which all the other personages added their voices. The lineage drawn here, which extended from the German tribes to the late nineteenth-century present, can be seen symbolically as a means of not merely attesting to historical continuity, but also recasting the masses of the present in pointedly antimodern imagery.

The ritualized pageantry that was widespread in the Weimar Republic[47] was intended as a theatrical means of expanding the present moment by presenting it in its historical dimensions. Here we can point to a number of formal landmarks, as Peter Sprengel has shown in his study *Die inszenierte Nation* (1991; *The Nation on Stage*):

- The pageants were always composed for a concrete occasion, that is, the literary or theatrical form served to publicly highlight a specific occasion and mark it as significant for the society. Pageants could be written to memorialize military victories as well as to launch public institutions or to honor prominent persons.

- Because of their pronounced ritualistic character, the pageants were understood as a public act of esteem and homage. Thus they often took place outside of conventional theaters, in symbolic places outdoors, for instance. In this sense, the pageant was one of the ways the (bourgeois) imagination pictured rites of acculturation that often harked back to ancient Greek precedents. The aggrandized appearance of allegorical figures can also be regarded as part of this imagination. For even on the (formal) level of setting up the figures, the pageant aimed at a refraction of all kinds of psychologization.

- In contrast to conventional drama, the pageant does not thrive on topical suggestion, but typically highlights the temporal difference between the performative moment and that of the event being represented or celebrated.

- The pageant was originally conceived for the general public and was often performed by primary and secondary school students or clubs and associations. In this form it was also a momentary participation in political life. This characteristic enables us to understand why it was such a widespread genre. There was hardly a school that failed to celebrate special events with specific pageantry.

- In keeping with their ritualistic character, most pageants demonstrated particular features that transcended the boundary between the actors and the audience that was constitutive for bourgeois theater. Of course, these features are to be understood less as adumbrations of a "theater of collaboration" than as clearly defined entities like pieces of music—in the sense that, for example, the German national anthem or "Die Wacht am Rhein" was sung in connection with the commemoration of a military victory. In this way, pageants were supposed to contribute to the consolidation of national identity and foster an immediate sense of community.

Max Reinhardt himself was involved in such a pageant in 1913 when, on the occasion of the 100-year jubilee of the beginning of the revolt against Napoleon in Breslau, he staged Gerhart Hauptmann's *Pageant in German Rhymes*.[48] This production, in which a cast of about 2,000 members played before an audience of 4,500–6,000 people,[49] displayed extraordinary pomp and set historical figures like Napoleon beside allegorical entities like "Athena Germany." Reinhardt collaborated with Hauptmann (1862–1946) and his set designer Ernst Stern (1876–1954) to create a performance that did in fact celebrate the German unification but showed a certain reserve with regard to militarism. Thus, in the finale a procession toward the German Athena contained not only soldiers, but representatives of various regions and professions as well. It is easy to imagine that the depiction of the legendary general Blücher (Marschall Vorwärts [Marshal Forward]) as a dismissable puppet did not strike the chord expected by Prussian elites. Although its first performances received nothing but positive reviews, the pageant had a short run and did not tour. Apparently Reinhardt's elaborate stage aesthetic clashed with the public's ceremonial expectations.[50]

Figure 16. Puppet of Blücher. Courtesy of the Theaterwissenschaftliche Sammlung of the University of Cologne.

Figure 17. Finale with the German Athena in the middle. *Illustrierte Zeitung*, June 13, 1913.

This rejection, due in no small part to political intrigue, tells us that pageants were understood as secular rituals that involved other expectations than those that pertained to theater in the classical sense. Erika Fischer-Lichte has shown that at the beginning of the twentieth century, there was a growing consciousness of (and need for) a specific performative quality of theater that—prompted by Nietsche's *Birth of Tragedy from the Spirit of Music* (1872)—placed a high premium on the connection between theater and ritual. Thus, Fischer-Lichte writes about the prevalent scholarly idea of theater represented by Max Herrmann (1865–1942):

> Rather, it [theater] is conceived as a physical process, set in motion by participating in the event, by perceiving not only through the eyes and the ears, but through the bodily sensations which affect the whole body. Thus, it is the bodies performing in space which constitute theatre—the bodies of the actors moving in and through the space and the bodies of the spectators experiencing the spatial dimensions of their common environment, the particular atmosphere of the space they share and their response to the bodily presence of the actors that articulates itself in particular physiological, affective, energetic and motoric impulses.[51]

This special physical quality was at the heart of the pageant experience, which was further strengthened by such active and activating features as communal singing. Underlying this activity was an idea of the people (*Volk*) that was consciously designed as an antimodern, *völkisch* antithesis to the modern conception of the masses. The pageant's target audience was the community, in Tönnies's sense of the term, which was to be at least temporarily regenerated through the theatrical experience. The *Festspiel* was to foster a revanchist perspective in which an ineluctable community could be seen to lie at the basis of a society that was ostensibly defined by chaos and loss. This vision was already in tune with fascist mass mobilization, which could only comprehend community in aggressive dissociation from others.

The many different ways of imagining the masses, which could only be presented sketchily by means of a few examples in the preceding discussion, underscore both the importance of the concept of the masses and the unrest it created. Having treated the conceptual formulation of the phenomenon and its various forms of representation/imagination, we will, in the following pages, explore the question of the place of the masses, understood as the place where discourse intersects with the imaginary.

The Place of the Masses

Behind the question of the place of the masses lay not only topographical or social concerns, but the fundamental realization that the growth of large cities required the creation of such mass locales in the first place. The architectural discourse of the time (or more specifically that of the burgeoning discipline of city planning) shows us that social changes had generated a sense of a need, both architectural and cultural, to design spaces and structures apart from purely "functional" entities like streets and railroad stations. The realization that traditional symbolic locales such as churches could not respond to an increasingly diverse society triggered a demand for new categories of public spaces. New building types would include primarily functional spaces like indoor market halls and department stores, as well as those that arose directly from an ongoing shift in cultural practices (or from the emergence of new ones), such as public swimming pools and sports stadiums.

A survey published in 1896 by the Architects Association of Berlin titled *Berlin und seine Bauten* (*Berlin and Its Buildings*) shows how much of a tension still existed in public spaces between traditional structures (schools, museums, churches) and newly developing types for which traditional forms were often being adapted. Of the latter, two were especially adapted to the conditions of a mass society: circuses and exhibition grounds.

Exhibition grounds are a good example of the overlap between cultural discourse and economic conditions. In addition to certain functional requirements (large exhibition space, bright lighting), favorable traffic access and the "sensation it [the exposition undertaking] creates in society—or better: among the masses"[52] are regularly mentioned. In this connection, Paquet shows that this necessary effect could only be achieved when the site's appearance was not dominated merely by its functional purpose. "Beyond its technical functionality, it is essential that the whole site be decisively characterized by certain aesthetic qualities—attractive grounds, monumentality, pleasingness—so that all aspects together create the impression of a unified showpiece, a cultural attraction."[53]

Thus we see that the exhibition grounds presented in *Berlin und seine Bauten* were characterized by an impressive park with diverse pavilions and other attractions, in addition to proper exhibition spaces. Also interesting is the adaptation of classical building and ornamentation forms.

> The grounds [of a panorama building] were intended to give visitors a picture of the excavation results from Olympia and Pergamum and have achieved this end brilliantly. The terrace facades display replicas of the finest parts of the famous altar frieze (the Gigantomachy). In the building behind the temple one could see, at the time of the Jubilee Exhibition, a painting by artists Kips and Koch that was based on the sketches of the architect Bohn, representing a restored vista of the city of Pergamum.[54]

The use of images from antiquity invested the space with the requisite bourgeois-cultural prestige and made it something of a museum.[55] This "masquerade" fulfilled an important social function by integrating the masses of visitors into traditional interpretive models of their social composition.

Theaters were often part of the exhibition complex. Max Reinhardt deliberately used such places for guest performances—the Musikfesthalle in Munich, for example, or the site of the aerostatics exhibition in Frankfurt.[56] His choice of these places was not justifiable on practical grounds alone; he was obviously looking into the idea of staging his mass- or festival-theater productions within the established context of exhibition practices. And we should keep in mind, if we accept Paquet's thesis, that the exhibitions for their part could only profit from the spectacular nature of Reinhardt's undertakings.

In contrast to exhibitions, which were, organizationally and functionally, closely linked with industry, the circus belonged solely to the domain of entertainment culture. Of course, we have to remember that the circus of this period was nothing like the marginal traveling show of our own age. It was a firm fixture of the bourgeois cultural repertoire. Admittedly, the tradition experienced a dramatic decline at the beginning of the twentieth century. In Europe around 1900, there were still approximately 200 large and medium-sized circuses in operation; by 1912, the number had fallen to about 70.[57]

But it was not just in terms of quantitative distribution that the circus had a different meaning then than it does today; it had, in a literal sense, a very different place in society. There were, of course, companies that visited various cities in tents, but more important was the stationary circus permanently attached to a specific building. Although the theoretical architectural publications emphasized that Germany was different from other European countries in having very few well-equipped circus grounds,[58] within a short time there developed an independent type of building in terms of both technical construction and disposition of space, on a scale that continued to outdo the size of theaters.[59]

Figure 18. The Circus Busch. Postcard circa 1900, Raphael Tuck & Sons.

The programs offered by circus companies, however, show considerable overlap with the theater, as Eduard Schmitt explains in his *Handbuch der Architektur (Architectural Handbook)*:

> In the last quarter of the 19th century, scenic and mimetic performances, which are half drama and half ballet, have been added to equestrian and gymnastic acts. Large-scale, expensive pantomimes with all the accoutrements are often a major factor in today's better circus programs. The major effect of such balletic pantomimes lies in their massive development of human materials, which is why they consist of ensemble dances that take place in the ring, with or without a stage.[60]

The overlap between circus and theater can also be inferred from the number of buildings Schmitt cites that were designed in such a way that they could be used both as a circus (with an arena) and as a theater (with a stage). Examples are the Apollo Theater in Düsseldorf and the Zirkus Schumann in Frankfurt am Main.[61] These adaptable buildings, seating from 1,500 to 5,000 people, tell us how low the threshhold between circus and theater really was in the domain of popular culture. It is hardly surprising or extraordinary, then, that Reinhardt used circus buildings after 1910 to realize his idea of a theater for the masses.

A small book by S. Sturmhoefel with the title *Scene der Alten und Bühne der Neuzeit* (1889; *Scene of the Ancients and Stage of the Modern Period*) generated a debate in connection with these mass structures of popular culture. The book was greeted with a number of responses in the architectural journal *Deutsche Bauzeitung*, some of them quite vehement.[62]

Sturmhoefel, who as councillor of city construction was involved in the erection and administration of the Stadttheater in Magdeburg, points out in his very introduction the social need for a national theater that exceeds the seating capacity of any existing theaters: "The question of national theaters has come to the foreground in all the major cities of our time. The poorer classes and even the majority of the middle class see themselves excluded from the theater, which should be a place of education and culture for the whole population."[63] Sturmhoefel puts the need for a theater affordable to broad levels of the population in the same category with other achievements of civilization like sewer systems, running water, and the education of children.[64] In this connection, he projects a theater that, with 4,250–5,000 seats, would well exceed the average seating capacity.[65] His argument is completely in keeping with the modernization discourses of his time. Sturmhoefel also explicitly uses the argument that such a theater is necessary for the metropolis as a social space and that only the metropolis can guarantee the organizational and financial success of such a project.[66]

Sturmhoefel's suggestion—although the majority of his professional contemporaries objected—found a delayed echo in a series of designs, submitted by various architects to *Die Bauwelt* (*Architectural World*) in 1911, of a mass theater for Max Reinhardt.[67] Common to all these designs, and reflecting Sturmhoefel's interest in increasing seating capacity, is the fact that they extend the stage well out into the auditorium, thus avoiding the conventional separation of these two spatial domains. And if we look more closely at August Zeh's design for a "Theater of Five Thousand," for instance, we notice too that there is no longer any attempt to hierarchize the seating (with boxes, for example) in the auditorium itself.

These designs, which were not all realized, show that Reinhardt's experiments with the circus, though they were thoroughly innovative, by no means represented a categorical break, as we tend to think today. We should think of them instead as a shift, a deliberate "protrusion" into the sphere of popular culture. In their basic structure, as Sturmhoefel's book shows, these visions should always be seen as reflecting the experience of the modernizing metropolis.

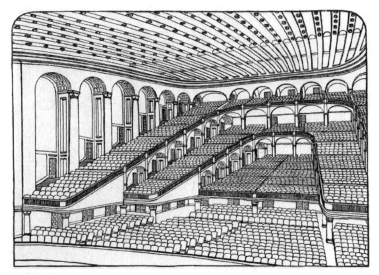

Figure 19. August Zeh, interior design for a "Theater of Five Thousand," *Die Bauwelt*, 1911.

Reinhardt himself began officially pursuing his plan for a permanent mass theater, which he himself called a "theater of five thousand," in 1911,[68] partly supported by an initiative to "establish German national pageants [*Volksfestspiele*]."[69] In 1914 he finally received the license to rebuild the Zirkus Schumann in Berlin, with the condition that the construction not begin until six months after any peace agreement at the earliest. While this condition is proof of the naive and chauvinistic attitude with which German authorities entered into the Great War, the fact that the work did not start before 1918 is also true to the course of history.

The Zirkus Schumann, which Reinhardt had already used in 1910 for his *Oedipus the King*, was situated, tellingly, between the Neues Theater and the Deutsches Theater. In terms of access, this meant it was very close to the Friedrichstrasse railroad station and a number of central streets. Just as Reinhardt took pains to find a central location topographically, he also sought to establish numerous social connections for his new theatrical undertaking. Heinrich Braulich has proven that Reinhardt was already, in 1914, holding discussions with the trade unions and the Social Democratic Party to build a secure subscription base.[70] At the opening of the Grosses Schauspielhaus, as the Zirkus Schumann was called after 1919, Reinhardt could point to an impressive list of 130,000 subscribers.[71]

The building itself recalls a history as varied as it is rich in associations. Erected in 1867 as one of Berlin's first indoor market halls, it became the Zirkus Schumann in the early 1870s and stayed that way until Reinhardt took it over. The reconstruction of the building entered the decisive phase when—after a series of designs and various initial attempts—Hans Poelzig (1869–1936) took over the implementation of the project in 1918. By this time there were already a ground plan and external walls in place, so that Poelzig's chief responsibility was the working out of the interior space.

The decision to hire Poelzig can certainly be understood as programmatic and direction-setting. Poelzig at this stage had already appeared as the architect of several major projects that explicitly dealt with the conditions and consequences of modernization. Indicative of his work was his membership in the German Werkbund, which had been cofounded by Peter Behrens, the architect of Schall und Rauch. This association, which was in its heyday between 1907 and 1934, was dedicated to humanizing the *Lebenswelt* of modern society through new architectural forms, but also in the design of everyday objects. Unlike other representatives of similar reform movements, Poelzig, who served as chairman of the German Werkbund (work federation of architects and builders) in 1919, insisted on a link between art and craft in modern design and expressly understood this combination as antithetical to modern industry and its methods of production. Design, Poelzig held, should be the expression of a higher truth and in this capacity lay claim to a moral authority: "The Werkbund must become the conscience of the nation."[72]

With this in mind, it is hardly surprising that Poelzig's designs show none of the austerity and clarity of line that is so typical, for example, of the Bauhaus movement, which appeared almost at the same time. Poelzig focuses instead on symbolic decor.

A large cupola extending over the arena and forestage forms the center of the Grosses Schauspielhaus. This feature, originating in a wish expressed by Reinhardt and connecting the theater formally with circus architecture, dominated the spatial structure, but it presented an enormous acoustical problem, which Poelzig compensated for by a special construction: "The cupola therefore acquired a tiered form, with hanging conical shapes that dispersed the sound waves and blocked the echoing in the auditorium."[73]

But when we look at the pictures of the interior space, our visual impression doesn't really correspond to Poelzig's reservedly neutral choice of words ("hanging conical shapes"). Quite the opposite, the space evokes—and this simile gained currency almost immediately—a limestone cavern with hanging stalactites.

> The huge circle is vaulted over with a kind of limestone cupola where light trickles down the uneven stalactites to the great tripartite and tri-tiered stage. A touch of the finger suffices to convert this flood of

light into a star-studded nocturnal sky, to compel the entire space and its murmuring audience to an awed silence.[74]

Paul Weiglin conveys a similar impression: "Pölzig has vaulted a huge cupola over the arena from which lights hang down as if on regularly placed stalactites, and when the house darkens they give the impression of a star-studded sky."[75]

Figure 20. Interior of the Grosses Schauspielhaus. Photograph by Zander & Labisch. Courtesy of the Theaterwissenschaftliche Sammlung of the University of Cologne.

This suggestion corresponds to the "barbaric monumentality"[76] that was typical of Poelzig and which Karl Scheffler describes as expressionistic:

> He pushes one too high in a primitive and romantic sense; there is a Gothicism in him; he strives for pathos of expression and colossal dimensions; he seems to break with all stylistic imitation and to introduce something quite new; he comes across as folksy, needs the masses, and thinks in stony exclamations and manifestos.[77]

Indeed, this decorative idealization is a cover-up, a "full-scale mock-up made of Rabitz plastering,"[78] for Poelzig came to the project so late that the wall design could only amount to a revetment covering what was already there. The decor, with its ostensibly natural forms, fitted the programmatic intent to make the space into a symbolic site of collective experience. Poelzig clearly sought to evoke the topos of the grotto as a place of mystical or transcendent experience.

But the configuration of the stage and the cupola with its lighting effects also had further associations. The reference to ancient Greek theater was made abundantly clear by the conversion of the former circus ring into a semicircular "orchestral" space before the elevated stage, but the artificial nocturnal sky likewise recalled the fact that performances in the ancient theater took place outdoors.

These two resonant spaces with their associations not only complemented each other in the effects they produced, but also, taken together, signified a rejection of the metropolis from which the theater, both in its organization and in its program, so clearly arose. In this sense, the architectural, atmospheric design placed the Grosses Schauspielhaus in a negative referential relation to its social environment.

But this very strategy of seeming to locate the design features of the new house outside of its urban context all the more obviously evoked the *genius loci* of the former circus in the eyes of many critics. Thus the mocking tone of Friedrich Düsel, who was otherwise very taken by the building:

> Outside, of course, in the atrium and walkways, where not too long ago horses stamped and lions roared, it's a frightful scene. You think you've been invited to a "fairy grotto" or a "pleasure palace" when you are greeted by the shimmering iridescent light play of the stylized palm trees, into which the coquettish taste of certain electrotechnicians has transformed the iron support pillars.[79]

In his polemic titled *Zirkus Reinhardt* (1920), Franz Ferdinand Baumgarten (1880–1927) writes: "The auditorium with its suspended cupola and artificial stalactites is a perfectly styled grotto for an ice palace with artificial ice and 'n——r songs.' The stalactite cupola is long familiar from the windows of many confectionery shops."[80] Even Poelzig's simple facade design, which stands out only through diverse tones of red, is a monument to failure in Baumgarten's eyes: "There, where Berlin's ugliness has become something spectral, in a narrow street on the Schiffbauerdamm, a firewall painted in an unbroken red screams out at you. This is the Grosses Schauspielhaus! Berlin's ugliest and most pretentious facade, a gigantic shack out of an anxiety dream."[81]

Apart from this polemic, which is directed at least as much at the undertaking as at the building itself, it remains to be noted that the Grosses Schauspielhaus was a modern theater that not only had the newest stage technology at its disposal, but was also a model in the variability of its stage space. Besides this, with its 3,200 seats it was much more spacious than the Deutsches Theater, with its approximately 1,000 seats.[82]

With the Grosses Schauspielhaus Max Reinhardt had realized his ideal of a "triad" of theater forms. The building brought him little luck, however. It was not just that the large stage required a very specific repertoire and placed great performative demands on the actors, few of whom were up to the job; the necessary long-term public response was also missing. We might say that the *genius loci* had the last laugh, considering that in the 1920s the house was used primarily for spectacular revues, thus reverting in the end to popular culture.

Giving Shape to the Masses

If social change was the moving force behind the creation of new sites for large crowds of people, there was a corresponding need to give these masses an appropriate shape (*Gestalt*). If there was a reluctance to adhere to the political metaphor of liberation for the working-class masses, it was equally impermissible to fall back on religious metaphors, since these were hardly in line with the heterogeneous composition of modern society.

It was in this connection that the cultural bourgeoisie's predilection for Greek antiquity and the humanistic heritage—both central elements of the educational system of the time—took on new significance. This was not just an intellectual tradition; it also offered a store of images that could be used to think about and represent social contexts.

It is in fact striking that the ancient Greek tragedies experienced a renaissance at the beginning of the twentieth century. This was initiated by both a growing interest in myth—as articulated, for instance, in psychoanalytic discourse—and individual reworkings of mythical material. The discourse of classical philology played a role here as well. For example, Ulrich von Wilamowitz-Moellendorf (1848–1931), the son-in-law of the legendary historian Theodor Mommsen (1817–1903), furthered the staging of classical drama with his translations and concrete assistance.[83]

This overlapping of theater and university ultimately produced the Akademische Verein für Kunst und Literatur (Academic Union for Art and Literature), which in February 1900 presented Sophocles's *Oedipus the King* in Wilamowitz's translation under the direction of Hans Oberländer.[84] This was by no means a purely literary "theater of declamation," for the production also utilized visual resources that would have been impossible in the stage practice of Naturalism. "The performance was not confined to the verbal text, but also included attitude, gesture, and dance. It was, to be sure, 'grand' illusionistic theater for the cultural bourgeoisie of the beginning of the century, but in the most skillful form."[85]

Besides decor and the use of music and dance, ancient drama also made it possible to thematize the masses in ways that had been missing in bourgeois theater since the eighteenth century. For, although the latter brought the focus on the actions of the individual subject to its consummation, it was precisely the chorus—so foreign to bourgeois drama—that enabled productions of Greek tragedy to conceive the masses in a way that transcended the conditions of modern society. Here, though it still needed to be worked out aesthetically, the collective entered the stage in a form that corresponded to the bourgeois image of society: as the ethically constituted polis.

And so in Reinhardt's first experiments with mass theater the role of the chorus, or the mass population, was central. This was not merely an aesthetic challenge; it also decisively broadened the spectrum of scenic possibilities. For it corresponded to a shift in theater's semiotic system, a shift that was typical of the theatrical reform movements of the early twentieth century and amounted to a strengthening of its visual components to the detriment of the literary text. To work out the aesthetic aspects of what he was doing, Reinhardt engaged his old friend Bertold Held (1868–1931), who was also the director of the theater school connected with the Deutsches Theater. Held was a specialist in crowd scenes and had developed a systematic "choreography" for staging them that went far beyond the prevailing praxis.[86]

Thematically, mass theater seemed all but forced to deal with mythic subjects. Reinhardt had staged these already in other theatrical formats—Hofmannsthal's *Elektra*, for example, at the Kleines Theater. But in that production, hardly any attention was paid to the aesthetic demands of staging a chorus. The first of Reinhardt's productions to take on this creative task fully was his *Oedipus the King* of 1910, also translated by Hofmannsthal.

When we examine the contemporary criticism of this production, the first thing that strikes us is the extent to which it centers on the adaptation of the circus space in the Zirkus Schumann.[87] Despite all reservations, expressed and unexpressed, the general feeling is positive, as we see in the case of Friedrich Düsel:

> Reinhardt has seen that the chief characteristic, the secret, of staging ancient theater lies in the expansion of space, both of the stage area and the circular auditorium . . . Here [in the Circus] he had the enormous space, which, though it couldn't handle the thirty thousand spectators of ancient Athens, was still capable of seating five or six thousand; here he had the amphitheater with ascending seats, which is the only way of providing a sounding board that gives the impression of sending the actors' voices echoing through the whole populace; and here in the former circus ring he had the orchestra that would be impossible to adjoin to any of our other modern stages.[88]

Düsel describes how completely Reinhardt had transformed the circus space into a theatrical space. The circus cupola was hung with an oversize cloth that muted the light descending to the arena, and an equally oversize set of stairs led from the orchestra (the transformed circus ring) to the stage:

A lowered ceiling in the form of a dark-brownish tent cloth veils the cupola, while curious violet and mixed-color beams from the spotlights flood the area below . . . The threefold Athenian proscenium has been replaced by a high free-standing set of stairs that descends to the orchestra circle (circus ring). The altar of the Greek theater is placed halfway up the stairs and gives the scene a natural articulation, a fulcrum for the play's action. Oedipus and his household are bathed in the bright glow of a spotlight on the high threshold of the palace and at the steps of the altar, a light that pitilessly presses into the depths of a terrible and painful destiny. The world besides, the thousand-voiced populace, remains in the half-darkness that is filled with muted shifting colors.[89]

Hermann Conrad's description reveals how much of the space was filled by the stage decor:

The impression rests on the grandeur of the setting and then, and of course mostly, on the grandeur of the action, which requires such a grand setting. The mere sight of the tall, broad, cyclopean stairs, of the six gigantic columns to which they lead, of the noble but simple portal, of the single entrance to the palace awakens the feeling of sublimity, of grandeur.[90]

Figure 21. Offering of Iocaste from *Oedipus Rex* (Berlin, 1910). Photograph by Zander & Labisch. Courtesy of the Theaterwissenschaftliche Sammlung of the University of Cologne.

Reinhardt's construction emphasized expansiveness and, therefore, contrast to a conventional theater space. Because of the division between stage and arena, a free surface was created on which masses of people had room to move:

> Opposite the palace and on both sides of the orchestra, two streets, emerging from distant, invisible depths, enter the circle. From the other side of these gates we hear the booming and swelling of a thousand voices; bands of people pour like torrents through the streets and convulse the air in a corybantic rush of tragic distress. Men, women, and the aged in motley garments that flutter in confusion when many hundreds of arms fly up under cries of woe. Handsome youths with torches, naked but for a cloth covering their slender loins.[91]

Hugo von Hofmannsthal (1874–1929) too had made the populace of Thebes a central protagonist in his translation, which was really more of an adaptation. One can see this in the very first scene, where he describes the people with the imagery of a catastrophically gushing torrent of water:

> A muted uproar becoming louder and louder. Faces first at the margins, looking backward; then, pressed from behind, they stream in like a torrent; all at once, they flood the stage to the palace stairs. Their eyes are fixed on the door, their lips repeating as in a litany: "Oedipus, help us! Help us, O King!" They are all young men, youths, and boys, with a few old men mixed in.
> ONE VOICE louder than the rest: Oedipus—King—help us!
> The heavy door of the palace opens suddenly. A stillness.—Oedipus steps out hastily. All arms stretch out to him.[92]

This first entrance of the populace—to describe which the critics repeatedly drew on Hofmannsthal's text—immediately displayed the largeness of the space through quick and copious movement and created an antagonism between Oedipus and the populace that was already adumbrated by the layout of the stage and the lighting. This effect is described by most reviewers as a central moment of the production: "This graphic representation of a people ravaged by plague and famine, hundreds of people lifting their naked arms to their king and begging for help, was the most effective piece of staging that I have ever witnessed, and thousands of others felt as I did."[93] Or as Hermann Conrad wrote:

> The beginning is just as marvelously worked out, a low rising sound in the distance, the swell and finally the roaring burst of the populace flooding onto the scene, the plague-ridden and the healthy, till they fill the whole arena and gather on the palace stairs, begging their strong king for help.[94]

Figure 22. Tilla Durieux as Iocaste in *Oedipus Rex* (Berlin, 1910). Photograph by Becker & Maas. Courtesy of the Theaterwissenschaftliche Sammlung of the University of Cologne.

Fritz Engel too translates the impression this makes into natural images:

> The populace throngs ahead to the palace to beg the king for help against the plague. The crowd stays always in the violet light that streams aslant from above, more shadow than actual light. Only Oedipus, the prince, and those closest to him who are moving on the stairs are bathed in the royal sunlight. A stroke of genius: symbolizing the great social divide with the help of spotlights. The masses of the people surge and ebb sonically too. Now we hear them thunder behind the hills, now like the booming of the sea, and again like a storm subsiding.[95]

Figure 23. E. v. Winterstein as Creon (*left*) and Paul Wegener as Oedipus (*top right*) in *Oedipus Rex* (Berlin, 1910). Photograph by Zander & Labisch. Courtesy of the Theaterwissenschaftliche Sammlung of the University of Cologne.

Reinhardt had divided the chorus into two parts, following Hofmannsthal's directions, those who had a speaking role and a host of extras, for which 300 students were engaged.[96] But this shift not only created the described aesthetic effect; it ultimately represented a new interpretation of the text, as Karl Frenzel notes:

> The real act of violence that Hofmannsthal perpetrates on Sophocles consists in the democratization of the tragedy. He makes a revolutionary drama out of it. The dark mass of the people of Thebes, which Sophocles represents as a modest chorus of aged citizens, becomes a vital presence in Hofmannsthal.[97]

We might supplement Frenzel's remarks by saying that the vitality of the "dark masses" only comes about because Reinhardt gives it an appropriate place in the scenic space so that it can then enter the spectators' consciousness.

The effect on the audience was strengthened by the fact that the half-darkness of the stage lighting brought together the arena stage and the rows of seats that (nearly) surrounded it, thus blurring the boundary between actors and spectators: "For the first time, we felt, in this enormous space holding 5,000 spectators, what tragic mass-effect is and what resonance Greek tragedy gains from the breadth and height of the space."[98] Fritz Engel connects this spatial effect with the cultural idea of the masses:

> But the individual is of no importance here. In this half-light only the crowd has any function. It dawns on us what is meant by the "audience." That is: what Reinhardt needs. For other directors would have nothing against five thousand spectators. But for him the crowd is everything, both subject and object. He thanks the five thousand attendees by showing them a troupe of what looks like ten thousand. He shows the masses to the masses. He shows them themselves in enhanced forms of passion and dress.[99]

Engel's reading opens up the staging of themes from classical antiquity to a contemporary figure of thought by identifying both audience and chorus as the masses. This is all the more surprising because the concept of the masses, as Erika Fischer-Lichte explains,[100] had distinctly pejorative overtones in the bourgeois context. For Fischer-Lichte, the special significance of the production lies in the fact that Reinhardt made no claim to establish a solid sense of community, but wanted rather to connect the audience and the actors together in a specific atmosphere.

> Since the sense of community did not arise through a common symbolism which explicitly referred to beliefs, ideologies etc. shared by all spectators—or, at least, by a majority of them—but to very special physical effects brought about by the presence of the masses in the space and by the frequently changing atmosphere, it cannot be regarded as a political, national, religious or ideological community . . . I shall call it a theatrical community. A theatrical community is not only a temporary community, as transitory and ephemeral as any performance. It exists, at best, throughout the whole course of the performance and dissolves, at its latest, at the very end. Moreover, it is a community which is not based on common beliefs and shared ideologies—not even on shared meanings; it can do without them.[101]

This aspect of community in aesthetic experience can be seen as an answer to the heterogeneity of society in the process of modernization. In this sense it also entails an aspect of visionary breakthrough:

> Reinhardt's productions of *Oedipus Rex* and the *Oresteia* succeeded in collapsing dichotomies between individual and community, between mind and body which were deeply rooted in Christian culture . . . This also implied the collapse of another opposition—that between elitist and popular culture. By using the most "sacred" texts from the cultural tradition of the elite on the one hand and, on the other, by playing in a circus which emphasized the body, providing "thrill" and "entertainment," Reinhardt bridged the gap between elitist and popular culture. In fact, a new people's theatre was created

in which members of all social groups, classes and strata met and formed a community together.[102]

This utopian element was singled out by Reinhardt's contemporaries at the opening of the Grosses Schauspielhaus as one of its aspirations:

> The new home of German dramatic art is meant as a place of collective experience that is lifted above daily life. Not just for a few hundred or thousand people, most of whom can give themselves the pleasure because they have the financial means. It is consecrated to the people. More than three thousand people can get together in common feeling without having to make a great sacrifice. And this fact at the deepest level means a "reawakening of Greek drama," which is the common heritage of all.[103]

Figure 24. Paul Wegener as Oedipus. Courtesy of the Theaterwissenschaftliche Sammlung of the University of Cologne.

With all this in mind, we still have to ask about the shape that Reinhardt gave to the masses in his production. Clearly the image he conveys is not aligned with a (more or less kitschy) historicism, but rather emphasizes, in the way the actors are dressed, for example, the unfamiliar or alien. This—from the European bourgeoisie's point of view—civilizational amorphousness has mostly to do with the chorus, which Arnold Neuweiler calls the "representational mass" in his short book *Massenregie* (1919; *Directing the Masses*).[104] The representational mass, he explains, has nothing to do with "humanity" (*Menschlichkeit*) in the stricter sense of the term.[105]

This loss of "humanity" is further stressed by Reinhardt's lighting and segmentation of space: the crowd becomes a unity of many bodies that are not clearly demarcated from those of the audience. As Fischer-Lichte insists, the masses are not presented as a formation defined by values or ideas, but rather correspond in their form to the idea of the "mass ornament" that Kracauer saw represented in the Tiller Girls: a self-sufficient aesthetic transformation that serves no immediate purpose and whose individual members have meaning not in their particularity, but only in the collective aspect they present as members of the masses.

But whereas Kracauer sees the Tiller Girls as a reflection of the capitalist economic system, Reinhardt's mass ornament has another point of reference. It imagines the masses as Greek polis in a free adaptation of the cultural bourgeoisie's imaginary and gives them an impressive aesthetic embodiment that exorcizes the terror of a free fall into the chaos of big-city mass society. Here we can see the dialectical point of Engel's formulation: "He shows the masses to the masses": Reinhardt's great project, which in its form and organizational configuration is both influenced by and steeped in the modernized society of his time, imagines a "beyond" to this modernity in order to give society an image of cultural continuity.

When this idea finally took hold in Berlin society in 1919, Kurt Pinthus, still under the influence of the most recent political events, described it as a basis for cultural self-reflection:

> The new society and the new national theater can only arise through a complete renewal from the bottom up and the inside out. Thus the national theater of the future will be able to organize itself not on the basis of a principle forced on it from without, but only through common longing, common enthusiasm, and will. Now, however, the combination of a degenerate economy, an ossified social system, and a stifling science and technology has blown itself to pieces. The spurious culture of a society which had no idea that its mightiest movements were only agonized convulsions has now collapsed—and the masses rise up and draw nigh, united in their misery and their longing for a better future and a new ordering of humanity. The national theater of the future can only be a theater for these masses,

who will also ultimately absorb the exploded remnants of the old society.[106]

In hindsight, it was predictable that Reinhardt's project was doomed to fail. His aesthetic concept was not sufficient to the demands of the time,[107] his image of the masses was no longer in line with the demands of the Weimar Republic. So we must see it as a symbolic act that it was Erwin Piscator (1893–1966), in his political revue *Trotz Alledem* (1925; *Despite Everything*), who came up with a new aesthetic and programmatic image of the masses in the same Grosses Schauspielhaus—at a time, to be sure, when the National Socialist movement in the streets was already preparing to permanently recast the image of the masses in the twentieth century.[108]

Siegfried Jacobsohn, for whom the mass productions signaled the beginning of a long, gradual break with Reinhardt, described the 1920 production of *Hamlet* in the Grosses Schauspielhaus as an act of physical overload that made aesthetic apprehension impossible:

> The physical strain of piecing together the text of the drama from shreds of sound—this alone would inhibit any kind of aesthetic impression. Added to this, the unbearable torturing of the nervus opticus. I don't mean just the garish beams of the spotlights, dancing around like will-o'-the-wisps . . . : fitted into the middle of the proscenium's sopraporta is a powerful cone of yellow light which Berlin's ophthalmologists will have to thank for the fact that their office hours will be as sold out as the Grosses Schauspielhaus for the next few weeks . . . At the end of the third act I was at the end of my rope. To hold up through this barrage, one would need the physical constitution of a barbarian; and to take pleasure in it, one would need a barbarian's taste.[109]

This arch dismissal shows both how hard it was to keep such a large theatrical space filled with a suitable repertoire and how quickly the momentum of the sensation aroused by the first experiments began to falter. The space Reinhardt designed for a mass theater proved to be, aesthetically and culturally, much too unstable.

This instability was observable not only in Reinhardt's own productions, but to an even greater extent in those of the many adepts who zealously hastened to emulate his circus experiments. As early as 1911, we hear Hermann Kienzl groaning, "Fashion is consuming itself again,"[110] as he reports on the staging of Fritz Helmer's *Oresteia*. But the culmination of such epigonism was reached in Shakespeare's *Richard III* as staged by Ferdinand

Bonn (1861–1933),[111] the P. T. Barnum of the German theater.[112] Bonn, who had made his fortune with theatrical adaptations of Sherlock Holmes stories, played the Shakespearean villain for the better part of the performance on horseback. Friedrich Düsel sums it up: "The main problem here is not the writer, not the director, not the actor, not even the chorus, but the circus ring and the leaping and galloping of the caparisoned nags."[113] If it was still possible for Reinhardt to attract a broad public consisting of all social levels,[114] Bonn's whimsical use of the space was reduced in the eyes of the critics to pure sensationalism:

> Let's be just! A city of three million obviously has quite a few boarders, and an audience of 6,000 represents an intellectual mix very similar to the social mix of people walking the streets; which immediately provokes the remark that the Bonn- and horse-act enthusiasts were by no means to be seen exclusively in the cheap seats.[115]

Here the *genius loci* has gotten the upper hand—an example that also shows how precarious it was to find the balance that would permit a complex negotiation of space, masses, cultural tradition, and audience to develop in the context of playing in a circus.

But not even Reinhardt's experiments met with undivided approval. They too experienced vehement rejection to some extent. Thus, for example, Franz Ferdinand Baumgarten believed he saw in them the signs of a general cultural decline:

> The bourgeois cities of the 19th century have become American colonies. The brutal instincts of the newly arrived cultural parvenus have undermined and superficialized the bourgeoisie as the sponsors and sustainers of culture . . . In the major cities, boulevard theaters, degraded by capitalist competion to a mere scrambling after effects, have appeared alongside the court and state theaters.[116]

Thus Baumgarten reads the circus experiment as a *mene tekel*:

> Since he [Reinhardt] is too weak to develop a style, his unbridled temperament can only shatter all style. Now he annihilates theater through the circus. He is the producer-director of the Wilhelminian baroque. His circus is the hara-kiri of the Wilhelminian theater. The features of this theater are market-hawked, dolled-up classics that have been abused to the point of department store kitsch, sexual allurements and scenographic jokes, the breeding of a snobbish premiere-riffraff, and the degeneration of sequel performances.[117]

Siegfried Jacobsohn likewise rejected the circus, but explained it on entirely different grounds:

> What corresponds to the amphitheater in our culture is not the circus but the theater we are perfectly familiar with already. If *Oedipus the King* were a new play it would be performed nowhere else than in the Deutsches Theater, and if Reinhardt is tempted to revive this old *Oedipus the King* he should make do with the conditions of his own stage.[118]

But behind this philippic lies a basic misunderstanding of the relationship between cultural tradition and the masses. Max Reinhardt's experiment was grounded in the conviction that the bourgeois theater was no longer up to the task of giving shape to the masses. By merging popular culture with cultural tradition and high-quality acting with mass productions, Reinhardt was trying to create a space that could provide an answer to the "dark mass of the people of Thebes"—an aesthetic and theatrical answer, however, that was just as unstable as the cultural space in which he sought it.

Chapter 4

✦

"Reinhardt Goes Global!"
Tours, Guest Performances, Expansions

The preceding chapters have shown not only how Reinhardt's programmatic pluralism led him to adopt diverse spatial formats and theatrical styles, but also how these different forms enabled him to define the social and cultural position of his theater within bourgeois society at the start of the twentieth century. The following chapters will more closely investigate the organizational structure of Reinhardt's "theatrical empire," as well as his working methods, in light of these findings. This does not mean that we shall undertake an analytical study of its internal workings as a business; our purpose is rather to show how this complex apparatus developed into an art form that consistently moved beyond the horizon of a national, bourgeois art.

Reinhardt had announced as early as 1901 that he had very pragmatic reasons for wanting to break out of a constricted social and cultural milieu:

> Meanwhile, we need to travel from time to time, of course, and I mean repeatedly. We need to take what we have gained in a narrow sphere and have it corroborated in other cities, other countries, other continents. In order not to relax and ossify in the assured appreciation of an all too familiar audience; in order to be forced to renew ourselves before new ears, new people, who know nothing about us other than their immediate impression; in order to hear the echo of foreign languages, which the art of theater needs once it feels seasoned enough to conquer the world. And then, too, because I personally feel more comfortable on the road than I do anywhere else.[1]

From this perspective, it seems that the extensive touring Reinhardt undertook soon afterward was a step consistent with his artistic self-assurance and self-criticism. His contemporaries, however, took a much more critical and dismissive view of it. Siegfried Jacobsohn, for instance, warned that Reinhardt ran the risk of becoming a "circuit tour director" (*Rundreiseregisseur*):[2] "It [Reinhardt's work] has fallen off since the success of *Oedipus*.

Since then, Europe has become Reinhardt's fatherland, the world his garden, and Berlin a backwater that he passes through rather reluctantly several times a year."[3]

The tone of an offended Berlin patriotism is hard to miss in this dressing-down—a resentment that Reinhardt himself felt for other reasons when he let it be known, about the same time he began the guest tours, that he was thinking of stepping down from the directorship of his Berlin theaters because he continually felt hindered in his work by critics and government authorities.

But if we look past these details and take a larger historical view, Reinhardt's tours appear in a different light. Mobility and travel have been a hallmark of European theater through the course of its history.[4] We only have to think of the foundation myth of Thespis's wagon, which still functions as a theatrical metaphor. And when we look closer at hand, we quickly realize that there is no development in the history of European theater that does not go back to concrete instances of exchange. Which makes it all the more puzzling that Reinhardt's plans were met with such condemnation and were vilified as simple lust for profit.

And so before going into more detail about the basic features of Reinhardt's production methods, using the example of *The Miracle*, I would like to present some pivotal ideas about the significance of tours in the history of twentieth-century theater.

Significance of Touring for Twentieth-Century Theater

It becomes obvious, when we take a closer look at European—and particularly German—theatrical history, that traveling actors and ensembles have made decisive contributions to the development of theater, even if this fact is sometimes hidden behind the facade of nationally oriented historiographies. Yet the development of Germanophone theater in the seventeenth century was as much indebted to wandering players from England, Italy, and the Netherlands, as French theater was to the influence of the commedia dell'arte.[5] And tours and exchanges have been the motor force and linchpin of European theater up to the present time.[6] We need only think of the festival culture that has been evolving, since the end of the nineteenth century, into what amounts to an institutionalization of such cultural exchange.[7]

Of course, the social frameworks have undergone considerable change over the course of time. Though we can still speak of an international aristocratic culture well into the eighteenth century, in which the courts were the predominant venues and sponsors of the theatrical system, a permanent shift—though not a radical break—took place in the nineteenth century, due to the influence and significance of the rising bourgeois classes.

As mentioned in the introduction, the theatrical landscape of the nineteenth century was marked by virtuosity, that is, by traveling actors and actresses who appeared in various theaters to perform "their" special roles. In the second half of the nineteenth century, this development was further marked by a strong trend toward internationalization. Guest appearances in foreign countries were no longer targeted solely at "countrymen" who attended the so-called "foreign theaters" in their new land of residence.[8] Instead, the virtuoso actors and actresses increasingly performed before audiences that spoke other languages. Thus, for example, the guest appearances of Eleonora Duse (1858–1924) in Berlin starting in the 1890s,[9] or the numerous world tours of Sarah Bernhardt (1844–1923), were events that became fixed reference points in the cultural discourse.[10] Guest performances were financially attractive to these artists, and they were worthwhile for the audience because actors' individual interpretations had increasingly become its dominant interest.

This development was furthered in the North German Confederation by the massive boom in private theaters once the free-trade laws were passed in 1869. Often the founders of these theaters had neither a resident troupe nor a diverse repertoire at their disposal. To lower operating costs and increase the rate of seat occupancy, they often rented out their houses for guest performances that alternated with their own productions. Houses that did have their own ensembles would regularly employ this same practice during the off-season: owners could meet their regular costs by renting out their stages to guest artists, while for many actors this kind of "summer theater" was a necessary source of income, since their contracts ran only to the end of a season and they were not paid during the off-season.[11]

A significant innovation in this practice was introduced by the guest appearances of the Meiningen troupe, which gave approximately 2,500 performances on the road within just sixteen years (1874–1890). In contrast to other traveling players, the Meiningen group's tours were not an extra, but were structurally and artistically a fixed component of the group's basic conception and economy. It is not hard to imagine that a small city like Meiningen could not really have supported such a lavish theatrical operation, even if the productions had been able to find enough of a local audience. Although other theaters in a similar situation tried to make themselves interesting to the public by offering a large number of productions, the Duke of Meiningen, Georg II, took the opposite approach. The individual productions were artistically too elaborate and too costly financially not to show them to a broader audience than could be found in the small town. Thus aesthetic policy and guest performances were inherently interrelated from the very start.

But even more important than the Meiningen troupe's "internal" motivation is the reception their performances got; for, in contrast to the reigning practice, the accent was on group achievement of a high aesthetic caliber rather than the celebration of a few great virtuosos. And so within a very short time, the Meiningen troupe came to epitomize a new theatrical aesthetic based on concern for historical accuracy on the one hand and ensemble performance on the other.

It is surely no accident that the autobiography of Konstantin S. Stanislavski himself (1863–1938), the founder of the Moscow Art Theater, describes his attendance at a performance of the Meiningen troupe as an "artistic awakening experience." Its new performance style gave him ideas for his own theater: "I never missed a performance and didn't just watch, but really studied them."[12]

With the Meiningen ensemble began a new level of cultural exchange and a process that was ultimately aimed at the establishment of international standards for the art of theater. There began an epoch of "global players" who were firmly rooted in the cities and regions they came from on the one hand, but who were oriented toward an audience beyond those boundaries on the other.

We can also see a continuance of the Meiningen influence in Stanislavski's work in this respect, for he and his Moscow Art Theater undertook extensive tours through Europe and the United States. In the process he propagated the theory of acting he developed and taught, in addition to his specific theatrical aesthetic. This form of psychological realism—which according to Stanislavski is not an expression of individual talent, but rather a product of precise training and artistic practice—developed into a standard model of bourgeois art. The Moscow Art Theater became a veritable model for the United States and Europe in the first third of the twentieth century, and its aftereffects are still being felt today. With the founding of the Actors Studio in New York (1947), associated with its long-term director Lee Strasberg (1901–1982), who became its director in 1952, Stanislavski's teaching method not only found a permanent home in the United States, but also became the central and virtually obligatory paradigm of the art of acting in that country to the present day. There is hardly a well-known American actor who was not trained in this school or has not been strongly influenced by it.[13] In this sense one can say (at least in terms of pervasiveness and acceptance) that Stanislavski gave bourgeois theater a form that enjoyed, and largely continues to enjoy, an international currency and prestige.

Beyond their common ground in terms of artistic views and practices, Stanislavski and Max Reinhardt also had a personal relationship with each other. In 1906, one year after Reinhardt assumed direction of the Deutsches Theater, the Moscow Art Theater made its first visit to Berlin. Its guest performances left a lasting impression on the theatrical discourse of the time,[14] a striking feature of which was the broad correspondence of repertoire between the Moscow Art Theater and the Deutsches Theater. If the production of Gorky's *Lower Depths* had been one of the crucial steps in the development of the Kleines Theater, the Moscow troupe's repertoire, for its part, included the works of Gerhart Hauptmann and others. The affinity demonstrates that this form of bourgeois theater was by no means a phenomenon limited to Germany; but, more than this, it was also one of the basic conditions for the success of guest performances, for only a correspondence of repertoire permitted nuanced comparisons and prevented cultural differences—especially in language—from becoming a barrier to reception.[15]

In 1928, Reinhardt made Stanislavski an honorary member of the Deutsches Theater, a distinction that had hitherto been granted only once. This honor should be understood as the outward expression of an inner solidarity, for in fact both directors seemed to be working on the project of an international theater.

With the Meiningen troupe there also began a practice that changed the perception of theater beyond the individual case. If the appearances of virtuosos (increasingly performing in a foreign language) were grounded in a shift of interest away from the understanding of a literary text toward individual theatrical interpretation, this same process of the de-literarization of theater[16] was continued in the new form of guest appearances. It is true that most productions were still based on a literary foundation, but it was the staging itself that now moved into the foreground as the benchmark of aesthetic appreciation. These guest performances, therefore, participated in a developmental process that was characteristic of early twentieth-century theater as a whole.

The internationalization that resulted from guest appearances, however, was by no means limited to "serious" theater (*Höhenkammtheater*). Our brief examination of exhibition spaces in the preceding chapter has already shown that a new level of international exchange was becoming the norm on that front, but we can add to this that popular culture itself was functioning as a (cultural) catalyst. This was especially true for the transatlantic axis. Thus the guest appearances of the legendary circuses of P. T. Barnum (1810–1891) and James Bailey (1847–1906) influenced the development of the European circus, just as the guest appearances of the Wild West Show of Buffalo Bill (1846–1917) occupied an important place in the entertainment culture that was becoming established in the European metropolises.[17]

Thus Max Reinhardt was by no means breaking new ground with his tours, but rather showing his openness to a cultural development that was already prevalent in a different social sphere and adapting it to the theater to an extent that was so far unprecedented. Max Epstein (1874–1948) was critical of this development: "No German director does guest appearances to the extent that Max Reinhardt does."[18] Heinz Herald, one of Reinhardt's most important collaborators, ascribed programmatic significance to it:

> It [the tour] has become one of Reinhardt's most effective resources, important both artistically and economically to the successful operation of his theater. It conveys to thousands of people who are spatially removed from the place of his creative work an idea of his art, to which they would otherwise have no access.[19]

Heinrich Braulich, in his study *Max Reinhardt. Zwischen Traum und Wirklichkeit* (1969; *Max Reinhardt: Between Dream and Reality*), has tried to explain the guest appearances mainly on the basis of the way Reinhardt's theaters were set up economically:

> It was no longer the individual virtuoso selling his or her individual achievement; it was the "business theater"—ultimately the theatrical company as the ensemble of economic relations—that now sold the ensemble achievement at top prices by regularly going on the road year after year, relying mostly on the draw of its stars. The first and most successful theater operation to demonstrate this method, remunerative in terms of both fame and fortune, was Max Reinhardt's.[20]

The same tempestuous intensity Reinhardt had shown in conquering his place in the Berlin theater landscape he now showed again by expanding beyond Berlin through guest appearances, as well as through the temporary acquisition of theaters such as the Münchner Künstlertheater (Munich Art Theater).[21] Within a relatively short time, the name Max Reinhardt was a "brand"[22] that was not only known throughout the whole of Germany, but was also intensively and aggressively used in the promotion of events. Epstein groused about this: "This traveling all over the globe, this currying favor with all sorts of journalists and officials, doesn't in the least fit the image of the quiet thinker so many think Reinhardt to be. He really must have an overpowering inclination to this kind of self-promotion."[23] Behind the criticism of Reinhardt's tours are various interlocking motives. The tours were understood as an expression of the growing economic orientation of theater and as the pure maximization of profit without intrinsic artistic value.[24] At the same time, these arguments demonstrate an implicit critique of the modernization of daily life. The talk of self-promotion and journalists can be read as codewords for modernization, in which art always functions as the object and disposable product of economic structures that run counter to its "intrinsic purpose."

With respect to guest appearances in Germany there is an alternative, less moralizing interpretation: that the expansion and "multiple use" of stage productions were a guarantee of the economic stability and continuity of the Reinhardtian theaters. The dual system of presenting regular repertoire and making guest appearances was the consequence of a permanent paradigm shift by which bourgeois theater was making greater efforts to free itself from a system that had arisen out of the conditions of the court and the later state theaters. If economic leeway was not ensured by sovereign protectorates or state subventions, then theater had no choice but to adapt its forms of production to the new situation. In this sense, Reinhardt appears as the representative of a modernization that had to try to overstep spatial and social boundaries in order to secure for itself the largest possible audience. The adjacent caricature gives expression to this need for and dream of a corresponding ubiquity.

"Reinhardt Goes Global!" 91

Figure 25. Caricature by Walter Herzberg titled "Lord of the World" depicting Reinhardt and the French secretary of state Briand. Reinhardt: "No, Monsieur Briand, I can't be fully enthusiastic about your pan-European plans—it is too small for my touring plans."

But whereas the early guest performances, for all their increase in scope, moved within the framework of what was hitherto normal practice, Reinhardt's production of *The Miracle* marked a radical caesura in his work. In both scope and expenditure, but also in its aesthetic structure, it was planned from the start as a "touring" production. Thus in the following pages we shall trace its contours at its two most important venues: London (1911) and New York (1923).

The Miracle in London (1911)

In 1911, Max Reinhardt intensified his efforts to gain a foothold in London, at that time Europe's most important theater capital.[25] The English public's attitude was marked by curiosity and interest. After all, his name was firmly established in Europe, although it rested more on hearsay than on personal experience: "The name of Max Reinhardt is not as well known in England as it should be."[26]

By the end of 1912 Reinhardt had presented four productions in London: *Sumurûn*, a pantomime based on a script by Friedrich Freksa (1882–1955); an adaptation of *Oedipus Rex*; and two pantomimes by Karl Vollmoeller (1878–1948), *Venetian Night* and *The Miracle*.

The success of *Sumurûn*, a production that Reinhardt imported from the Kammerspiele in Berlin, was so great that after its first six-week run the term "Rheinhardtism" had gained currency as a catchword for his theater aesthetic.[27]

It wasn't just the sheer visual opulence, but rather the coordination of all theatrical elements together that left a deep impression on the English public. This becomes especially clear in the way Reinhardt was contrasted with Herbert Tree (1853–1917), London's most important and best-known theater director up to that time.[28] John Palmer describes the difference between them as follows:

> Sir Herbert and his men would insist that you should see, not with the mind but with the eye; and that what you saw should make it impossible for your imagination to go roving behind the gross confines of unlovely stones and trees. It has always been the aim of these producers to fill the vision, not to direct it; to thwart, and not to encourage, the imagination. The method of Professor Reinhardt is precisely converse. He plays with the imagination as with a familiar. He knows the things it will see, and not see.[29]

Sumurûn's success prompted the impresario Charles B. Cochran (1872–1951) to commission Reinhardt to create a pantomime especially for London. The venue was to be Olympia Hall, an exhibition space that was also used as a circus and a hippodrome. The showing of *The Miracle* there on December 12, 1911,[30] surpassed all previous standards. If Reinhardt had played before 5,000 spectators in the Zirkus Schumann, the number at Olympia Hall was approximately 30,000, and the staging area had room for about 1,800 extras.[31] A special attraction of the production was the versatile and extensive lighting, for which a crew of 56 electrical and 82 mechanical technicians was required. The total expenses ran to 1.4 million marks according to Huesmann, which meant that the production had to gross 20,000 marks per performance to cover the costs.[32]

For the plot of *The Miracle*, Karl Vollmoeller drew on the same legendary material for the pantomime that Maurice Maeterlinck (1862–1949) had already used for his play *Sister Beatrice*. It centers on the young nun Megildis, who has been designated by the abbess to succeed the cloister's hundred-year-old sacristine and for that reason has the key to the Muenster. In the middle of the cloister stands the miraculous statue of the Madonna. Because Megildis has been led to neglect her duties by a minstrel and dancing children, she has to spend a night of vigil in prayer as a penance.

As she lies prostrate in prayer before the holy statue, there comes a knocking at the church door—it is the minstrel, who is revealed in the course of the action to be a demonic tempter. He has brought a knight with him who falls in love with the nun at first sight. Megildis lays her habit and her key before the statue and follows the knight out into the world. At this moment the Madonna descends from the altar, removes her own crown and mantle, and takes the place of the nun. When the other sisters come to early mass, they notice that the holy statue is missing. The old sacristine, however, recognizes the Madonna in the nun's clothing, and the sisters break into jubilant song.

At this juncture an interior sequence of five tableaux that depict Megildis's travels through the world is inserted into the action. She is kidnapped by a robber knight, who for his part loses her in gambling to a prince. The latter is stabbed to death incognito by his father, who has fallen in love with Megildis at first sight and seeks to protect her. The father then loses his mind as a consequence. Finally Megildis—after a court scene in which the crowd falls into a collective twitching[33]—is carried off as a whore by mercenaries. The fifth tableau depicts her in the mercenaries' train holding a dead child in her arm. As Megildis falls exhausted in the snow, the minstrel reappears, leading a *danse macabre* of her dead lovers, a scenic recapitulation of the entire inserted sequence.

> When the procession is over, the minstrel steps toward the woman, who stands there trembling, to drag her with him after the others. At this moment the great cloister bell rings out from very close nearby and we hear children and nuns singing. A bright, warm light, as from the opened portal of a bright Weihnachtskirche [Christmas church], falls on the snow. Megildis tears herself free and hastens, clutching her child to her, toward the nearby sound and light.[34]

The Madonna, now back in her own garments, takes the dead child from Megildis and cradles it in her arms like the child Jesus. Then she returns to her old place above the altar. The room darkens, and in the last tableau we see Megildis lying before the statue as she wakens from a long dream.

Vollmoeller's adaptation of the material is not really oriented to the religious kernel of the legend, as was critically noted on the occasion of its Berlin performance in 1914.[35] Instead, Vollmoeller uses its framework to evoke a teeming world of images from the Middle Ages that turn on the tension between sanctity, represented by the Madonna, and sensuality and sin, represented by the minstrel. The conflict is carried out in the body of the young nun, as we clearly gather from Vollmoeller's description: "The young nun can no longer withstand the enticing melody, her whole body begins to sway unconsciously to the beat, her feet begin to glide, and the young sacristine forgets office and key for a light, delicate spring dance."[36]

Figure 26. The nuns hail the Madonna in *The Miracle* (London, 1911). Photograph by Wilhelm Willinger. Courtesy of the Theaterwissenschaftliche Sammlung of the University of Cologne.

This opposition corresponds to the opposition in Vollmoeller's script between the interior of the cloister church and the colorful but merciless world of daily life outside the church portal. The medieval ambience of the fable makes it possible to depict the liturgical splendor of the religious sphere and to evoke the world of knights and courtly life in equal measure. Reinhardt's scenic designer Ernst Stern (1876–1954), who was responsible for the spatial design and costumes, describes in his diary how the imagery was pervaded by familiar precedents in the history of European art:

"Reinhardt Goes Global!"

> Suddenly a bishop stands before me in the full splendor of his regalia.—Michael Pacher had painted him in 1457. Now he is in the "Olympia"... The knight in armor riding toward me owes his appearance to a statuette of St. George by the old master Hans Mutscher... And then I sketch the women with their colored veils wafting on their tall hennins. The cut and material of their long-trained garments forces them to take positions that have been immortalized by the master Froissart in his miniatures.[37]

The key element of the staging was the transformation of the acting space by the architect Hermann Dernburg (1868–1935) according to Ernst Stern's sketches. If Olympia Hall at the start of the work could be called a "railway station of glass and iron with a chaos of automobiles inside,"[38] the whole space was nevertheless converted into a Gothic cathedral within a short period of time.

Figure 27. Sketch by Ernst Stern of the set design for *The Miracle* (London, 1911). Courtesy of the Theaterwissenschaftliche Sammlung of the University of Cologne.

The sketch of the set design shows that the audience was integrated into the imaginary space of the cathedral; in other words, the conventional separation between stage and audience was annulled, so that the audience was seated within the stage decor. The entire space became scenic space. At the same time Reinhardt had elaborate stage machinery built, for example, a stage wagon twenty meters long and eighteen meters wide that had room for 1,400 extras. There were also various lowering and transforming mechanisms. Not only did the lighting setup make it possible to create different moods with color, which made light a constitutive factor of the whole production, but the large, bright-colored Gothic windows too were correspondingly lit to full advantage. Immense pains were taken with the scenic elements to create the desired illusion. The imaginary cathedral's rosette alone had a diameter three times the size of the one in the Notre Dame cathedral in Paris.[39]

Figure 28. Sketch by Ernst Stern of processional entry through the main door in *The Miracle* (London, 1911). Courtesy of the Theaterwissenschaftliche Sammlung of the University of Cologne.

But the gigantic space was brought to life not only by technical means; the crowd-handling aesthetic for which Reinhardt was by now famous was also put to use. The critics constantly cited the scenes that were brought to life by huge masses of people. Thus, for instance, the opening scene, showing a procession of pilgrims to the holy statue, the high point of which was the miraculous healing of a cripple, had an especially great effect on the audience, as a reviewer from the *Nation* notes: "In the first [scene] you witness the glory of the miraculous Virgin, dispensing curses and blessings to the throng of worshippers that surges in, the guardian nuns and ecclesiastics through the east door, the people through the west."[40]

In his discussion of the play, John Palmer remarks that Reinhardt succeeded in directing the audience's attention less through the actual arrangement of the space than through an intensity of atmosphere, a concept also used by Herald to describe Reinhardt's aesthetic. Only in this way, Palmer argues, was it possible for the cathedral decor, which also incorporated the audience space, to be neutralized in places where it would have been irrelevant.

> There is a moment of darkness; the great cathedral door glides open; a small but "practicable" hillside rumbles in through the opening; and, when the light returns, the walls of the cathedral have vanished. Physically you can see them, if you really wish it. But who would strain the physical eye to discern in the shadow something impertinent to the story when the producer has forcibly suggested to your imagination the thing he wants you with your whole heart to see?[41]

Palmer's description enables us to guess how successful Reinhardt was at filling the gigantic dimensions of the space with a host of extras and a series of spectacular effects, including clusters of knights and a pack of hounds.[42] Through the interaction of images that one clearly recognizes as deriving from the collective imagination, through a coordination of all elements of staging and a dramaturgy of atmosphere, Reinhardt created an impressive stage work that—as the reviewers constantly attested—did not belie its "German provenance," but rather used this "foreignness" as an aesthetic stimulus. "Movement, spectacle, mass, impression by color and changing panorama, and the sentimental religious appeal—the whole fortified by some real scholarship and the studious German imagination—these are the substantial ends and agencies of Herr Reinhardt's production."[43]

With *The Miracle* Reinhardt had given new form to his mass productions and created a new genre, the "monster pantomime," whose roots lay equally in artistic pantomime, circus pantomime, and the tradition of English pageants, a form of community theater in which local history was theatrically (re)called to mind.[44] And since the early nineteenth century, the "Christmas panto(mime)" had been a fixture of the English holiday customs.

At the same time, this new form indicated a turning away from the artistic resources of bourgeois theater, which in this instance was marked not only by the annulment of the separation between audience and stage, but also by a new definition of the actor's status. The omission of speech as a creative resource reduced it to a visual sign—a procedure that aroused objections.

Already with *Sumurûn* one critic had expressed doubts about the genre of pantomime, because it was unfair to the actor:

> Why, after all, should it be dumb-show? Why should the actor be docked of his faculty of speech? . . . Are the passions concerned too delicate, too subtle, too evanescent for speech to convey? . . . No; the truth is that Reinhardt rejoiced in thus dealing with dumb puppets—that he could mould them to his purpose as a "producer" easier so that with their full scope [*sic*].[45]

Figure 29. The Knight sees the Nun in *The Miracle* (New York, 1923). Photographer unknown. Courtesy of the Theaterwissenschaftliche Sammlung of the University of Cologne.

This mistrust of the director's new "omnipotence" can also be regarded as an echo of a book by Edward Gordon Craig (1872–1966) that had just been published in 1911. Craig's concept of the "über-marionette" was often interpreted in the sense of a "dehumanization" of the actor. Palmer's essay "Footlights and the Super-Doll" (1912) makes an explict connection between Craig and Reinhardt by affirming Reinhardt's aesthetic pragmatism against Craig's theoretical rigorism. Referring to *The Miracle*, Palmer gives this description of the successful shift in acting style:

> The moments when "The Miracle" fails as a production are moments when the whole burden of the conception is put upon an individual player—I am thinking of Mlle. Trouhanowa [Megildis]—who is not content to be an agent, but consciously feels impelled to exploit her personality. The playing of the Spielmann [minstrel] is perfect because Herr Pallenberg is content to be the perfect puppet in pose and gesture; his playing is throughout symbolic, independent of any idiosyncrasy of manner and feature. This applies equally to the suave, gracious figure of the Virgin.[46]

The "marionettish" quality of the acting is grounded in the dimensions of the space, which required a very physical style of acting and exaggerated gestures.[47] On the other hand, the shift in acting style was an indication that the staging in its dramaturgy was no longer oriented to the idea of plot development but organized instead as a succession of tableaux: "The great public success the performance enjoyed was based exclusively on the ravishing beauty, for the notions of that time, of the tableaux vivants."[48]

Compared with the other Reinhardt productions shown in London, *The Miracle* was the most successful one. This may have had to do with the fact that the external conditions were most favorable here—Reinhardt had all the technical means he wanted at his disposal and was less restricted by the space (leaving aside its size) than he was with the other productions, which took place in already existing theaters. At the same time, Vollmoeller, Reinhardt, and Engelbert Humperdinck (1854–1921), who composed the music for the piece, had succeeded in putting together a well-coordinated mix of recognizable themes and images and German local color. Thus the *Times* singled out Vollmoeller's "external" view of the legendary material: "Naturally, for this great spectacle Dr. Vollmoeller has chosen an external, a spectacular, treatment."[49]

If we keep from too hastily reading this notice, which also relates to Reinhardt's staging, as a verdict of decay, we may recognize that the spectacular, external approach was the crucial guarantee of the work's success. The play's thematic foreignness, to which the costumes and decor added an aspect of historical distance, underlined the fact that it was not trying to be an affirmative restaging of salvation history and the Christian belief in miracles. The production aimed rather at a collective aesthetic experience that permitted the appropriation of a common European legacy under the auspices and conditions of a modernized, and partly secularized, society. *The Miracle* offered a "pre-view" of an international, metropolitan art that did not seek refuge in an absence of history,[50] but rather placed its appropriation in plain view.

That this event got its start and found its place in London was by no means either accidental or irrelevant. London was the model of a modern European metropolis, one that was more strongly influenced by international exchange than even Paris. Reinhardt himself was fully cognizant of London as the specific starting point for this production, as we can infer from a letter to Berthold Held in 1912. In it he speaks skeptically of the possibility of a guest appearance in Vienna:

> And for another thing, the Viennese are marvelously spoiled as far as ecclesiastical pomp goes. (Corpus Christi processions with the Kaiser etc., and all the more now with the Eucharistic Congress, and all kinds of jubilee processions to boot.) Our chances are poor enough therefore. Protestant, sober, gray, naive London, with its ridiculous theater, can't be compared to Vienna.[51]

Reinhardt's discomfort about placing his theater in direct competition with a living liturgical and baroque-courtly culture shows his awareness of the fact that his projected appropriation of the cultural legacy ultimately required that its forms be divested of their original context (and of their hegemonic claims).

After the great success in London, Reinhardt's *The Miracle* did find its way to Vienna (1912), as well as Frankfurt, Dresden, Leipzig, Breslau, and Prague (1913), before finally coming to Berlin in 1914 at the Zirkus Busch. Reinhardt also had a guest appearance in New York planned for the latter year, which did not take place, however—and this was true of further appearances in London—because the war had broken out.

In this regard, *The Miracle* and its "itinerary" teach a twofold historical lesson. Its success attests to the fundamental "porousness" of European cultures at this time: they were nowhere near as hostile and closed off as the march of historical events might have made one believe. On the other hand, the interruption of the itinerary shows how narrow the scope for the utopian project of a metropolitan art that consistently ignored national boundaries really was.

The Miracle in New York (1923)

If the guest residency in London in 1911 marked an important step from the German-speaking wings onto the international stage, a guest stay in the United States, the "leap across the Atlantic," still remained a logical challenge.

Of course, a trip like this was still an expensive undertaking at the beginning of the twentieth century, but New York was an especially popular travel destination, because it had a large and lively German-speaking community that was only gradually abandoning its native language as a result of the United States' entry into the war on the side of the Triple Entente.

If we keep this in mind, it is not difficult to understand why there was already a strong cultural connection between Germany and the United States that drew a broad spectrum of artists to New York in the nineteenth century. A few examples are Bogumil Dawison (1818–1872), Adolf von Sonnenthal (1834–1909), and the Schlierseer Bauerntheater (the Schliersee Farmers Theater). Reinhardt's ambition to take such a trip was perfectly consistent with a tradition that had existed for several decades.

It was a prudent move to choose *Sumurûn* for his first guest appearance there in 1912. Not only had it already proved a success in London, but as a pantomime it could appeal to an audience that far exceeded the segment of the population that could speak or at least understand German.

Because of extensive coverage in both the German- and English-language[52] newspapers, Reinhardt was an even better known personality in New York, and his theater work more famous, than was the case in London. Ever since his London success Reinhardt and his style had become a byword. By the way, Reinhardt did not travel himself but merely sent the productions with an assistant director.

Just as with the London press, the New York reviewers were soon measuring Reinhardt against one of the city's best-known directors. In London it had been Herbert Tree; now his work was being juxtaposed with the perfectionist realism of David Belasco (1853–1931).[53] Here too, there was express praise for Reinhardt's innovative direction based on stylization and the creation of a holistic stage atmosphere.

A guest performance run of *The Miracle*—following the series of performances in Berlin—was already in the works for December 1914 in New York,[54] but had to be canceled when the war broke out. One of the most important initiators of this enterprise was Otto H. Kahn (1867–1934), a Mannheim-born banker whose financial patronage made him an almost legendary figure in the early twentieth-century cultural history of New York or even the United States generally.[55] Kahn was not simply planning a temporally limited guest appearance; he was much more interested in settling Max Reinhardt and his theater permanently in New York, as we see in a letter from Reinhardt to Kahn dated January 13, 1913. For an opportunity like this, Reinhardt was ready to radically alter his modus operandi up to that time:

> In practice it would work out that I would sacrifice the many guest performances the Deutsches Theater puts on every year in Bucharest, Vienna, Petersburg, Moscow, and London, by reducing them significantly or giving them up altogether, in order to limit my activity

> essentially to Berlin and New York. I would have to take steps to get one or two pieces ready at the beginning of each season for 6–8 weeks in New York, although I expect that in the first years the stay would possibly be longer or a second visit might turn out to be necessary. A permanent agent who was completely familiar with all my intentions and stayed in constant contact with me would manage the New York house artistically for the whole year.[56]

In another part of the letter, Reinhardt also explains the attraction such a transatlantic modus operandi held for him:

> The essence of our task seems to me to be to make the theater great and monumental again, to recapture the fundamental thought behind ancient and Renaissance theater, so that it is suitable for presenting the great works of world literature: . . . I firmly believe that this kind of theater most corresponds to the American spirit, the whole character of the American way of life . . . Why should America repeat this whole laborious development of the present-day European showcase theater out of Italian ballet with all this narrowness and confinement, why shouldn't it begin with the present phase of the process that best corresponds to the nature of the country?[57]

Numerous points emerge in his argument that had already been named in connection with the Grosses Schauspielhaus, especially the idea of bringing the theater, as a place of collective experience, back to the center of social and cultural life.

Reinhardt's conception of American society must be seen as a pure projection of his European experience, not just because he had never been in the United States before, but also because he himself could hardly speak English.[58] He used New York as the epitome of metropolitan culture, for which the historylessness of the United States—all too often used as a reproach—represented less of a lack than an opportunity. From today's perspective, it seems very symbolic that Reinhardt's plans, the visionary kernel of which we can hardly deny, were blocked by the outbreak of the First World War.

When the guest appearance plans were taken up again in the 1920s, both Kahn's financial patronage[59] and, especially, the hiring of Morris Gest (1881–1942), who as impresario took charge of the overall management of the production as well as the associated tour through the United States, were important for their success.

Gest, born Moses Gershonovitch near Vilna, had come to the United States while still a young man and had been working as a theatrical producer in New York since 1905. From 1917—partly with Kahn's support—he ran his own house, the Century Theater. Having gained connections to different levels of the New York theater scene as the result of his marriage to David

Belasco's daughter, he soon became a "specialist" in organizing guest performances of European artists. Thus, for example, he organized a tour of the Ballet Russe in the 1910s, engaged Michel Fokine (1880–1942) to come to the United States, and planned the 1923–24 farewell tour of Eleonora Duse in the United States. Besides *The Miracle*, he was best known in the United States for planning and implementing the tour of the Moscow Art Theater there under Stanislavski between 1923 and 1925.

If we want to see guest performances as doing more than just providing actors with increased earning opportunities, we will need to pay more attention to what "agents" like Morris Gest accomplished. Such people are mostly forgotten today, but it was their activity in the first place that produced the itineraries that made it possible for metropolitan culture (to avoid the loaded and ambiguous term "modernity") to become established.[60] In light of the current discussion about the risks and dangers of migration, it might be worth noting the extent to which the development of modernism and modernity in the West depended on people with a migratory background. Gest's achievements in introducing the United States to the pinnacle of European performance art (with a strong emphasis on Russian artists) were clearly rooted in the personal cultural versatility that predestined him to be a cultural go-between.

Whereas Max Reinhardt himself was hesitant to show *The Miracle* in New York because he felt the organizational and financial problems were insuperable, it was Gest who pressed insistently, and successfully, for precisely this major production. By the beginning of 1923 the newspapers could finally report that Reinhardt was coming to New York for the first time to concretize the vague plans.

In contrast to the London production, which could and had to appropriate a practically empty space, it was quickly determined that in New York the play would take place in the Century Theater. Since Stern's designs were no longer relevant to the new space, the industrial and theatrical designer Norman Bel Geddes (1893–1958) was hired. The technical expenses for the production were in no way inferior to what they had been in London. Again it came to a "battle" of superlatives, gleefully publicized by the newspapers.[61]

Geddes too created a cathedral in the theater, though his solution was different than Stern's. Adapting the spatial conditions of the house, he constructed an interior space that turned the stage into the apse of a Gothic church. Whereas in Stern's arrangement the audience sat on the two long sides of the hall facing each other (in seating that remotely suggested choir stalls), in Geddes's arrangement the audience looked ahead as if sitting in the church's nave. Although Geddes extended the forestage further into the auditorium and bridged the distance with several steps, the separation between the two spatial spheres was fundamentally maintained. In this respect, his design seemed to revoke some of the theater-aesthetical innovations implemented by Stern for the London performance. On the other hand, the cathedral aspect of the theatrical space was intensified by having the lobbies and aisles decorated and transformed into a cloister. Geddes even went so far as to dress the loge attendants as nuns.[62]

The reviewers expressly praised the spatial configuration: "Thus the theatre has been literally lined with a cathedral not a mere contrivance of canvas and paint but a solid structure of wood and iron and concrete and seeming stone."[63] And in another review we read: "Indeed, the impression of being in church is so perfect that the greatest incongruity is the sight of men and women in the audience in evening clothes. The *Sun* critic suggests that impresario Ray Comstock and Gest make a rule forbidding this."[64]

The costumes too were redesigned by Geddes. Whereas Stern had turned to historical and art-historical models, Geddes felt free enough to fashion costumes that stood out for their markedly severe style. The differences become obvious when we compare the way the two Madonna figures are conceived, especially in the choice of the materials for the mantle. Stern's mantle with its sumptuous pattern has a very structured look, whereas Geddes's mantle has a more sculptural form, which is further emphasized by the statue's interplay with the pillars behind it, particularly in the fall of the folds, whose artificiality strikes the eye because of the mantle's single color. At the moment in the play when the statue comes to life, the sculptural quality of the costume enhances the whole effect of the scene, as the reviews repeatedly emphasized: "By common consent the most exquisite moment of the play is that when the Madonna is vivified, steps down from her statued place and puts on the garment left there by the recreant Nun."[65]

Stern had played with historical and art-historical associations, which was certainly significant for the play's European reception, but Geddes's designs aimed more at a uniform solution that created a cohesive atmosphere. To that extent, some of his costuming had more grotesquely fantastical features and seemed to comment more powerfully on the characters than was the case with Stern.

The differences between the two productions were not just confined to stage design and costume. Reinhardt also reworked the plot to clarify the basic outline of the story. In the London version, the figure of the minstrel, who introduces the repeated dance motif, oscillates between an actual character and an allegory of death or sin, which is invoked in an allusion to the medieval *danse macabre*. For the New York version, Reinhardt wanted to strengthen this double meaning by creating a new figure, a kind of shadow figure, who makes the relationship between the minstrel and death more explicit.

Furthermore, the dream character of the inserted plot was now given stronger emphasis in the scenic realization. Thus Geddes had a machine installed on the apron of the stage that could produce a smoke screen. This served to replace an actual curtain, but it also visually set the dream scenes apart from the frame narrative.

Interestingly, the dream was interpreted in a psychoanalytic sense in the New York reviews, as, for example, when we read in the *New York Times* about "that Nun's Freudian dream." This was an interpretation that never surfaced in London in 1911, but one that gave another meaning to the inserted plot: "Whether it was in fact the outer world or only a cloistered dream of the libido, rioting ashamed in revels of the flesh, was not quite clear."[66]

Figure 30. Maria Carni as Madonna in Ernst Stern's costume for *The Miracle* (London, 1911). Photograph by Zander & Labisch. Courtesy of the Theaterwissenschaftliche Sammlung of the University of Cologne.

As in London, the coordinated interplay of elements succeeded in creating a thick atmosphere that enveloped members of the audience as soon as they entered the auditorium, so that the performance had no clear boundary, no specific moment when one could say it began:

> There is no curtain nor any division between the stage and the rest of the theater, for the stage has become the apse of the cathedral in

which the audience is sitting . . . A smell of incense fills the house, drifting up through the worn medieval standards that hang from the galleries, by the magnificent rose windows, into the darkness of the vault above. The whole place has an air of solidity, of mellow age, and impressive beautiful dignity. No one knows when the play begins, as movements seem to be continual and natural. A young man in a black robe wanders swinging a golden censer in the apse and through the aisles among the arriving spectators.[67]

The crossing of boundaries between the two spheres was not just the result of the stage design and the smell of incense, for Reinhardt had created a comparable effect in 1905 with *A Midsummer Night's Dream*. The presence of costumed extras in the auditorium was also a factor.

The reactions to the show ranged from completely positive to enthusiastic:

> The audience at yesterday evening's gala premiere was carried breathlessly from one emotional reaction to another. As soon as they entered the theater—which is no longer a theater, but the most imposing cathedral in New York City, more authentically medieval and gothic in its architecture than all our other churches—people received an impression of astonishment that commands fear . . . Never before outside of real life . . . has it been granted to us to witness such a moment of seething and furious human passions.[68]

Michael Monahan wrote of the production in the *New York Times*:

> Spectacularly, "The Miracle" is the grandest dramatic production ever attempted in America, and not merely attempted but carried out with a unity of artistic purpose and a completeness of ensemble to satisfy the most exacting critic . . . In our cosmopolitan New York—metropolis of all creeds and all peoples—one is, above all, impressed with the religious emotion of this grand evocation of the medieval past—I would say the emotion inherent in the play to which our cosmopolitan audience is, beyond expectation, so prompt and sympathetic in its response.[69]

The show's success in evoking a religious ambience is revealed by the fact that many members of the audience were unsure how to react, as John Corbin remarks: "Probably because of the religious nature of scene and stage, there was no great outburst of applause. Enthusiasm took the form of a series of calls at the close for those chiefly responsible for the production."[70]

There were only a few isolated voices that expressed criticism of the spectacular appropriation of religious forms[71] or saw the pantomime as too weak an echo of the original legend. The reviewer of the *Independent* cites this ambivalence:

> Processions of great beauty are directed with marvelous skill and the various phases of religious and secular life are multitudinously presented. The general effect is, of course, very different from that produced by the medieval legend. With Reinhardt the religion of the Church has become a figure of speech, a rich decoration with infinite facets, holy if exotic in its atmosphere; with the medieval monk it was simple, direct, and consuming.[72]

This process of appropriating historical and religious forms as "figures of speech" leaned more strongly toward an appropriation of history in the London production through the historical citations in the stage design and costumes. This approach would certainly have miscarried with the heterogeneous, metropolitan New York audience. Monahan, who explicitly refers to the heterogeneity of the "cosmopolitan" audience in his discussion of the work, expressly praises this outward treatment because it addressed a broad audience and brought a spiritual longing to expression in aesthetic experience.

> Perhaps in the deeply moved and genuine response which the Century crowds make nightly to this touching legend, there is manifest a yearning for the old simple religion of duty and sacrifice, which has so little place in our present-day world. In this regard "The Miracle" may claim attention as something more and higher than mere dramatic entertainment. It is significant that the intense Catholic mise en scène and atmosphere of the play seem to attract equally all classes of theatregoers.[73]

The opulence of the production and its atmospheric density—if we can extend Monahan's line of thought in this way—not only made up for the missing common historical heritage that Stern was able to draw on and suggest in his costumes. It also helped overcome ethnic and religious differences through aesthetic experience.

The show was remarkably successful. Between January and November 1924, *The Miracle* was played 289 times in New York. This was followed by a long tour through the United States that extended into 1930. The show not only made back its production costs, estimated at around $600,000, but turned a clear profit.[74] In both aesthetic and financial terms it was a complete success.

In 1927 Reinhardt returned to the United States for a lengthy period to show seven of his Berlin plays with the original cast and scenery between November 1927 and January 1928. It was, as Heinrich Braulich remarks, the first guest appearance in the United States of a German-speaking ensemble since the end of the war.[75] He also describes it as the opposite of *The Miracle*:

> In contrast to *The Miracle* as entertainment fare that would sell well in the United States, the American audience was now offered the best artistic repertory and ensemble theater . . . Old culture-rich Europe showed here, shortly before the world financial crisis . . . , what remained of the former and still shining glory of its bourgeois theater.[76]

Even if this appraisal of *The Miracle* is certainly too one-sided, we can still agree with Braulich's characterization of bourgeois theater. In fact, *The Miracle* represented a radical shift in the artistic production process of bourgeois theater. For to make such a production successful, Reinhardt had to come up with a work method based on the idea that the costs would only be recovered through lengthy runs. The expensiveness of the stage design meant that presenting a repertoire of alternating productions was unthinkable in the first place. For this work, then, touring was a constitutive, necessary component of its concept and feasibility.

The guest tour of 1927–28 gave Reinhardt the chance to demonstrate his artistic versatility to the American public.[77] Remarkably, the language barrier did not hinder the plays' success. This may certainly have been due to the relatively large number of German immigrants in New York, but it was also because the name Reinhardt was widely considered a guarantee of an exquisite theater aesthetic. The American audience was in any case used to guest performances in a foreign language—we need only think of Stanislavski's tour. But it was also obvious that literature could no longer claim an unquestioned primacy over theatrical presentation when it came to aesthetic appreciation.

Reinhardt's presence in the United States in the 1920s resuscitated the idea of building him a theater in New York. Joseph Urban submitted a series of designs for it. But it is characteristic of the later course of events that the project never came to fruition, and when Reinhardt returned to the United States as an emigrant in the 1930s, he found it very difficult to make a place for himself in the theater scene.

◆

There exists a photograph from the year 1923, taken in New York, that shows David Belasco, Konstantin Stanislavski, and Max Reinhardt side by side. It is no exaggeration to see this fortuitous document, which in its poor quality radiates the always somewhat embarrassing charm of posed pictures, as a symbolic expression of *Regietheater* (directorial theater) at the beginning of the twentieth century. All three figures represent a specific concept and a particular system of theater that marked their time. The photograph thus represents practically the whole spectrum of European-American theater art in the early twentieth century.

The juxtaposition of these three theater luminaries can also be seen as a physical expression of the fact that theatrical forms did not exist in isolation: there was an international exchange that gradually gave shape to norms and approaches of a culture that transcended national boundaries. But more important than their mutual influence on one another was their effect on an entire generation of theater people who (sometimes more, sometimes less epigonally) looked to them as models.

Theater as "spatial art," as Max Herrmann defined it, requires, unlike literature and film, for example, special itineraries to create such an exchange. On these itineraries, the prosperous metropolitan centers—with their good, though still cumbersome, transportation systems, their large potential audiences, and their available capital—were important stations and milestones. But beyond this infrastructure, the large cities primarily offered a climate of aesthetic and cultural openness and curiosity, too often denounced as a sensationalist craving, that was the most important prerequisite for experiments like these.

But the photograph is just as expressive in what it does not show as in what it does. The view of the famous artists in the spotlight leaves the many organizers and enablers of these itineraries in the shadows. The invisibility of Morris Gest, whom it is not difficult to imagine as the guiding spirit of this meeting, is paradigmatic of a theater historiography that in its concentration on essentials loses sight of the "mundane" underpinnings of its object. Only when we take the trouble to include these supposed "banalities" in our account can we properly understand the special dynamics of the modernizing European-American world, with its opportunities and crises.

The Miracle can be seen as a classic example of the attempt to create a metropolitan culture that understood internationalization and mobility not as side effects, but as the motor force of its art. In this connection, Rudolf Kommer has pointed to the fact that the various guest appearances were in no way mere reproductions: "These seventeen productions [of *The Miracle* in Europe] do not represent the activities of a touring company, they were seventeen entirely different, extremely individualized presentations."[78]

Indeed, this new theatrical form can hardly still be comprehended by means of traditional ideas of bourgeois theater, whose horizons were always limited to a city or a nation—though some of the more negative German criticism still evinces this trait. For Reinhardt, it was simply true that "the world was his garden," as Siegfried Jacobsohn stated (see page 86 of this book). Metropolitan culture, with its roots in history, the cultural canon, and popular culture, on all of which it fed, but which it freely adapted to its own purposes, promised—despite indisputable weaknesses that are worthy of criticism—a culture of aesthetic experience for which national, ethnic, and religious boundaries were secondary.

Chapter 5

♦

Reinhardt and Film

A Missed Rendezvous?

When we think of Reinhardt's theater aesthetic, which showed itself characteristically open and flexible with regard to new forms, and of the organization of his theatrical enterprise, which provided this diversity with a locus and a foundation, we might assume that Reinhardt, more than any other artist of his time, was destined to take on the new medium of film, which had been growing in significance since the 1890s, and develop it into a further "playground."

In reality, however, film occupies a marginal position in Reinhardt's oeuvre. Compared with the abundance of his theatrical productions, the five films ascribed to him seem a negligible quantity. Reinhardt himself expressly justified this marginal position as late as 1924; for him film was still in the beginning stage of its development and had a "parasitical status": "The art of film in its present form is not developing from its own resources and strengths, though both are present in great abundance. It has taken root and lives on foreign soil. It is a parasite (and incidentally a dangerous parasite) of theater, literature, painting, and so on."[1] Now that film has become a dominant medium in aesthetic, but also in economic and organizational, terms, such an appraisal appears almost naive—especially when we remember that film, though it was still a relatively young art in 1924, had already experienced a first blossoming, and precisely in Germany. Besides this—and Reinhardt's parenthetical remark shows his clear awareness of the fact—cinema was entering into ever stiffer competition with theater.

In the following pages we shall take a closer look at this ostensible naivete, for Reinhardt's peculiarly negative relationship to film promises interesting conclusions with respect to both his understanding of aesthetics and the situation of two media that were becoming increasingly independent of each other but still overlapped.

Max Reinhardt's Films

As mentioned above, Max Reinhardt's film oeuvre is easily surveyed:

1910 *Sumurûn*
1912 *The Miracle*
1913 *Isle of the Blessed (Insel der Seligen)*
1914 *Venetian Night (Venetianische Nacht)*
1935 *A Midsummer Night's Dream*

The first two are film versions of plays in the narrow sense; in other words, in each case the film was based on a (successful) play and only small modifications were made for the transposition into film. The film version of *Sumurûn* received special attention because, with its length of several hours, it was promoted as one of the first films to really fill an entire evening.[2] Henning von Kügelgen noted in a short essay on the film that the idea of doing film versions of plays could be traced back to earlier prototypes. Thus, for example, in 1908, Sarah Bernhardt and colleagues from the Comédie-Française founded the association Film d'Art to produce artistically sophisticated films based on theatrical productions.

The affinity with theater was also stressed in *Sumurûn*'s marketing—obviously the production company was trying to exploit Reinhardt's prestige as director by continual reference to his participation. This strategy backfired, however, for the direct comparison of film with play was an indictment of the former. Not just the way the film was shot—it was a straightforward filming of the staged version in the Deutsches Theater—but the more important limitation of black and white reproduction was described as a loss of vital aspects of the staged version (Stern's colorful scenography).

Although the film is at least mentioned in passing in various accounts, it probably had only three public showings altogether.[3] But what weighs more heavily from the theater-historiographic point of view is the fact that the film versions of *Sumurûn* and *The Miracle* have not survived—at least no copies have surfaced up to the present. For, regardless of their cinematic value, they would have been of great interest as documents of Reinhardt's directorial style.

In 1913, Reinhardt signed a contract with Projektions-AG Union (PAGU), one of the most important movie theater and film production companies in Germany at the time, whose head, Paul Davidsohn (1871–1927), can be considered one of the most influential film producers of the still very young and—compared with other countries—still underdeveloped German film industry.[4] The contract required Reinhardt to deliver four film dramas a year until 1916.[5]

The time and the content of the contract match the picture we have hitherto gained of Reinhardt's theatrical enterprise. Since 1911 he had been intensifying efforts to internationalize his work; thus it seems consistent that he was now pursuing active involvement in a new medium and the industry that supported it.

We can also detect an interest on PAGU's part in cultivating an active dialogue between film and theater, for Reinhardt's first film was shown with great fanfare on October 13, 1913, on the occasion of the opening of the eighth PAGU cinema on Kurfürstendamm, a fancy locale in Berlin. The prominent situation of the house, combined with Reinhardt's renown, represented an effort to "ennoble" cinema, which still stood in the twilight.

Isle of the Blessed *(1913)*

Reinhardt's first film production for PAGU already shows the difficulties and misunderstandings that still plagued the two spheres—theater and film—as they moved toward each other in a way that was virtually paradigmatic. Although Reinhardt was initially thinking (solely) about filming his international successes, Davidsohn soon pressed for independent projects whose aesthetic and narrative structure was to be explicitly tailored to the film medium. The fiasco with *Sumurûn* had certainly served as a warning for special caution in this respect.

Isle of the Blessed, Reinhardt's third film, was meant to accomplish this purpose. The textual base came from Arthur Kahane, Reinhardt's dramaturg of many years and one of his most loyal collaborators.[6] The uncertainties (and lack of models) that attended the project are already evinced by the film's awkward subtitle: "A jovial flicker-show [*heiteres Flimmerspiel*] in four acts."

The film's plot is easily rehearsed. The fathers of two young women want them to marry men they do not love and refuse to hear about the men they actually do love. The girls escape to an island—pursued, of course, by all involved. Here, after all sorts of complications and confusions, and with the assistance (or through the shenanigans) of the gods and sprites, the true lovers eventually find their way to each other. The echoes of Shakespeare's *Midsummer Night's Dream*, which as a sensational theatrical production was the basis of Reinhardt's fame as a director, are unmistakable in terms of plot, setting, and the figures associated with that setting (nature and nature spirits).

The film develops two main thematic threads. On the one hand, it presents a critique of bourgeois philistinism, which emerges from the opposition between nature and a very peculiar idea of "culture." The naturalness of the landscape not only forms a visual background to the behavior of the two fathers, it becomes their virtual antagonist.

But this opposition is not confined just to the father figures. The film consistently uses encounters with nature to define the characters. The naturalness and freedom of the bathing girls stands in marked contrast to the somatophobic caricature of the bourgeois philistine, whose peculiar bathing costume and the card game he plays on the beach pointedly demonstrate his denial of everything natural. This portrayal can also be understood in relation to the anti-bourgeois satire that we have encountered in the early cabaret. To be sure, the critique is made not in a radical, revolutionary spirit, but rather with a sympathetic wink of the eye, which ensured the film's—economically indispensable—acceptance on a broad basis.

The other thread is the fairy world, represented by mythological set pieces, which as an antithesis to bourgeois philistinism embody sensuality and pleasure in a form uncramped by civilization. Beyond internal thematic references, these mythological citations can also be understood with reference to Reinhardt's own "directorial biography," in the course of which he constantly drew on mythological material.[7]

But the film also shows another hallmark of Reinhardt's aesthetic: the innovative use of space as a meaningful environment for the plot. *Isle of the Blessed* presents extensive shots of nature and makes use of the specific materiality and visuality of water to convey through its multifaceted movements the active and animate character of nature.

The film seems to multiply the potential for spatial representation—nature does not need to be artificially "produced," but can be directly presented. Yet precisely this potential seems to turn against the intended aesthetic. Whereas Reinhardt could impress his audience by conjuring up a meticulously constructed forest in the artificial framing of a theater stage, the photographic representation of "actual nature" lacked this allure—even more so as the pictures were still rather shaky and blurred. Thus we find in one review: "The glorious images of the landscape, rendered with photographic enchantment, cannot camouflage the tortured content."[8]

Lastly, we have to note that Reinhardt's great successes on stage were invariably marked by effects that had less to do with an individual actor's achievement than with an interplay of disparate elements in which the "amazement" generated by technical solutions played a key role—we need only think of the revolving stage or the sophisticated lighting. *Isle of the Blessed* displays a number of such effects, although their technical unwieldiness strikes the twenty-first-century viewer as almost comical: the transformation of nature into the mythic forms of the fairy world through dissolves or simple cuts, for example.

Despite these efforts, however, critics used Reinhardt's own prestige against him and the film:

> So we have to speak plainly! We have to raise an objection when an actress of the caliber of Mary Dietrich has to play Galatea as a confectioner's image of a goddess in a short, sopping scrap of silk. We have to state for the record that the dreadfully forced farcicality the film occasionally resorts to cannot coax a smile even from a truly undiscriminating "moving pictures" audience. We have to say that the demand for cupids with clapped-on wings and other such jokes

has already been fully met by the rest of the industry. And we must protest above all, and with vehemence, when we see that a man with Max Reinhardt's history and eminent talent squanders his energy and reputation with such kitsch, kitsch, and more kitsch.[9]

Venetian Night (1914)

With *Venetian Night*, Reinhardt returned to the filming of an internationally successful pantomime: as already mentioned, he had already made a success of it on the London stage. The script was by Karl Vollmoeller, one of Reinhardt's inner circle of collaborators.

The short pantomime's plot focuses on a dream. The young student Anselmus Aselmeyer satisfies his craving for Italy with a trip to Venice.[10] Once arrived, he first tours the labyrinth of its canals and eventually witnesses the marriage of a rich groom to an impoverished beauty of noble descent. The girl, however, is actually in love with a young officer, and by a process of mistaken identity Aselmeyer becomes involved in a ménage à trois. When he goes to sleep that night he dreams that he kills the officer in a fight for the lovely woman's favor. Then in order to hide the body, he sets out on an eerie trip through Venice and ends up being pursued by an army of ghosts. When he wakes up from this nightmare the following morning, he is confronted by an altogether different situation: dumbfounded, he sees the newlyweds (including the officer) departing in a gondola and realizes he has been completely excluded.

Figure 31. Ride in the gondola; still from *Venetian Night* (1914).

The pantomime's guest performance in London as well as the subsequent performances at the Deutsches Theater in Berlin were distinct successes—although the weakness of the material was repeatedly noted. For one thing, its moral indeterminacy came under fire,[11] but a special target of criticism was the quality of Vollmoeller's script. The story seemed to oscillate between comedy and ghostly grotesquerie, an ambivalence that hindered an affirmative reception. By contrast, the production's elaborate stage design was singled out for praise.

The shooting on original location in Venice began in May 1913, though the film was not released until 1914. Margot Berthold and Uwe Vogt believe the reason for the delay was the meager success of *Isle of the Blessed*:

> Could they make a profit with the quality brand Professor Max Reinhardt? Evidently there was little promise of the proceeds covering production costs. This consideration was probably one of the reasons the astute businessman . . . Paul Davidsohn withheld *Venetian Night* for a while. We cannot exclude the idea that the rather discouraging financial aspects of the situation overshadowed the good understanding he had with Max Reinhardt. They also ultimately led to the termination of the three-year contract of spring 1913 between PAGU and Reinhardt by mutual agreement after just one year.[12]

But not even the temporal delay could ensure the film's success. Most of the reviews, which compared the film to the stage production, discussed it almost exclusively in terms of its deficiencies.

Figure 32. Dream sequence; still from *Venetian Night* (1914).

On the other hand, critics singled out the "original location" as one of the film's strengths. The gondola trip at the beginning of the film, especially, was sensationally innovative compared to the usual shots from a stationary camera position in a studio.

From today's perspective—including our experience with the contemporary film, television, and video aesthetic—the film's character development often seems grotesquely exaggerated, so that the very sequences in which the action intensifies come across as caricatured distortions.

As with *Isle of the Blessed*, Reinhardt was also seeking in this film to resolve points of dramaturgical complication by means of spectacular visual effects. Of special interest in this regard are the dream sequences. For these, Reinhardt found the optically convincing solution he was looking for in double exposures or dissolves. He did not draw on the possibilities familiar to him from the stage, but specifically sought forms of presentation that only film could offer. The scene deploying the army of specters is a good indication of this. Again the technical solution was a double exposure that showed the spectral bodies as half-transparent. As mentioned, this film too met with only modest success, which eventually led to the dissolution of the contract between Reinhardt and PAGU. In the years that followed, Reinhardt was always working on one film project or another, but none of them came to fruition until the mid-1930s.

A Midsummer Night's Dream *(1935)*

To conclude this discussion, we have to mention the late production of *A Midsummer Night's Dream* that Reinhardt did in a film version for Warner Bros. in 1935.[13] The project was preceded by a stage production in Hollywood with which Reinhardt scored one of the greatest successes of his emigration years in the United States. From a theater-historical perspective, the film seems to complete the circle that had begun almost exactly thirty years earlier, in 1905, with the play's legendary success in Berlin.

But although we recognize the Reinhardt touch in many ways, the film is rather disappointing. There are no points of reference to the legendary success of 1905. Quite the contrary, the film is completely dominated by the Hollywood aesthetic, which comes across as kitsch in comparison with the stage version. The film incidentally met with the same fate as the others. Although reviewers praised it unanimously, it was economically a disaster, and Warner Bros. terminated the contract that was originally set for three films after just this one. And yet, the film might be worth a fresh look; if one reads it not in light of Reinhardt's theatrical work but in the context of the emerging genre of fantastic film, one might get a different perspective.

The Film-Historical Context

The early years of the twentieth century, but primarily the 1910s, are regarded generally—and this is especially true of German film—as a consolidation or transition phase during which the characteristic features and specific potential of the new medium were beginning to become recognizable. But precisely this marginal status in the history of film justifies a twofold interest for our present discussion. The ostensible coincidence of the fact that Max Reinhardt experimented fairly extensively with film during this phase tells us that the openness of the medium, or of the border between film and theater, appealed to him. As we have seen, both parties to the contracts had a keen interest in occupying and exploiting the area of the overlap between theater and film, an overlap that was not just confined to aesthetic matters, but also involved the cultural position of theater and film or playhouse and movie theater.

Thomas Elsaesser highlights the extensive restructuring of film and its production during this phase in his periodization of the early history of cinema:[14]

1895–1903: Early phase of cinema

Film showings during this phase primarily took place in "traveling theaters" (*Wanderkinos*) or in the context of carnivals. In terms of subject, narrative was entirely secondary to the display of the "wonders of cinematography."[15]

1903–1907 or 1909: Consolidation of cinema

A system of stationary cinemas developed, often so-called "storefront theaters" (*Ladenkinos*). On the production level, a specialized system of production and distribution took shape. The resulting short films were no longer sold, as in the early phase, but lent out.

1907–1917: Transition from storefront theater to movie palace (*Kinopalast*)

Cinema moved increasingly into premises that were often oriented to the pomp of bourgeois theaters in their form and character—a development connected with the claim to a higher level of social prestige. There was a simultaneous shift in offered product to the evening-long feature film.

According to Elsaesser, the early period of cinematic history was an epoch of social and cultural "ascent" for both films and movie theaters—one externally marked by the shift from storefront theater to film palace. Before this, film showings were not considered to be an independent art form; they were mostly part of a broader revue program, worked into the variety show's "number" system. With the move to film palace, film gained an independent cultural position and also established—thanks to new distribution systems—a new cultural praxis: "The emergence of a national cinema was primarily a matter of the institutionalization of theater attendance. It was a process in which the role of film production was merely to ensure that people didn't come just occasionally to see this or that film, but returned to the movie theaters week after week."[16]

This process of institutionalization also included an attempt to win broader levels of the public to the new medium. Research to date—influenced by the historical discourse of the 1910s[17]—has assumed that it was primarily the working class that went to the cinema. This interpretation resulted from the (still current) differentiation between "serious" ("high") and "entertainment" ("low") culture, "entertainment" being the pejorative designation for the lack of an explicit educational discourse.

More recent investigations—and a parallel development can be found in the work on entertainment theater—suggest that early films in no way represented a special form as "popular entertainments" (*Vorstadtvergnügungen*), but were part of a general entertainment culture and that the bourgeois classes (tacitly) supported them.[18] The growing localization of movie theaters (as contrasted to "traveling theaters"), as well as their occupation of prestigious premises, were major factors in the strategy to increase the social value of film consumption.

In her study *Frühe deutsche Kinematographie* (1994; *Early German Cinematography*), Corinna Müller has shown that the shift from storefront theater to film palace was not a reaction to evolved audience standards. It was rather born of a dynamic whose roots lay in the area of film or entertainment culture itself:

> Competition was the mechanism that drove the history of German cinema . . . The motor force was not, as some want us to believe, a reaction to "raised" expectations in the public. It was rather the film industry that created these standards by providing an (ever larger) supply. Because supply here was not driven by demand, but governed by the interplay of trade competitors—one imitating what the other had just done—it was bound to come to the irritating situation that the behavior of German cinema did not coincide with the wishes of its clientele . . . The development from "storefront theater to film palace" was not target group–oriented but rather conditioned by competition and merely a matter of time.[19]

Thus it was largely PAGU and its director, Paul Davidsohn, that played the decisive role in this development, since PAGU was initially active in the venue sector and only later developed its film production. Its growing involvement in other levels of production made it possible for PAGU both to control the market and to introduce a crucial development: the new theater framework required a new film format to suit it.

Davidsohn developed a number of strategies for putting his enterprise in a particularly favorable position:

- The most important method was the so-called "monopoly film," a term that indicates a business procedure rather than a type of film: "The system of monopoly distribution was based on giving the rights to handle a film to a single contractor, so that a legal monopoly resulted."[20] The monopoly existed not simply between the producer and distributor, but could also be

extended to the individual theater owner, so that certain films could only be seen in a specific theater.
- Davidsohn was one of the first entrepreneurs in Germany who deliberately contracted well-known stars and had them work within the framework of the monopoly film. The best-known examples are Asta Nielsen (1881–1972) and Ernst Lubitsch (1892–1947), as well as Max Reinhardt.
- A further element was the deliberate upgrading of the theaters. The remarkable thing about this is that PAGU did not, in the first instance, link the move with a rise in prices; on the contrary, it offered an enhanced product at reasonable prices.

Reinhardt's 1913 contract with PAGU can be seen as a textbook case in light of these strategic considerations. It could be expected that the hiring of a theatrical personage who was as famous as he was respected would mean that his renown (and also his success) would rub off on the company's products. Even the fact that it did not produce the desired effect is no argument against the intention. Reinhardt's mere readiness to engage with the new medium represented a distinct ennobling of film and cinemas in the still-pejorative film discourse of the 1910s.

Film and Theater: Two Media in Interaction

Thomas Elsaesser's call for a "history of cinema" instead of a "history of film" draws attention to the latter's real social context (*Sitz im Leben*): whereas a history of film focuses on film as an artwork, expanding the focus to the cinema house as the central place of viewing films (at least at the beginning of the twentieth century) allows us both to consider the medium's social and cultural circumstances and to discuss production, reception, mise-en-scène, and dramaturgy in relation to the cultural practices inscribed in cinema, along with the economic models that gave rise to it.

The relations between film and theater also influenced the internal structure of films. Thus Elsaesser can show, for example, from the instructions for how projectors were to be set up that early films imitated the look and experience of theater, because the projected figures were not supposed to be larger than in real life:

> This means that before 1915 the relation of the viewer to the projected image sought to imitate the relations of theater, variety show, and cabaret. Later—in other words, during the transition to "classical" narrative cinema—cinema wanted to create its own feeling of space, the most important aspect of which was the construction of a single perspective for all viewers independent of where they sat in the room.[21]

Elsaesser goes a step further in his discussion of the relationship between theater and film when he investigates, for example, the structure of the gaze in early films and determines that the figures in them often deliberately make eye contact with the camera or even make an actual bow in its direction. Traditionally, such moments were regarded as intrusive and were blamed on inexperience with the still young medium—elements that were "outgrown" as an autonomous film aesthetic became more established.

Elsaesser, however, argues that these elements had a constitutive significance for early film, recognizing them as residues of theatrical practices. He describes early film as a medium that presents things visually instead of recounting them in terms of a complex narrative structure.[22] The communicative aspect of narration arises from performance practice, by means of a live interpreter, for example. Elsaesser understands this connection as a performative feature of early film.

> This implies, if not altogether proves, that such films—almost as directly as those whose protagonists glance at the camera—imagine their audience as likewise physically present in the room. By directly addressing the audience in order to annul the separation inherent in the spatial constellation, they resort to the stylistic and performative resources of theater (direct eye contact is the most evident of these), which in turn makes their supposed "naivete" all the more drastically apparent.[23]

In this perspective, early film—Elsaesser sets the boundary at 1915—seems to be marked by the adoption of theatrical elements to a much greater degree than we are typically aware of even today. But this "elective affinity" also shows that we need to be skeptical about historiographic approaches that are primarily oriented toward technological development. The supposed semiotic constitutives that categorically separate different media from one another prove on second sight to be culturally constructed to a very large extent.

A key aspect of the relationship of displacement or differentiation that existed between film and theater can be seen in the opening sequence of films. They were often constructed as symbolic introductions and, as such, copied such theatrical practices as stepping out in front of the curtain to address the audience. A particular example of this is the introductory sequence of *Venetian Night*. The film presents a circular vignette of Max Reinhardt himself in profile; after a few seconds he rolls his eyes, puffs on a cigarette, and blows the smoke out slowly before reassuming the portrait's starting position.

Figure 33. Introductory scene starring Max Reinhardt, smoking; stills from *Venetian Night* (1914).

In this sequence Reinhardt not only plays with the theatrical convention of commentary *ad spectatores* (here through eye contact), he also implicitly thematizes the variable state of visual representation. By rolling his eyes, and so on, he dramatizes the subtle interrelationship between motion and stasis, and thus between the moving and stationary image. It is especially significant that it is Reinhardt's image that oscillates between photography, film, and theater, thus demonstrating—in this prominent position for any film—the permeability of the different media.

The relationship between theater and film, however, should by no means be understood as a one-way street, with the older medium disciplining the younger and showing it its place. On the contrary, there is a reciprocity that forces theater too into a new position. Whereas many conventional historiographic models run on a tacit assumption of a quasi-evolutionary logic by which the preexisting is ousted by the new, models of cultural history have recently discussed phenomena of residues and anachronisms. With respect to media history, Jay David Bolter and Richard Grusin's concept of "remediation"—originally developed to historicize digital media—has been used to describe the fact that media are in a continual state of interrelation and that the emergence of new media (and modes of representation) calls on preexisting forms to reorganize themselves aesthetically, as well as in their epistemological claims and economic structure.[24]

We can also see a reflection of such reciprocity in Reinhardt's interest in pantomime. Although pantomime apparently appealed to him first and foremost as an aesthetic experiment on the borderlines of theater, he also soon came to the pragmatic realization that, because the genre was not bound to language, it promised a greater mobility, and he took advantage of this, as we have seen.

We have already noted in connection with the mass productions and *The Miracle* that large-scale pantomimes had an established role in nineteenth-century circus culture—a role, incidentally, that cinema made use of, as Klaus Kreimeier notes: "In the cinema everything was melted down and born anew: burlesque, acrobatics, water ballet, circus, and variety show."[25]

But pantomime was also related to early film in its semiotic constitution, as A. Nicholas Vardac explains in his study *Stage to Screen* (1949). The genre of pantomime—even more popular in England and the United States than it was in Germany—was distinguished by its excessive use of fantastic and spectacular effects.[26] Thus Vardac sees film developing from the stage practices of pantomime: "Apparently, the pantomime-spectacle, because of the limitations of stage equipment more a metropolitan than a provincial form, had begun to cry out for a [more] fluid and spectacular pictorial medium than that of the stage."[27]

In this light, film seems the better, because simpler and cheaper, solution:

> Not only was the film able to include a larger number of effects, but these effects were more fantastic. At the same time the motion-picture theatre, with a simple screen opposing a projection machine at the end of a hall, was able to replace the elaborate metropolitan stage machine and thereby vastly enlarge its potential audience. Production costs were decreased while box office receipts were increased. The motion picture was, from the start, the more practical and economical medium for the pantomime-spectacle.[28]

Vardac's argument is grounded in the specifically visual, spectacular quality of pantomime. Indeed, we have to acknowledge an important analogy a priori between the two formats, inasmuch as they both sought to impress their audience through opulent visual effects. But we also need to bear in mind—to dispense with a widespread misconception—that neither was as soundless as we might assume. Pantomimes were no more silent than silent films. The latter were acoustically complemented and narratively connected by live interpreters, music, and so on, and pantomimes were after all provided with musical accompaniments, which in Reinhardt's case were specially written by notable composers like Victor Hollaender and Engelbert Humperdinck. Furthermore, contemporary sources constantly allude to the fact that the noises made by the actors on stage had a decisive influence on the audience.

However, we should not, as Vardac implies, understand this affinity between pantomime and film in the sense of a coherent or even evolutionary chain of internal necessities. Rather, we can already trace divergent tendencies in the 1910s themselves. Thus we cannot say that film simply superseded pantomime. After all, the scant success of the film versions of *Sumurûn* and *The Miracle* also proves—in contrast to Vardac's theory—that simply transferring pantomime to film by no means satisfied the expectations of the audience.[29]

In their study *Theatre to Cinema* (1997), Ben Brewster and Lea Jacobs have explicitly argued against such an equation.[30] Starting with the central position of the visual in nineteenth-century theater,[31] they refer to the importance of the mise-en-scène: "Although the sensation scene in nineteenth-century drama is linked to the plot as the depiction of a particular sort of situation, it is also characterized by specialized staging that often corresponded very closely with the magical transformations of the *féerie*."[32] These "magical transformations" in the last clause—the reference is to scene transformations on the open stage—seem particularly pertinent to Reinhardt's staging style, if we think, for example, of his use of the revolving stage or the elaborate stage technology of *The Miracle*.

Pantomime and film, with all their parallels, cannot be lumped together or understood as "forerunner" and "end point" respectively in an inevitable developmental history. In the interdependence of the two genres, there arose an "in-between realm" that was characterized on the one hand by a close affinity of forms and a similarity of aesthetic means, but on the other hand by a tension between two self-differentiating media, each with its own logic and dynamic.

These tensions appear clearly in the contemporary theater reviews of the *Sumurûn* pantomime. The author Friedrich Freksa had already tried to categorically distinguish pantomime from film in an article of 1912: "One thing was clear to me from the start: that artistic pantomimes have to be played differently than the old market-fair pantomimes whose remains have been preserved in cinema."[33]

But the theater critics who were clearly "madly in love" with dramatic theater did not appreciate this experiment. Friedrich Düsel described the production as a "kaleidoscope of lively scenes awash in gay oriental colors," which in the last analysis, however, could offer nothing more than an "overfeeding of the senses to the detriment of heart, soul, and intelligence."[34] Only Maximilian Harden, who began his review with extensive historical observations, saw in the sensuousness of the pantomime's rich imagery a special aesthetic, and even emancipatory, potential:

> The combination of pantomime and ballet could save us, change the stage from a debating platform to a place of celebration. The gate of grace opens here to gods and fools, angels and thugs; the heavens open over the thick smoke of factory chimneys, high above the aeroplanes of an industrious humanity; the young Macedonian Alexander strides across the rainbow bridge to enter a field flashing with modern weapons and artillery; Hagen espies the gold minted in the Rhineland over a thousand streams of fire; and in the air, on the earth, in the waters, sinuous maidens' bodies wreathe together in roundelay. Make haste! Otherwise the cinematograph will capture the customers.[35]

In Harden's interpretation, pantomime offered the opportunity of an aesthetically sensuous experience that decidedly extends the living space of a modernized society or even transcends it. But at the same time this possibility is threatened by cinema.

Max Reinhardt seems to have taken this "warning" to heart, for with *The Miracle* during the 1920s in the United States he had almost defiantly championed the theatrical form against film. Moreover, in 1925 he also wanted to give it a firm organizational framework with the foundation of the International Pantomime Association (Internationale Pantomimen-Gesellschaft). Heinz Herald describes the organization's goals:

> The International Pantomime Association was founded as an attempt to create a new kind of theater for Germany . . . It wishes only to set beside the developed and firmly established form of contemporary theater a variant form which, by specialization in a limited sphere, will do what the regular theater, because of its versatility and all-embracing character (which is its strength), is in no position to develop in that special sphere. The new association wishes to cultivate activity in two areas, the pantomime and the tour.[36]

Two points in this declaration are of special interest. The first is the programmatic claim of establishing a new theatrical form—although it is somewhat relativized by the fact that the new genre will seek to avoid any direct competition with existing theatrical forms. The second is the direct relation of pantomime to touring. What comes into view here is an economic structure not unlike that of film. In both cases, the production costs are so high that profit is only possible with an elaborate distribution system. The conjunction also indicates the extent to which Reinhardt at the beginning of the twentieth century had deliberately planned large-scale pantomime as a mobile theatrical form.

Max Reinhardt's reaction to the introduction of sound films in 1928, outlined here by Gusti Adler, his secretary of many years, makes it clear how much he believed in the aesthetic superiority of theater:

> Previously, films of general interest—effectively international therefore—exercised their profound influence across the boundaries of language. This internationally intelligible art form has been limited by language-bound sound films. Film was previously an independent art form. Now, in talking films, plays with dialogue were to be brought to the screen. This made the art of film into a variety of theater, a theater-substitute to take the place of an art form in its own right.[37]

The close affinity between the two aesthetic forms, as well as film's superiority in terms of production costs, was the framework condition within which Reinhardt's abortive rendezvous with film played out. The sense of the spectacular, the atmospheric density: Reinhardt saw all of this—completed by the physical presence of the actor—ideally represented in theater. This was why he believed he could create a bit of metropolitan culture with pantomime. That film with its more favorable cost schedule and its technically simpler distribution—to say nothing of the technical possibilities familiar to us today—was in a better starting position from the very beginning he either could not or would not see from his stage-oriented vantage.

Ending Credits

Although Max Reinhardt himelf never managed to enter into an independent, innovative, or even commercially successful relationship with film, the principles of his artistic staging had great influence on its further development. In her famous study *L'Écran démoniaque* (1952; *The Haunted Screen*), Lotte H. Eisner (1896–1983) expressly took up the question of this influence and was able to show the relation between Reinhardt's work and German films of the 1920s in such areas as use of light, the direction of large groups of actors, and the creation of atmosphere.[38]

Any closer study of these influences leads to the work of Ernst Lubitsch, who after his beginnings as an actor with Reinhardt soon became one of the most important directors of early German films. In 1920 he created his own monument to Reinhardt's influence with a lavish film version of *Sumurûn*—the last film he appeared in as an actor. Yet this direct quotation brings out the differences all the more clearly. For when we compare this film with Reinhardt's stage production (and the reports of his own film version), it becomes apparent that Lubitsch's work was strongly marked by an attempt to find a solution that was adequate to the technical and artistic possibilities of film. Lubitsch made a masterful use of technical resources, such as cutting and camera perspective, to generate a defining rhythm for the film. This example shows, precisely in its distance from Reinhardt, how his aesthetic resources enriched film. But that the road to film had to lead away from the stage is indicated by the fact that by 1922 Lubitsch was already settled in Hollywood.

Chapter 6

✦

Reinhardt & Co.

The Economy of a Theater Concern

It was not just Max Reinhardt's aesthetic program that defined the social and cultural position of his theater. Its economic character was at least equally crucial. From today's perspective, it hardly seems imaginable that such ambitious theater could exist without any kind of state subvention and still turn a profit. We in Germany have long been used to a system of "theatrical full provision" (*theatrale Vollversorgung*) that not only requires public support, but would be completely unviable without it.

That Max Reinhardt himself ascribed special significance to the economic basis of his theater is revealed by an ostensibly incidental remark he made in a letter of June 16, 1933,[1] to the National Socialist government, where he explains his departure and hands over the Deutsches Theater to the public:[2]

> But the time when one could run such institutions privately is over. In the future it will no longer be possible to run an artistic enterprise without state guarantees. Nevertheless, I can point to the fact that in all those early years, as long as the Deutsches Theater and the stages connected with it were under my direction, I was able to maintain them and handle the constantly increasing tax burden without any subvention and without the rich possibilities that the state as entrepreneur has at its disposal as a matter of course.[3]

Obviously Reinhardt recognized in the National Socialist seizure of power not only a political and personal-biographical rupture, but a cultural shift that eliminated the social and economic latitude that his own work was rooted in.

The fact that he explicitly refers to the economic consequences of this political development should not be misunderstood as liberal-economic nostalgia. Economic conditions supported and influenced his work in a way that went far beyond its purely financial organization. This close connection between culture and the economy is so foreign to our German point of view that we can only reconstruct it with difficulty. Thus, at this point in our study we wish to undertake a kind of cultural "archaeology" that will enable us to describe the cultural and economic principles behind Reinhardt's aesthetic products and programs.

Remarks on the Relationship between Culture, Art, and the Economy

In bourgeois society, culture, art, and the economy are like the polar elements of a force field: they exist in close and necessary correlation yet are always in an (at least latent) tension with one another. Art and the economy—art and commerce, to use a catchphrase—form something of a dichotomous axis in the continuum of bourgeois thought. Art is almost by definition the sphere of societal life that is distinguished by its categorical independence of the banalities of the economy.

This attitude is not confined just to the eighteenth or nineteenth centuries; it is a twentieth-century phenomenon as well. Of course, Karl Marx (1818–1883) tried to incorporate art and culture into his economic model of society, but he limited himself to asserting their dependence on prevailing economic conditions. He saw art and culture as a decorative *superstructure* resting on a factually determinative economic *base*.

The critical theory of the Frankfurt school that took shape in Marx's wake maintained this antagonism. Thus the influential theory of Theodor W. Adorno (1903–1969) and Max Horkheimer (1895–1973) is marked by the opposition between art, which is characterized by an inherent potential for insight and emancipation,[4] and the *culture industry*, which Adorno and Horkheimer identify as the social sphere that is permeated and contaminated by the logic of the economy.

> The only escape from the work process in factory and office is through the adaptation to it in leisure time. This is the incurable sickness of all entertainment. Amusement congeals into boredom, since, to be amusement, it must cost no effort and therefore moves strictly along the well-worn grooves of association. The spectator must need no thoughts of his own: the product prescribes each reaction, not through any actual coherence—which collapses once exposed to thought—but through signals.[5]

This reformulation of the bourgeois opposition between art and the economy uses the concept of the culture industry to confirm the boundary between high and popular culture, which allows all profit-oriented forms to fall subject to the verdict of pure commercialism.

To think that artistic and economic concerns could coincide, as they did in Reinhardt's theater, is not possible in this model. It is therefore no accident that the question has been surrounded by a certain historiographic oblivion that marginalizes economic and organizational details in order to retain the "memory" of "pure" art.

In order to escape such coercion, we need to find a figure of thought that, instead of understanding the two spheres as antagonistic, allows them to be described as overlapping and mutually conditioned.

In his book *Philosophie des Geldes* (1900; *Philosophy of Money*), Georg Simmel tries to develop an alternative figure of thought that allows him to question the meaning and function of money for social and individual experience. The key point of his discussion is that money can only achieve its full significance in the context of a fully differentiated society marked by a broad-scale division of labor, for it acts as an intermediary between various spheres of life and production and so permits intensive social exchange on different levels. Looked at in this way, differentiation is not only the precondition for money's growing significance; differentiation requires money for its own part to generate an internal social coherence in the first place:

> This formal autonomy, this inner compulsion, which unifies cultural contents into a mirror-image of the natural context, can be realized only through money. On the one hand, money functions as the system of articulations in this organism, enabling its elements to be shifted, establishing a relationship of mutual dependence of the elements, and transmitting all impulses through the system. On the other hand, money can be compared to the bloodstream whose continuous circulation permeates all the intricacies of the body's organs and unifies their functions by feeding them all to an equal extent.[6]

These two central metaphors, the articular and circulatory systems, sketch the picture of an organic society in the broadest sense. At the same time, the metaphor of blood implies a dynamic that is societally constitutive. This idea of society as a dynamic context whose parts or elements must constantly be brokered against one another also goes back to Karl Marx, who takes up the question of the movement of capital in the second volume of *Capital* (1867–94). There he outlines the economic process as a circulation of capital in which labor power is bought and commodities sold in return.

But as much as Simmel's metaphors tie into such established ideas, he also breaks free of them. His reflections rescind the categorical separation between superstructure and base, and instead describe culture and economy as an interrelationship. This is already evident in the introductory chapter of *Philosophy of Money*, where he shows that objects do not have an intrinsic value: "The value of objects, thoughts and events can never be inferred from their mere natural existence and content, and their ranking according to value diverges widely from their natural ordering."[7] The assignment of value is rather the result of social interaction:

> The fact of economic exchange, therefore, frees the objects from their bondage to the mere subjectivity of the subjects and allows them to determine themselves reciprocally, by investing the economic function in them. The object acquires its practical value not only by being in demand itself but through the demand for another object.[8]

Value and significance are always related to the social and cultural context in which they are placed. Hence Simmel rejects any kind of idealistic worldview and adopts a view of culture that recognizes the centrality of economic elements in all cultural transactions. The assignment of economic value takes place not beyond or in opposition to cultural values but always in relation to them. This process, too, only takes place through the use of money; in other words, the significance of objects and processes can also be measured by the amount of money they raise.

The French sociologist Pierre Bourdieu (1930–2002) has tried to characterize the relationship between culture and economy in a similar way. He suggests that the concept of capital not be limited to just money; other societal spheres can also be described in terms of the types of capital that are proper to them. Thus Bourdieu distinguishes:

- economic capital
- social capital (relatives, relationships, friends, etc.)
- cultural capital (education, titles, linguistic competence)
- symbolic capital (gestures, clothing)[9]

Concepts like cultural and symbolic capital indicate that, for example, art and education are not ideal spheres outside economic reality, but rather, there is a constant exchange of various types of capital. Along with this extension of the notion of capital the concept of society also changes, as Bourdieu himself explains with explicit reference to Marx:

> The inadequacies of the Marxist theory of classes . . . stems from the fact that, in reducing the social world to the economic field alone, it is forced to define social position solely in terms of position in the relations of economic production and consequently ignores positions in the different fields and sub-fields, particularly in the relations of cultural production, as well as all the oppositions that structure the social field, which are irreducible to the opposition between owners and non-owners of the means of economic production.[10]

The border between the economy and education/art/culture is made permeable in Bourdieu's perspective, and the different social spheres are logically related to one another.

For the historiography of theater, this means that history cannot be described merely as the history of ideas, artistic achievements, and aesthetic blueprints. Theater is rather to be regarded as an institution of social discourse that is also part of the economic system.

With respect to the pre-bourgeois, courtly theater system, such a conclusion is immediately evident. For in the context of a social order that constitutes itself essentially through symbolic representation, the maintenance and sponsorship of theater presented a singular opportunity to highlight the potentate's significance and claim to power in the social sphere. The bourgeois idea of art, however, created an antagonism that disguised this connection. This is all the more surprising in that the cultural rise of the bourgeoisie took place parallel with the rise of theater as a commercial business and stood in close interrelationship with it. We must begin our search for the interrelationship of economy and theater in bourgeois society with this contradiction and opposition in mind.

Max Reinhardt is such a suitable object of study for this purpose because he was obviously very good—as his many years of success demonstrate—at reconciling or at least withstanding these contradictions.

Theater as "Economic Sector" between 1869 and 1933

The introduction of free trade in 1869 and 1871 not only brought about far-reaching quantitative changes in Germany's theatrical system; its main thrust was a qualitative restructuring. This latter involved, for one thing, the emergence of a genuinely bourgeois theater, as we have explained earlier, but it also—and even especially—involved its economic structure. One could now speak of theater as an economic sector proper, even if it was of secondary importance in the national economy because of its small scale, as Max Epstein noted: "Because of the proportionately small number of establishments, it follows that theater can play no major role as a factor in the national economy."[11] The chief feature of this new sector, besides the emergence of new theaters, was increasing diversification and specialization in their various domains. The typical relationship between "producer" and audience was extended into different intermediate levels and supplemented by a number of institutions that were just getting started.

The chart on the next page attempts to outline this process. The central feature of the diversification was the appearance of all kinds of intermediaries—publishers, agents, designers—who stepped into the theater production process and soon had a decisive influence on it. The new versatility of the theater scene and the needs that grew out of it created new players who were not involved in the theatrical act proper, but supplied its "component parts" (actors, dramas, costumes, and scenery).

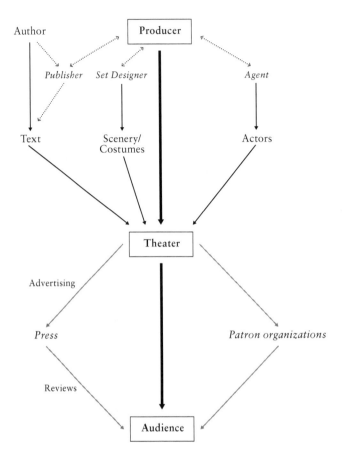

An especially telling example of this was the agency or placement system for actors.[12] Research literature on theatrical agents is still sparse, but using the figures provided by Petra Hildebrand in her essay "Theateragenten im deutschsprachigen Raum des 19. Jarhunderts" (2000; "Theatrical Agents in the German-Speaking World of the 19th Century"), we can at least get an approximate idea of the growth and extent of this sector. As the number of theaters grew from 50 in 1836 to over 300 in 1885, the number of agencies rose from 19 (in 1840) to about 139 (in 1890). But the really remarkable thing is Hildebrand's finding that most of the placement agencies had an average lifespan of only two years. The agencies that can be traced over a longer period of time were known for their versatility. They not only placed actors, they sold theatrical texts and published their own theatrical journals.[13]

Agents kept the German-speaking theater system dynamic by satisfying its apparently insatiable demand for young actors and actresses. There is hardly a major actor who has failed to allude to the services of such "career helpers" in his or her memoirs, even if mostly in subordinate clauses.

Meanwhile, the liberalization of the theatrical landscape had generated such a proliferation of agencies that employer and employee organizations formed very early on in an attempt to guide work relations along certain paths.[14] Agents had become the epitome of unscrupulous profiteering, against whose power social reforms in the theatrical sphere were directed. In 1922 the Employment Agency Act (*Arbeitsnachweisgesetz*) was passed, which went into effect on January 1, 1931, and prohibited all such private placement agencies. These were replaced from 1930 on by a government agency.

Professionalization also occurred in the area of scenic design, with the establishment of companies that specialized entirely in the production of costumes or—more seldom—stage scenery.[15] This kind of "outsourcing" made it possible for theaters to lower their costs by not having to maintain their own workshops. The existence of such scenographic companies allows us to draw interesting conclusions about the performance practices of the time: most plays were performed with standard scenes and costumes that were not designed for any particular play.

The scenographic sector is also a good example of vertical integration, that is, the economic engagement of a company on different levels of the production process.[16] In his *Theater als Geschäft* (1911; *Theater as Business*), one of the few comprehensive studies of theater's economic dimension, Max Epstein shows that costume and scenery companies often had a role in the establishment of theaters. They seldom contributed cash, however; instead they gave discounts on their wares—in return for a guarantee of steady orders—which were then carried over as an investment in the newly founded theater association.[17] In this way, costume and scenery businesses guaranteed themselves sales and could share in the net increase in value that accompanied the theater's success, with comparatively small risk.

One of the most important companies in this sector was the Berlin firm Hugo Baruch & Co., which had produced all possible kinds of theater decor since the end of the nineteenth century. Baruch also operated branches in London and New York and expressly used this internationalism in its advertising. In 1927 the company initiated bankruptcy proceedings, which Heike Stange sees as the expression of a broader development that was economically and structurally significant for scenographic companies in general.[18] Theaters were increasingly producing scenery in their own workshops.

This turn of events was not simply a matter of logistics; it reflected a newly developing set of aesthetic practices in which Max Reinhardt played a decisive role. With the growing importance of directorial originality, stage design acquired a new status. Reinhardt's constant collaboration with painters, for example, led to a change in artistic praxis. The use of prefabricated standard scenery was becoming more questionable, yet standardization was the sine qua non for the quasi-industrial production of stage sets and scenic elements.

With respect to the economic interrelations in this field, Epstein sees theatrical publishing houses as the prime example of vertical integration. The "crown witness" to this development was Adolf Sliwinski (1857–1916), the longtime managing director of the renowned Berlin theatrical publishing house Felix Bloch Erben. Sliwinski was not just a theatrical publisher, he was also financially involved in various theatrical undertakings, such as the Theater des Westens in Berlin and the Carl-Schulze-Theater in Hamburg. Besides this engagement in vertical integration, his business success also rested on the special practice of the allocation of staging rights. In order to get the rights to perform a box office smash, theater directors had to agree contractually to accept lesser known, "inferior" stage works as well. Epstein describes this "coupling" of plays[19] as follows: "This stipulation allowed him to have any play he wanted performed. It is perfectly obvious that anyone who can give a director a piece like *The Merry Widow* is in a position to set his own conditions."[20] One can well imagine that such an exercise of power was severely criticized by many of his contemporaries. Political pressure brought about the passing of an ordinance—Epstein calls it the "lex Sliwinski"[21]—that forbade the involvement of theatrical agencies in the establishment of theaters or the publishing of theatrical texts. Epstein himself opposed such legal limitations:

> The publisher must in a certain sense also be a theater director's advisor, he must select from among his manuscripts and should offer individual directors only the things he thinks are right for that particular theater... The more competent our publishers are, the more they will look for talents, for hits, for successes, and ultimately for artistic values.[22]

We should also mention here, parenthetically, that the differentiation and professonalization of the theater system also showed its effects in the sphere of "consumption." One thing we can mention in this regard is the increasing significance of the press, which likewise developed a spectrum of various reportage formats spurred by rapid quantitative growth in its own sector. Such reportage ranged from professional journals like *Bühne und Welt* (*Stage and World*) and *Die Schaubühne* (*Playhouse*) to theater columns in edifying magazines like *Westermanns Monatshefte* (*Westermann's Monthly*).

Patron organizations also grew in importance, whether these were associations like the Volksbühne (People's Theater), an initiative of the Social Democratic Party and the unions, or the subscription systems developed by individual theaters. Subscriptions could ensure a higher level of seat occupancy because there was a comparatively stable regular audience to count on.

Theater's economic structure becomes completely understandable only when we also examine expenditures. Here we get a very clear picture. Two-thirds of all costs went for personnel, mostly actors' salaries. The better known the actors, the greater the cost. "A theater that employs only new actors, like the Lessing Theater or the Deutsches Theater, works of course with a completely different salary budget than a theater that presents farces and other drolleries.

Such a theater pays out over 400,000 marks a year, or about 1,400 marks every day."[23] Of the remaining third, the biggest item was the rent or lease of the theater building. For the Neues Theater this amounted to 110,000 marks annually, according to Epstein. The other costs were for scenography, stage machinery and lighting, and authors' residuals. In view of these last, we might be justified in the suspicion that the growing popularity of classical dramas had something to do with the fact that they did not involve royalties.

Epstein caps his argument with a very remarkable example. For a small theater (about 500 seats) that did not use music we have the following calculation: "If a small theater has a daily budget of 900 marks and receives an average of 4 marks per seat, then it has to sell 225 seats in order to break even."[24] This means that, ideally, such a theater could cover its costs with an average seat occupancy of 45 percent. Of course, Epstein admits that the cost situation at larger theaters, especially if they maintain their own orchestra, is much more complicated.

Epstein's simplified example can serve as a reference point when we look at present-day theater. At the end of the 2002–03 season, Claus Peymann, the director of the Berliner Ensemble, gave a statement on the financial situation of his house (formerly the Neues Theater, with approximately 890 seats). Peymann proudly announced that they managed to cover about 25 percent of their expenses themselves, with a seat occupancy rate of 87.57 percent.[25]

The unfairness and historical unreliability of such a comparison is obvious. This is all the more true because such quotas actually make the Berliner Ensemble an exemplary case, as a glance at theater statistics confirms.[26] Nevertheless, the example of Peymann is indicative of the fact that in the current German system, a director—however successful and acclaimed he or she might be—would be far from breaking even financially.

Max Epstein juxtaposes the costs with the various means a theater has of generating income, the lion's share of course coming from ticket sales. But beyond these, he cites a number of possible and usual sources of income that cannot replace a good seat occupancy rate, but which contribute to economic stability:

- Leasing out the cloakroom; Epstein estimates this figure at about 60,000 marks for the Theater des Westens—although he says that this was the highest sum paid for such a lease in Germany. For the Deutsches Theater and the Kammerspiele together, the leases came to 65,000 marks.[27]
- Leasing out the program note concession; the program booklets, for the most part very simply put together, were made up and sold by third parties. This was an easy way for a theater to get supplementary income, which might not include income from advertising insertions.
- Leasing out restaurant operations if the space was available
- Advertising
- And lastly—*pecunia non olet*—leasing out the running of the toilet facilities

The various types of lease make us realize how deeply the theater sector's diversification had entered into the internal structure of individual theaters. The complexity of organization and economic calculations clearly shows that the private bourgeois theaters—irrespective of their aesthetic program—were by no means sublime temples of the Muses, but rather multifaceted undertakings that could function on a profitable basis with skilled management. Epstein sums up their significance for private investors:

> Anyone who invests in a theatrical undertaking should first take a careful look at the way it is managed and especially whether the basic principles I have set down in this chapter have been followed. If so, then theater is still one of the most lucrative businesses to get involved in. In a certain sense it is a speculative business, because it depends on good and bad plays and, unfortunately too, on good and bad weather.[28]

The Specifics of the Reinhardt Theaters

In order to take up the specifics of the Reinhardt theaters, it is important to bear in mind that the economic stability that allowed Reinhardt to withstand all economic and historical vicissitudes in the more than twenty-five years of his directorship was unparalleled in the theatrical history of both Berlin and Germany in general. Yet the successful management of the complex enterprise was not to his credit alone; it was first and foremost the achievement of his brother Edmund Reinhardt (1875–1929). Edmund looked after all his older brother's business affairs from the start, as Arthur Kahane (1872–1932), one of Max Reinhardt's most loyal associates, stressed in 1930:

> We say "Reinhardt," but we should say the "Reinhardts," for his brother Edmund stood beside him with equal authority—loyal to the point of self-extinction, ensconced unassumingly in his purely economic functions, his full equal in the anonymity he maintained with iron consistency—the invisible, but everywhere palpable, everywhere efficacious soul of the whole . . . Edmund Reinhardt gradually reached such a level of competence in the handling of theater finances that state and municipal institutions and authorities turned to him for advice, suggestions, and assessments on the financial rehabilitation of theaters and the organization of subscriptions.[29]

Edmund Reinhardt organized the business according to his brother's artistic ideas and needs, and the more of a luminary Max Reinhardt became, the more assiduously Edmund Reinhardt sought to remain in the shadows. When he died unexpectedly in 1929, there was no official photograph or portrait available for the obituary, so that the people concerned had to resort to a snapshot that only survived because Edmund knew nothing about it.[30]

The cometlike rise of Max Reinhardt's career and the emergence of his theatrical empire are all the more surprising when we remember that he began with practically no capital of his own. His success was only possible with the intellectual, social, and financial support of a wide circle of patrons. And here a modicum of theater-historical justice must be done to one of Reinhardt's most important patrons, without whom his career would probably have ended at a very early point, someone who today is almost completely unknown or is mentioned only marginally as an "unseemly old lady" (to use a Brechtian phrase).[31] The rich widow Emmy Loewenfeld (ca. 1841–1912) not only gave Max Reinhardt the 50,000 marks he needed to become the chief partner in Schall und Rauch,[32] but advanced him the 12,000 marks Otto Brahm demanded from the renegade actor for breach of contract.[33] She financially supported Reinhardt's theaters continually over a period of many years, until her far less arts-oriented family tried to have her declared legally incompetent for fear that she would donate her entire fortune to the theater.

Besides the launching of Schall und Rauch, the critical move for the whole Reinhardt undertaking was the purchase of the Deutsches Theater, including the real estate, for 2.47 million marks. For this a silent partnership of financiers was set up—the list of names recorded in the legendary "journal number 1," the first account book of the Deutsches Theater under Reinhardt, is as illustrious as it is impressive. Besides personalities from cultural life like Paul Cassirer, we find bankers like James Hardy and Robert von Mendelssohn, industrialists like the AEG (Allgemeine Elektricitäts-Gesellschaft [General Electric Company]) heir and later foreign minister Walther Rathenau, and August Huck, the publisher "king" of the *General-Anzeiger* (*General Gazette*).[34] For operating capital, a consortium invested in the theater and raised one million marks in shares: "It was truly astonishing how quickly the money was put together and what kind of credit Reinhardt must have had even with sober businessmen."[35]

This major support for Reinhardt from private investors was not simply based on hope of financial gain, although Epstein reports that Reinhardt was able to pay his shareholders a handsome dividend. Projects like the Metropol-Theater, which was run as a joint-stock company, were far more suitable for speculation.[36] It is not at all unlikely that an interest in social and cultural positioning lay behind the financial commitment. The example of the Kammerspiele, which adopted and fostered bourgeois salon culture (see chapter 2), shows the extent to which Reinhardt's theater created a stage for bourgeois self-presentation. The fact that he found enough supporters from the various layers of the successful (neo-)bourgeois class proves how well this strategy met an existing need.

Expansion

What strikes us when we consider the development of Reinhardt's theatrical enterprise is the large number of theaters that either operated on a permanent basis or had a relatively short duration. Expansion was not just a feature of his earliest undertakings (as evinced by the acquisition of the Neues Theater), it was his very trademark. In the preceding chapters we have focused on the aesthetic and programmatic dimension of the various forms and formats his theaters took, but now it is time to take up the question of the economic significance of this strategy.

For this, we first have to bear in mind that what is special about theater—the simultaneity of production and reception, as well as the transitory character of the artwork itself—is what determines its economic profile, because in view of these conditions, and in contrast to other mediums, it is hard to *increase* profits.[37] If we accept Epstein's findings, that a small theater (with no music) had to achieve a 45 percent seat occupancy in order to cover its costs, we see that it is in fact possible to realize a profit margin of about 55 percent, but only with a utopian 100 percent seat occupancy. And such considerations can only be applied to Reinhardt's theater in a limited way, since here the artistic expenses and production costs go far beyond the costs calculated by Epstein.

The production requirements at the Kleines Theater early in his directorial career can be taken as characteristic of the business constellation of the Reinhardt theaters in general. The success of *The Lower Depths* (1903), which had a total of 500 performances, meant a clear profit of 25,000 marks per month.[38] This profit, which was urgently needed to stabilize the undertaking, led de facto to a (semi-) *stagione* operation, wherein a single play was shown on successive nights for an extended period. But since this tied the Kleines Theater up, it was only expansion into the Neues Theater that generated the "excess capacity" needed to develop further productions. Such a strategy was necessary on economic grounds, in order to make efficient use of investment in *The Lower Depths* on the one hand, and on the other to generate sustainability by taking advantage of a period of economic success to work on what would bring a new success. This also explains why *The Lower Depths* had twelve performances in the Neues Theater—during which new productions were already being shown in the Kleines Theater.

The further history of the Reinhardt theaters demonstrates that such a strategy of duplication and expansion was necessary. For it was not until September 1903 that a first success at the Neues Theater could be entered into the books—with *Salome* under Max Reinhardt's own stage direction—though it could hardly be compared with the success of *The Lower Depths*. The decisive breakthrough had to wait until January 1905, with the staging of *A Midsummer Night's Dream*.

This example shows that smaller theaters were only prima facie a secure (or at least less risky) business. It is true that they could recover their costs sooner, in both relative and absolute numbers, but longer-term security could only be achieved with excess capacities that made the development of new productions possible. Thus expansion—at least to a certain size—seems to comply with an inherent logic and dynamic of theater as an economic sector.

Multiple Use

If we were to describe Reinhardt's success from a predominantly economic viewpoint, we would have to say that he managed to find a market niche and to fill it on the highest level. His specific aesthetic was, as we have shown, marked by great lavishness and a commitment to maximally consistent formal presentation. Thus he staged Ibsen's *Ghosts*, for example, not in the (typical) setting of a bourgeois salon; instead, he engaged one of the most notable painters of his time to design a set exclusively for this particular space. Such deviations from the conventional practice—in which even houses that regarded themselves as very demanding relied on what the scenographic firms were selling—certainly contributed in no small way to Reinhardt's peculiar success. But the example of the Kammerspiele should still be considered relatively minor in this connection compared with productions like *The Miracle*, which cost far more than the average yearly budget of a repertory theater.

Just as expansion was a necessary element of Reinhardt's economic strategy of survival and profit, so too a complex meshwork of multiple stagings had a central role in this system. The higher the initial investment and production costs, the more important it was to get full value from them in the subsequent stagings. Expansion served primarily to create excess capacity, whereas multiple use (*Mehrfachverwertung*) was meant to exploit existing productions to the largest extent possible, by keeping them in the repertoire for months or even years and staging them periodically, either at the home theater or on tour.

Multiple use can be described at various levels, both within individual productions and in relation to productions as a whole.

Within individual productions, it was primarily the system of double and multiple use that allowed Reinhardt to keep plays in the repertoire for years. Thus, for example, the *Hamlet* production of 1913 at the Deutsches Theater had been performed approximately a hundred times by 1924 (not counting guest performances and later performances in some of his other Berlin theaters). Heinrich Huesmann, in his listing of the Reinhardt productions, refers to nine different castings of the title role for this production alone.[39] For these multiple castings such different actors as Alexander Moissi, Albert Bassermann, and Eduard von Winterstein were called on. We can easily imagine how much broader the spectrum of actors must have been for smaller roles.

The production itself, as a "framework," remained largely unchanged; it was just the individual roles that were assumed by different actors.

The reason for multiple castings was mostly strategic. Although Reinhardt maintained a very large ensemble for the conditions of that time, he focused his chief attention on the premieres. For these performances he resorted to the biggest and most familiar names in his ensemble. But to avoid permanently tying up his best resources in grueling performances, he often planned from the start on alternating them so that he could do justice to the elaborate logistics of his various undertakings. Alexander Rudin described this system as follows:

> The sometimes chaotic aspect of the performance operation was a necessary consequence of Reinhardt's directorial work, which was always single-mindedly focused and oriented to extreme precision; his uncompromising drive to perfection crowded out any concern for what we might call normal theater operations . . . The pamphletist and other opponents who objected to the way things were done at Reinhardt's theaters didn't take into consideration the fact that a repertory theater with several stages, frequent guest tours, and numerous productions in its program (e.g., a total of 25 plays in 1905–06, and 54 in 1915–16), most of which had long runs, could be managed only if actors took on third and fourth roles. Otherwise, the ensemble would have to have been larger than what the company could handle economically.[40]

That the changing of roles might also affect the aesthetic structure of the plays, that the choice of the protagonist might affect the words he was speaking, seems to have played only a minor role in this strategy. Only in a few cases was such diversity explicitly used as a selling point; for the most part, it was simply left unmentioned.

The actor Fritz Kortner (1892–1970), who worked for Reinhardt at the beginning of his career, describes vividly how the principle of profit maximization and multiple use played out on the level of the performers. Kortner played one of the chorus leaders in *Oedipus the King*:

> One night during the performance, I was surprised to hear Profe, likewise one of the chorus leaders, speaking Danegger's big solo line, although Danegger was there performing with us. Afterward, Danegger explained that he had sold the line to the persnickety Profe, a mediocre talent who came from a well-to-do family, for 5 marks, or rather, Danegger owed him 10 marks, and this 5 counted against it. He was going to give him the line again and then he could hit him up a second time. But Profe wouldn't lend him any more. Instead he said he would pay him 3 marks every time he gave him the line. And so it

> happened that Danegger never spoke that line again. Finally another actor made an offer, and Danegger sold him the rest of his lines. For my big line Profe offered . . . 5 marks for each performance. After some serious wrestling with myself, and under great economic pressure and advancing squalor, I made the deal. In the end—like Danegger—I sold all my lines. For a while Danegger and I kept acting in the chorus. But then we would just come to the dressing room before the performance began, sell the lines, drive the prices up, and leave.[41]

The confusion generated by this bartering, which made higher demands and created gaps and glitches in the performance, soon met with negative comments in the reviews and contributed to the common complaint that Max Reinhardt worked only for the premieres, while the rest of the performances were marked by increasing attrition.

An important precondition for Reinhardt's particular form of efficiency enhancement was the introduction of exact prompt books that recorded the most important technical staging details as well as the basic features of the actors' direction. This directorial method, by which the majority of the work was already finalized before rehearsals began, made it possible for Reinhardt to revive productions, or for other theaters to present them, without a comprehensive rehearsal process. An effective system was likewise developed for adapting productions to local conditions. This was not necessarily handled by Reinhardt personally. On the contrary, there were many assistant directors within the Reinhardt empire whose primary duty it was to conduct such rehearsals in Reinhardt's absence. This allowed him to appear personally only for the final rehearsals.

In this way, the high "investment costs" of comprehensive preparation and elaborate scenographic furnishings could be continually used and amortized. Thus, comparatively long run times could be guaranteed and a large repertoire maintained without hindering the ongoing operations that were taking up most of the time.

But the most significant vehicle of multiple usage for Reinhardt was the numerous and extensive guest appearances the company made. As we have already explained, these tours were centrally important with respect both to the development of an international theater aesthetic (transcending the national cultural context) and to questions of international communication. Economically speaking, they represented a crucial support for the Reinhardtian theater enterprise.

It was precisely the experiments in mass theater—*The Miracle* is the perfect example—that made the tours necessary: the costs of these productions were so high that they could hardly have made a profit in one city even with long run times and good seat occupancy rates. The development of new audiences was indispensable.

The 1920s added a new dimension. The disastrous economic situation in Germany made guest appearances abroad especially attractive, because the money made would be in foreign currency. In another context, Reinhardt mentioned that most of his personal income during this period came from his activity in the United States.[42]

But there is another economic phenomenon involved in Reinhardt's touring, one that comes up in a good deal of discussion today in connection with electronic media: the so-called "economies of scale." Hans Kleinsteuber and Barbara Thomass describe how it works:

> The economic motivation for the expansion of media concerns into international markets is primarily economies of scale, which are especially operative in the area of the media, where the production costs are high but the reproduction costs are low. And so it is far more cost-effective to supply large markets than small markets.[43]

The economies-of-scale effect seems, at first sight, especially applicable to Reinhardt's guest performances. Although the costs of a production were relatively high, the follow-up costs of continuing performances were comparatively slight. Thus *The Miracle* at first ate up hundreds of thousands of dollars in New York, but could then be successfully shown for a year on Broadway and for years after that on tour in the United States.

But if we take a closer look at economies of scale, it becomes obvious that the concept was formulated with reference to film or electronic media. There, the follow-up costs of reproduction and distribution compared with production costs are truly negligible. Theater, however, seems by the specifics of its semiotic constitution—especially because of the necessary physical presence of the actors and the simultaneity of production and consumption—to be a counterexample of an economic structure in which profit can hardly be achieved in the area of distribution. For in order to repeat a performance at a later time and in a different place, the actors, scenery, and costumes have to be brought there—and even then, they can only be in one place at one time, in contrast to film, which in theory can be shown simultaneously at an unlimited number of theaters.

Nevertheless, there are indications that Max Reinhardt in his production methods was aware of these conditions and sought to take advantage of such profit effects. For example, his pantomime productions, such as *The Miracle*, show that he was looking for forms whose effect did not depend on the communication of linguistic information, but on the contrary could be received across linguistic and cultural boundaries. Thus, Reinhardt was able to cater to new and larger markets and potential audiences without the extra costs of adapting his productions linguistically, which would have meant working with a new cast.

Assuming the economies-of-scale effect, we can draw a further conclusion. Economic success can only emerge to a degree worth mentioning if the residual costs peculiar to theater—personnel and travel costs, essentially—are negligible. There is some evidence of this in Reinhardt's theater management. His extensive foreign tours to Denmark, the Netherlands, Norway, and Sweden during the First World War were made possibile by state subventions; in other words, the costs Reinhardt had to bear were reduced throughout.[44]

In an economic and organizational sense, we can speak here of a "post-bourgeois" theater, which sought its audience beyond national boundaries a priori. The Reinhardtian theaters thus freed themselves from a fixed social milieu, and this new orientation affected both the aesthetic focus, as shown with *The Miracle*, and the organizational structure, which was no longer directed at a specific audience, but—also through mixed financing—became more independent.

Reinhardt & Co. Inc.

The organizational structure of the Deutsches Theater—fully tailored to Reinhardt's work methods but with the risk cushioned by a "silent partnership"—was typical of private theaters at the turn of the century. Even though Reinhardt was the owner of the building and so preserved a certain independence, such autonomy was only possible because there were sponsors and investors in the background who supported this form of theater and Reinhardt's aesthetic.

Reinhardt's efforts to establish a people's theater, in the sense of a modern theater for the masses, called for a new form of organization, which he tried to achieve in the framework of a joint-stock company (*Aktiengesellschaft*). In July 1917, the Deutsches Nationaltheater Aktiengesellschaft was set up for the Deutsches Theater, with a capital stock of 1.6 million marks. The extent to which programmatic objectives merged with business form is indicated by the fact that Reinhardt had already signed a contract with Georg Fuchs (1868–1949) in 1916, by which the latter agreed to develop with Karl Vollmoeller a memorandum and concrete plans for the realization of the later Grosses Schauspielhaus.[45]

With the legal structure of a corporation—a comparable model, incidentally, was also planned for the Reinhardt Theater in New York—the involvement of third parties in German theater went a significant step further, in that Reinhardt now bound himself to increasing levels of accountability to his financial backers. The adoption of economic models in the cultural sphere shows how much Reinhardt's work methods were determined by the exchange of economic and cultural capital. The name Max Reinhardt had become a brand that carried economic weight. Christopher Balme clearly alludes to this process: "Reinhardt's example virtually forces us to rethink our traditional idea of the modern theater, to be far more nuanced in our interpretation of it. In this narrative, economic, social, and aesthetic perspectives are interwoven in a network of mutually conditioning factors."[46]

Advertising and Public Relations

> Max Reinhardt seemed to have thought it one of the main jobs of a theater director to surround himself with advisors. In this way, the Reinhardtian theater became, if not the most significant, then at least the most advised theater in living memory.
> —Goldmann 1908, 225–26

Although Max Reinhardt, whom many critics never forgave for his "patricide" of Brahm, had to put up with sometimes violent headwinds of theatrical criticism in the first years, his theater enterprise was ultimately based on the understanding that a private theater could only be run profitably if there were good relations with the press.

Paul Goldmann's dig at the large number of Reinhardt's assistants and advisors, however, fails to appreciate that this staff developed a "clout" (*Durchschlagskraft*) in advertising and public relations that was beyond comparison with anything previously known. Max Reinhardt went to great expense and deployed an abundant "arsenal" of fine-tuned resources to influence the "word city"—as Peter Fritzsche described the Berlin of the turn of the century.[47]

His most important assistant for this task was Felix Hollaender (1867–1931), who was already a known and respected novelist before his collaboration with Reinhardt. For Reinhardt he worked as a dramaturg and regisseur, and he directed the Deutsches Theater from 1920 to 1923, when Reinhardt withdrew from Berlin for a short time in the early 1920s. Hollaender worked continually on Reinhardt's celebrity, and he sometimes came up with distinctly original ideas in the process. Thus on January 12, 1904, he invited the then already eighty-nine-year-old painter Adolph von Menzel (1815–1905) to a rehearsal of *Minna von Barnhelm*, ostensibly to seek his expertise for the costumes. But in fact Menzel's visit primarily served to arouse interest in the still new directorship of the Neues Theater.[48] Max Epstein sums up Hollaender's activities as follows:

> This Felix Hollaender was a genius in the art of making Reinhardt popular. Today he would be dragging old Menzel to the rehearsals of *Minna von Barnhelm* as the chief connoisseur of the Frederician epoch; tomorrow he would be arranging an interview on Shakespeare for the master; and he always saw to it that the newspapers took due notice of these important events—all the while ensuring that the other theaters played hardly any role in the press at all.[49]

Reinhardt & Co.

The fact that August Huck (1849–1911), the "*General-Anzeiger* king," invested in the consortium was also largely Hollaender's achievement, once he had taken over the organization of subscription shares. And this very economic nexus seemed to strengthen contact with the press beyond the usual and permissible measure, as Epstein explains: "When you realize the kind of journalistic power this newspaper publisher, who controlled over fifty gazettes, possessed and passed on to his heirs, you can begin to assess what Reinhardt gained in influence over the press through the connection."[50]

But more important was the fact that Max Reinhardt himself was increasingly becoming a public personality. He was (self-)styled as an introverted genius—a legend who was subject to the rumors and captious criticism of his contemporaries. In fact, social occasions like premiere celebrations were increasingly set up for troupe members and critics, where the boundaries between the different spheres of interest were systematically blurred and overstepped.[51]

The carefully crafted public image of Max Reinhardt was an important part of his work and his operating capital, as Christopher Balme notes:

> In truth, Reinhardt can very well be regarded as the first star director in theater history, whose name stood for a specific high-quality art product. Like with some present-day film directors and fashion designers, the name Reinhardt was a kind of seal of quality that was used for advertising purposes, sometimes on the margins of legality.[52]

A further element of the public relations work—besides the publication of the theater's own irregularly appearing magazine, *Blätter des Deutschen Theaters*—was the contact with major personalities and opinion leaders who were not officially in Reinhardt's service but supported him out of personal sympathy or liking for his aesthetic program. The best-known figures in this connection were the critic Maximilian Harden (1861–1927), whose journal *Die Zukunft* (*Future*) always championed Reinhardt, and the already mentioned Harry Graf Kessler, who as Maecenas and benefactor produced a lot of social contacts for Reinhardt.[53]

Next to these positive effects, it should not go unmentioned that Reinhardt was always looking for more ways to exploit his growing theater organization in order to systematically expand his dominant position. The long-term allegiance of actors, artists, and authors belongs in this category. Epstein says about this: "His business operation has become so big that it's as hard to work against it as it would be to work against any large concern."[54]

◆

This look at the financial and organizational side of the Reinhardt enterprise—which must remain cursory here, though more penetrating scholarly study of the matter is a pressing need—shows that its artistic agenda did not emerge independently of its economic underpinnings, but rather that each mutually conditioned the other. The economic structure also reveals that Reinhardt's theater was so important and successful because it consciously intersected with the modernization of society and used modernization's dynamism as a motor force for its own work and development. One can be very critical of this, ridicule the obvious vanity of the protagonists, castigate the "almost pathological obsession with promotion,"[55] or bemoan the artistic sacrifices that accompanied such a full-throttle theatrical operation, but no one can deny its social relevance, its thorough involvement in the conscious life and lived experience of its contemporaries.

Chapter 7

Max Goldmann—Max Reinhardt

Between Participation and Exclusion

> For my part I wouldn't trade my pious grandmother for another if you gave me a "G-palace." Her face was lit up by the shrewdest and kindest eyes that only a Jewish grandmother can have, and the most magnificent tortes were baked in her house.
> —Max Reinhardt

The preceding chapters have tried to establish a comprehensive classification of Max Reinhardt's theatrical work by tracing its aesthetic, cultural, and organizational conditions. But a theater-historical perspective especially cannot content itself with a view directed only at the theater. Theater history as part of the larger project of cultural history also has to ask about the social and cultural conditions of its protagonists. In this sense, even a rough glance at the course of Reinhardt's life arouses our attention: born in the heyday of the Habsburg empire, making his career in Wilhelminian and Weimar Germany, and finally expelled by the Nazis, he died in New York while World War II and the Nazi terror were still raging in Europe. Although Reinhardt kept his religious convictions and his Jewish background rather private, it is also important to read his life and work in light of German-Jewish history in the twentieth century.

The influence of this history is already evident at the beginning of his career when he—like so many other actors—exchanged his birth name Goldmann for the more neutral-sounding Reinhardt.[1] This practice clearly reveals the discrimination faced by Jewish artists, but it need not be read as an act of hiding. On the contrary, for, as we can see in the case of Reinhardt, when they offered him the chance to become an "honorary Aryan," he straightforwardly declined the dubious honor and went into exile.[2]

Between these two events unfolds an unparalleled career that moved through the entire range of German-Jewish history in all its highs and lows. The path included equal rights and the various possibilities of cultural

149

participation and social engagement, as well as continuing discrimination, rejection, and finally expulsion.

As historians, however, we have to ask whether such a personal detail as his Jewishness, which Reinhardt himself never denied, but also did not publicly address, can be discussed within such a framework without making it unduly central.

In fact, this argument weighs heavily, because resonating in it is the fact that, by introducing a distinction that they themselves avoided, we are closing off an area of neutrality, flexibility, or leeway (*Spielraum*) that was so important to the protagonists of that time. Yet the only alternative to seeking out such traces is a timid discretion that in its "silence" risks idealizing a posteriori the actual complexity of that historical interrelationship. In any case, our knowledge of the Holocaust forces us to regard such an approach as untenable. As far back as 1964, the Jewish philosopher of religion Gershom Scholem (1897–1982) emphatically opposed the popular notion of a "German-Jewish symbiosis":

> The allegedly indestructible community of the German essence with the Jewish essence consisted, so long as these two essences really lived with each other, only of a chorus of Jewish voices and was, on the level of historical reality, never anything else than a fiction, a fiction of which you will permit me to say that too high a price was paid for it.[3]

Scholem's argument touches painfully on the key point of the official intellectual discourse. For how should we describe the so important cultural participation and collaboration of Jewish artists and intellectuals without segregating it, or at least relegating it to a marginal position?

In this context, the historian Shulamit Volkov has called for a historiographic perspective that is aware of the fact that the negotiation of cultural leeways and the interrelationships of different social groups are no special case, but rather a fundamental condition of modern, that is, heterogeneous, pluralistic societies:

> Therefore, a history of European countries that is free of nationalism and the ideal of a nation-state still needs to be written. Only therein would the story of minorities of all kinds come into its own right. Jewish history, a history that reproduces the whole scale of the various narratives, a prototype of all minority reportage, might then finally be rescued from its existence on the margins. In this new context, it might be instructive not only for Jews, but for all who seriously wish to reconsider modern history, for those who are ready to experiment with new ways of looking at things.[4]

In a nuanced historiographic perspective of this type, the thematization of *ethnicity*[5] becomes a factor in the social negotiation process that allows possibilities of participation or exclusion to be staked out. Harley Erdman has alluded to the significance of symbolic dramatizations in this connection:

> Ethnicity, as shaped by history, as lived in the moment, is all too real most of the time. The power of culture, as expressed in both the beauty of difference and the injustice of oppression, asserts itself continually. In fact, anti-essentialism ultimately foregrounds the importance of ethnicity since it posits difference as the ongoing creation of complex dynamics which can never be reduced to a gene visible under a microscope; it is a process for which we all bear an active responsibility for perpetuating, in both its positive and negative aspects, as we perform as both actors and audience members in daily encounters.[6]

In the following pages, then, we shall attempt to trace the public perception of Reinhardt—to the extent that available contemporary sources permit such an analysis—in order to be better able to describe the maneuvering spaces available to him as well as their limitations.

Max Reinhardt in the Eyes of His Contemporaries

> What was the self-made youth from Mosaic Vienna to do, if he wanted to get ahead in Berlin, but be receptive to everything that stirred around him?
> —G. Reinhardt 1973, 238 [This passage does not appear in Gottfried Reinhardt's own English-language version of his memoir.]

When Max Reinhardt came to Berlin in 1894 to take the job offered him by Otto Brahm, he was "traveling light." Although we know relatively little about his childhood and youth, we do know that he grew up in rather simple circumstances and by no means came from a learned or a theatrical family. His schooling is unlikely to have been very impressive, as many of his contemporaries never tired of emphasizing.[7]

The road to Berlin, which Walther Rathenau (self-)ironically called "Parvenupolis,"[8] promised abundant opportunities for advancement in a city whose social fabric had drastically changed in a very short period of time due to expansion and immigration. Though Reinhardt's cometlike rise, which made him one of the most important theater directors in Berlin within approximately ten years, was exemplary, it is also characteristic that disdainful references to his social background accompanied him like a shadow. Harry

Graf Kessler, for instance, who was one of his strongest backers, writes in a diary entry from February 6, 1909:

> Evening large dinner at Reinhardt's in his princely rooms Hinter den Zelten; mixture of court, literature, and theater, Chelius with aides-de-camp galloons in red dolman, since he was going to a ball afterward, Varnbülers, Frau v Hindenburg, Helene Nostitz, Gerhart Hauptmanns, Hofmannsthals, Vollmoellers, Theodor Wolffs etc. When I think that I connected Reinhardt with court society a mere two years ago, and that he was still playing the fleapits ten years ago, it's rather remarkable to be taking part in his dinner, which is hardly less elegant than at an elegant ambassador's.[9]

Kessler, whose background and education were the mirror opposite of Reinhardt's,[10] repeats here, in ironic astonishment, the prejudice against the social mobility that was so typical of the Berlin of the late nineteenth and early twentieth centuries. Reinhardt's acquisition of social prestige—he lived in a palace and cultivated a magnanimous, luxurious lifestyle—was the constant target of critical comments by his contemporaries, the reactions ranging from mild ridicule to biting contempt.

The discomfiture caused by the social shift found expression in references to Reinhardt's Jewish background. This "casual" anti-Semitism became a veritable identifying feature of the Wilhelminian empire, as Shulamit Volkov has noted:

> Wilhelminian society underwent a process of cultural polarization. While the activists were absorbed in quarrels and controversies about basic principles and tactics, there arose two main constellations of ideas, two ideological camps, two systems of norms and values, in short: two cultures. Two terms often served to symbolize and characterize them: anti-Semitism and emancipation . . . By the end of the 19th century, it [anti-Semitism] had become a "cultural code." To declare oneself an anti-Semite became a sign of cultural identity, of belonging to a specific cultural camp.[11]

Volkov says that the anti-Semitism of the empire, in contrast to that of the Weimar Republic, is to be understood not in the sense of a political agenda, but rather as an expression of social discontent. This argument should by no means be taken as an exoneration or a historical downplaying of these anti-Semitic sentiments, since it is only too easy to trace the connection between this "social code" and the National Socialist terror. But Volkov's argument does help us understand why liberal circles were not alarmed earlier at anti-Semitic currents and how few barriers stood in the way of adopting such lines of reasoning, if only out of sheer populism. Volkov's analysis of anti-Semitic discourse reveals the tensions that ran through Wilhelminian society.

Max Goldmann—Max Reinhardt   153

The political radicalization of the Weimar Republic may have begun at the "margins," but it found great resonance in a society torn from within and struggling in its "center" for the prerogative of interpreting various projected identities.

Figure 34. Caricature depicting Max Reinhardt in different roles. From *Bühne und Brettl*, 1905.

The adjacent caricature underscores the extent to which Max Reinhardt was perceived in such categories. It appeared in 1905—the very year in which he experienced one of the high points of his career, with the production of *A Midsummer Night's Dream* and his acquisition of the Deutsches Theater—in the journal *Bühne und Brettl* (*Stage and Cabaret*). The composition of the drawing follows the pattern of role portraits. The prominent, central position is occupied by an image of the artist himself, surrounded by smaller images that represent the spectrum of his roles. Under the title "A Famous Berlin

Theater Director and His Roles," the caricature shows, besides the just mentioned portrait of Reinhardt (labeled "R"), four more or less grotesque forms with the following captions: "Ha! Shareholder meeting and I / am soon a poor man, or I / take more energetic precautions. Yet / 31,000 Marks surplus! Brilliant speculation."

While the first three figures can be seen as allusions to theatrical roles—the figure top right, for example, is reminiscent in costume and expression of those naturalistic "old man" characters that Reinhardt played when he was with Brahm—the fourth figure (bottom right) deserves closer attention. The caricaturist's use of anti-Semitic stereotypes such as a hooked nose, a double chin, and a misshapen body[12] is unambiguous. Together with the other figures there emerges a thematic climax here: the genial (and smug) businessman enjoying the success of his "brilliant speculation" can only come across as the "real nucleus" of Reinhardt's multiform personality. The attached subliminal message is that Reinhardt is interested not in artistic values, but only in financial success.

The reference to his Jewish descent, which the caricature presents in passing, is also an echo of the widespread preconception that Jews were disproportionately involved in the theater. This topos, expressed by the malicious catchphrase "the jewification of the theater,"[13] was also constantly used with reference to Reinhardt. Thus, in his book *Max Reinhardt* (1918), Max Epstein writes about the theatrical situation in Berlin:

> Theatrical life in Berlin is dominated by Jewish directors, in the provinces by Christian-Germanic elements . . . But the anti-Semitic movement is solely responsible for the fact that artistic life in Berlin is inundated with Jews and that the very healthy withdrawal to the provinces cannot take place. Thus Jewish directors work almost exclusively in Berlin.[14]

Epstein, who repeatedly alludes to his own Jewish descent in this connection, confirms the preconception on the one hand, but wants to invalidate it on the other by stipulating anti-Semitism as the actual cause. The ostensibly rational point is, however, undercut by the fact that in his language Epstein himself supports the fundamentally negative evaluation of Jewish cultural involvement by using a term like "inundated" and opposing it to "healthy withdrawal." Epstein is ultimately caught up in the essentialism underlying his argumentation:

> It cannot be denied that Jews, as it were by nature, bring to the theater director's job exactly those qualities that are especially important to it. On the other hand, however, one should not fail to recognize that Jewry after all, like every other racial community, has a certain intellectual and therefore also artistic orientation; it thinks and feels in artistic questions also with a certain singularity.[15]

Epstein's appeal to nature and to the very common concept of race in his time claims an inherent inevitability for the extensive engagement of Jewish artists in the German theater. At the same time, however, he stipulates a certain alienation between these artists and their audience that is ultimately almost insuperable because it is biologically determined. The culmination comes with his statement that in view of such superior numbers a "German sensibility" cannot prevail.[16]

The extent to which Epstein's argument follows the lines of anti-Semitic discourse—possibly against his personal intentions—becomes clear in his judgment of Max Reinhardt. Indeed, he praises his talent, but states conclusively that Reinhardt is not capable of creating anything genuinely new; he is, rather, primarily "outstanding . . . in the broadening and improvement of already discovered paths."[17] This thesis of the supposed Jewish incapacity for independent artistic achievement had already been advocated in the nineteenth century by Richard Wagner[18] and Friedrich Nietzsche.[19] To explain Reinhardt's success, Epstein describes him as an ethnic hybrid: "Commercially speaking, he is sufficiently Semitic and artistic, but luckily so Germanically oriented at base that his successes are both possible and justified."[20]

The fact that Epstein believes it possible to discern the features of the two brothers'—Max's and Edmund's—characters with the help of physiognomy further demonstrates how much his reasoning is filled with stereotypes and clichés: "The same oriental desire for something new and striking in their gaze and the bearing of their heads."[21]

It would be idle to speculate here on the possibility of "Jewish self-hatred" to explain his use of such motifs.[22] More important for our purposes is that Epstein's argumentation is no isolated case, but rather an instance of a common figure of thought.

Thus, in 1906 Ernst Bergmann wrote his polemic *Der Fall Reinhardt oder Der künstlerische Bankerott des Deutschen Theaters zu Berlin* (*The Case of Reinhardt, or The Artistic Bankruptcy of the Deutsches Theater in Berlin*). Bergmann accuses Reinhardt of "decorative pomposity and aesthetic parvenuship,"[23] relying—like Epstein—on racist stereotypes: "For anyone who credits the study of facial features, Reinhardt's physiognomy is extremely informative, especially his profile. The nose dominates."[24]

Bergmann understands Reinhardt's style of staging as an expression of his ethnic identity, which is not capable of profound engagement: "Reinhardt's stagecraft is specifically an art of surfaces that has nothing to do with what is essential in the play being performed, nor does it wish to do so . . . I see in all these manifestations of Reinhardtian stagecraft a specific characteristic of an oriental imagination."[25]

With this identification of an "oriental imagination" Bergmann ultimately forecloses the idea of a pluralistic society, further describing Reinhardt's theater as a "blossoming of Semitic culture in the midst of German peoples."[26] Such a conclusion implies an ethnically homogeneous society. The use of the term "German peoples" exposes his roots in *völkisch* ideology. His concept of culture is based on the idea of a homogeneous community, thus placing itself in opposition to the enlightenment idea of a civil society (*aufgeklärtes, staatsbürgerliches Denken*). In such a perspective, the association of different groups and forces on an equal footing and the negotiation of social positions and leeways are always a marginal case or a sign of decline. Bergmann explains: "Nothing is further from our mind than a petty racial hatred. We do, however, want a clean separation. This Jewish cultural blossoming already encompasses all areas of art today . . . But this cultural blossom is not to be dressed up as a German one."[27] There is a reason why Bergmann's postulated "clean separation" reminds us of the language of National Socialism—it is a first step in the direction of a political policy.

Artur Dinter's *Welkrieg und Schaubühne* (1916; *World War and Theater*) represents an intensification of this line of argument. Dinter, who was close to the *völkisch* movement and, later, to the National Socialists, sees in the commercialization of theater a first manifestation of cultural decline, for which he blames Jewish artists: "The theater is business for this baleful class of human beings!"[28] Dinter regards the whole cultural landscape as dominated by "literary racketeering and fraudulence," which, it is true, he explicitly identifies as Jewish in only a few places, but the attributes that he lists allow no other conclusion.

It is characteristic of Dinter's antimodernist attitude that he speaks of a betrayal "that has been perpetrated for ten years now by un-German forces on the ancient German spiritual heritage."[29] The World War for him is the ultimate consequence and expression of a cultural conflict that is to be carried on within German society:

> These chaos-writers, who don't have a single drop of German blood in their veins . . . they and those of our own blood who have succumbed to their tribe and their spirit, they are the ones who dominate our theater in the current World War, which we wage for the survival or annihilation of the specific Geman character![30]

When we consider the aesthetic that Dinter finds reprehensible, we recognize a clear allusion to Reinhardt's stagecraft and its quest for an all-embracing atmosphere as the nucleus of aesthetic experience. "The oriental opulence and extravagance peculiar to this 'culture' has generated a mania for decor on German stages that has also contributed, in no insignificant way, to the placing of the whole German theatrical operation on economically shaky ground."[31] Dinter's criticism is aimed not at aesthetic phenomena or cultural manifestations, but at the idea of a heterogeneous society with diverse ways of seeing things. The "clean separation" advocated by Bergmann, which with him can still be understood as a conceptual problem, is finally translated into political terms by Dinter.

> If the German *Volk* does not succeed in pushing these elements back within the confines appropriate to their minority, then its most glorious victories will avail it nothing; then in the forseeable future, it will perish just as surely as the mighty Roman Empire, which succumbed to the same chaotic forces.[32]

With Dinter, anti-Semitism is no longer a "social code," as one may suspect it is for Epstein, but the central element of an aggressive political program, which the National Socialists finally converted into a horrifying reality starting in 1933.

Even if the opinions of the authors cited here represent extreme cases and were opposed by a large group of sympathetic critics, they still mark one pole of that political and cultural space in which Reinhardt's theater was situated. In their escalation, they underscore the forms taken by the conflict of two cultures described by Shulamit Volkov in this society and the areas in it was waged.

Reinhardt in the Mirror of Literature

Success soon made Max Reinhardt a prominent and colorful figure in Berlin's social life, which he very consciously linked to himself and his theater. The growing interest in his personality not only took the form of extensive coverage in the press but also generated various literary portraits. In the following pages I want to trace Reinhardt's persona in *Erwin Bernstein's Theatrical Calling* (1911) by Friedrich Freksa (1882–1955) and "The Magician" (1929) by Bruno Frank (1887–1945).

In 1911, there appeared a novel by a close associate of Max Reinhardt with the title *Erwin Bernsteins theatralische Sendung* (*Erwin Bernstein's Theatrical Calling*). The novel, which is almost completely unknown today, was nevertheless so successful in its own time that it quickly went through several printings. By genre, it is part Bildungsroman and part roman à clef. The author describes the rise (and rapid decline) of the minor actor Erwin Bernstein to the status of one of the most powerful theater directors in Berlin. The title itself alludes to the first German Bildungsroman, Goethe's *Wilhelm Meisters theatralische Sendung* (ca. 1776; *Wilhelm Meister's Theatrical Calling*).[33] This literary reference is the first instance of the author's ironic commentary, for it highlights the distance that separates Erwin Bernstein from the "formation" (*Bildung*) tradition. At the same time—and this aspect of the novel is clearly preponderant—Freksa is concerned with exposing the secrets of Max Reinhardt's success, it being easy to recognize Reinhardt behind the figure of Erwin Bernstein. It is altogether remarkable—and this is what makes the novel so interesting as part of the historical discourse on theater—how meticulously Freksa reproduces Reinhardt's theatrical system.[34]

The novel begins and ends in Berlin. The young and so far unsuccessful actor Erwin Bernstein—the very name identifies him clearly as a Jew—is hired for a guest performance thanks to the patronage of a more experienced actress named Minna Meister, a name that again suggests Goethe's novel. He makes himself so indispensable during his stay with the company that he is able to find work at a small municipal theater. From there, his journey takes him to Berlin, where he connects with a circle of renowned actors who aspire to take theater in a new direction. Erwin Bernstein's ascent begins with the estabishment of their own cabaret and finally culminates in the opening of a gigantic theater. At the conclusion, the Bernstein empire collapses. He loses his mind and now lives—again under the care of Minna Meister and now fully delusional—to play with a puppet theater.

There are two motifs that are specifically connected with the figure of Bernstein, who on his agent's advice has, suggestively, changed his name from Bernstein to German in order to achieve greater success. The first topos is his penchant for externalities, which is already shown by his inability as an actor to play real characters, only minor stereotyped roles,[35] and, as a director, by his chasing after external effects.

This superficiality (a topos also for Bergmann and Dinter), which will soon be unmasked as lack of psychological depth, corresponds to a further central motif that defines German: his unrestrained sensuality, which is conveyed to the reader at the beginning of the novel by a casual encounter with a maidservant: "When she [the maid] met the steady gaze of his gray eyes, which seemed to penetrate her clothes and lay her bare, she blushed, smiled, and turned as if her shoulders had been tickled."[36] The look that can penetrate clothing returns as a leitmotif throughout the novel. It therefore corresponds to the novel's logic that the various stages of the plot are marked by numerous affairs, all distinguished by German-Bernstein's mere exploitation of his paramour. "The greed for life and the compulsion to make people his own took him from woman to woman."[37]

German-Bernstein is a character without substance, whose energy—on the intellectual, physical, and economic levels—is always drawn from others without producing any like service in return. Bernstein is presented as dominated by his undisciplined (Jewish) body, which never conforms to the standards of the non-Jewish environment. Freksa describes him as a destructive factor of societal development. The underlying motif of the parasite—if not the vampire—has been a fixture in the repertoire of anti-Semitic metaphors.

The second topos defining the character is his relation to the city or, more exactly, the metropolis, which is always described as an environment hostile to human life. Its phantasmagoria is contrasted to a "healthy" way of life, one fit, that is, for human beings to live in. The first sentence of the novel typifies this conceit:

> The long stone walls of the buildings stretched higher, as if threatening to cover the last meager strip of sky that people could still glimpse. In the gray of the November daylight, the alleys of the metropolis resembled the ravines of a primeval world. They seemed to wait mutely for a fateful hour when they would close over all the weak, etiolated life in its caves and chasms.[38]

In the course of the book, the title character and the city seem to fuse ever more into a single entity, until they are finally all but coterminous. Thus Bernstein-German is characterized by another figure:

> He sometimes appeared to me as the spirit of this city ... for whom all intellectual and technical values have the sole significance of sensation. Read the Berlin reviews. Someone who is hailed as a god today is tomorrow's muck. This city is more American than America, for there at least they are proud of men who have created sensations, whereas here people are vain only about the sensations themselves.[39]

Bernstein-German is stylized into a figure symbolic of a superficially understood modernism. He appears as an unscrupulous character whose success is due merely to the harsh conditions of metropolitan life. And so the two already named points of reference yield a third one that typifies Bernstein's whole character: he appears as the prototype of the parvenu,[40] the social climber who finds success by chance—not at all through any competence on his part. At the same time he is presented as a driven figure, unable to control his appetites and without feeling for anything that does not have to do with achieving a goal: "According to the predispositions of his nature, nothing he had achieved was as valuable to him as what was still left to achieve."[41]

These interlocking qualities are especially evident in the description of the start of his love affair with a duchess:

> This woman became his prey, which he pursued with a cool resolve. The hope that she would win him influence at court was mixed with the parvenu's desire for an adventure with a duchess. Perhaps he acted from the dark instinct that drives rebellious slaves to violate the wives and daughters of their masters. He enjoyed the tension of blood that existed between him, the lowly draper's son from Kronstadt, and this woman, whose veins flowed with the blood of Europe's kings.[42]

Freksa describes German's desire as an aggressive act intended to transgress a cultural and biological boundary ("tension of blood"). Yet at the same time—and this seems more far-reaching still—he stages the whole situation as a scene of revolution and voluptuous disorder that overthrows and secretly undermines the existing order from within, an order that, as antithesis to Bernstein's own designs, is repeatedly described as value-oriented, substantial, and ultimately inaccessible to German.

Bernstein-German's decline is represented in this narrative dramatization as a self-purification process for society. This is made especially clear through the contrast between Bernstein-German and the actor Reuter, who turns his back on the metropolis in order to move to the countryside:

> But what had the strongest effect on German were the expressions Reuter used to give his views on the theater. Reuter spoke of it as a world in which only vain half-lunatics and ingenious swindlers could feel at home. In the long run, any healthy person would have to develop an antipathy for the whole enterprise, which was nothing really but mental prostitution. And so Reuter had carried out what he had always set as his life's goal and did in fact live as a farmer.[43]

Freksa's horizon of values unfolds in this juxtaposition of Bernstein-German and Reuter, who represent the urban and rural spheres of life respectively. Behind his settling of accounts with Max Reinhardt we discover an antimodern worldview that rejects the metropolis as the epitome of a pluralistic society that is threatening, unnatural, and unhealthy. That Freksa has chosen a Jewish figure for this parable cannot be explained simply by reference to Max Reinhardt. The passage on the relationship with the duchess reveals that Freksa sees modern culture as aggression and appropriation, if not an act of revenge on Europe's dominant cultural elite. Thus Freksa's parable departs from the individual code of the roman à clef in order to portray Reinhardt's theater as the symptom of a general cultural collapse.

But Freksa's roman à clef—although its exactness of detail and obsession with exposé are clearly personally motivated—is no isolated phenomenon. Reinhardt's fame seems to have encouraged the desire to shatter or at least profane the myth—even by authors who did not share the political agenda of Freksa and his ilk. In 1929 Bruno Frank, the son-in-law of the opera diva Fritzi Massary and the (Reinhardt) actor Max Pallenberg, published his story "Der Magier" ("The Magician"), which also unmistakably targets Max Reinhardt.

The story's plot centers on a production of Racine's *Phaedra*. Meskart, the name of Reinhardt's literary alter ego, stages the play in an intimate garden theater at his Schloss Oldenberg.[44] But when its great success fails to make any impression on him inwardly, he sails precipitately to New Orleans, where he rehearses a play with an unknown "Negro troupe" and goes on tour.

Bruno Frank, who imagines the African American communities in the American South as the antithesis of Western cultural discourse,[45] likewise describes Meskart as a parvenu whose art is able to give expression to his age's sense of life: "Then suddenly he was in Berlin. Here was a public to be won, brittle, hard, greedy of novelty; and they seemed to be waiting for him. A brilliant and noisy period, the official manifestations of which were apt to offend the sensitive, here found its representative artist of impeccable taste."[46] Meskart spends the night before his "flight," after the premiere of *Phaedra*, with the princess Anna, whose fascinating grace and beauty are described as a leitmotif in the first part of the story. As with Freksa, here too the erotic encounter with a woman of the nobility is an occasion to bring up the subject of Meskart's ethnic background:

> This love-night and many others like it were but a ceremonial of fame and nothing more. He imagined how he might have entered the bedroom of this granddaughter of the Albas, he, Meskart, but not as a well-groomed gentleman with a great name in his dark silk . . . but in another form which also would have been true—as a bent and aging Jew with side curls, in another long garment, the kaftan, which Jews still wear in the East. How she would have started back in horror from her pillows![47]

Frank has Meskart "dream through" the anti-Semitic (anxiety) fantasy of a Jewish takeover of European culture in the image of a love-night. This image would also be true, as the narrator affirms. But, unlike in Freksa's novel, with Frank it appears not as an act of aggression, but more as a shadow side of cultural participation, hidden behind the mask of cultivation and the "great name." By contrasting Meskart's emotional coldness vis-à-vis the beautiful princess with his enthusiasm for the unbridled vitality of the African American "pariahs,"[48] Frank also identifies Meskart as a "foreign body" in European culture. His flight is not merely an expression of ennui with respect to a smug and rigidified culture that craves ever more sophisticated enjoyments. Because of Meskart's Jewishness, the flight—or the insufficient, inward participation in that culture that underlies it—becomes the expression of a categorical foreignness. The fact that he can only be satisfied by the singing, dancing, and acting of these despised former slaves[49] reveals him too as a pariah whose cultural participation amounts to a mere masquerade.

If we gather together the different public and literary conceptions of Max Reinhardt, we quickly realize the extent to which the public persona served as a projection screen for hopes and expectations, as well as fear, envy, and uneasiness. It is very telling that critics and adversaries took it as a matter of course not only to oppose his art or his economic activities, but to make allusions to his Jewish background in their criticism. The very casualness of this anti-Semitism shows how much it was a part of society and its discourse.

For all their diversity of interests and purposes—not to mention their political implications—we recognize certain points of anti-Semitic focus behind the different thematizations:

- *The commercialization of theater.* Reinhardt appears as the protagonist of commercial theater, understood as standing in sharp opposition to the "true interiority" of the bourgeois, "German" theater of culture (*Bildungstheater*).
- *The externalization of art.* Reinhardt's staging style is described as an (oriental) predisposition to externality—a line of argument that opposes such art to value-oriented interiority. Visual opulence seems mere effect-mongering, disguising a lack of ideas.
- *Physicality and sensuality.* In the superimposition of private life and public persona, the (Jewish) body becomes the expression and epitome of an all too insufficiently restrained sensuality and sexuality. Nor is this an end in itself; it is dramatized in the cultural debate as an act of appropriation.
- *Metropolis and modernity.* The metropolis is the "crime scene" of cultural collapse and as such is opposed to an ideal, homogeneous community. The unhealthy hecticness and greed for sensation of the "parvenupolis" is identified as the breeding ground of the kind of art that is connected with Reinhardt's name.

Max Reinhardt's Shylock: An Answer from the Stage?

Max Reinhardt rarely spoke about his Jewishness—and Jewish themes occupied no special position in the repertoires of his various theaters. It is true that he performed *God of Vengeance* by Sholem Asch (1880–1957) after having it translated from the Yiddish, and he also promoted the young Arnold Zweig (1887–1968). But there was no special emphasis involved.

On the other hand, it is striking how often Reinhardt staged Shakespeare's *Merchant of Venice*, whose Shylock could be taken as the archetypal thematization of Jewish life in a predominantly Christian society. The character of Red Itzig in *The Count of Charolais* (1904) by Richard Beer-Hofmann (1866–1945), a role that Reinhardt himself repeatedly played, can be seen in the same tradition.[50]

Of all the productions of *The Merchant of Venice*, that of 1913 stands out especially. In it the role of Shylock was alternately played by Rudolf Schildkraut (1862–1930) and Albert Bassermann (1867–1952).

While double castings were justified on practical grounds in Reinhardt's plays, in this case the two actors were so different that it seems to have had programmatic significance. Albert Bassermann, who came from a well-known, non-Jewish Mannheim family, was famous for his heroic roles, which he acted with force and dignity. Rudolf Schildkraut was better known for comic or grotesque roles. Schildkraut's persona was a myth in itself. What was known of his background, to which reviewers constantly referred, was based on rumor rather than reliable sources. Reputedly born in Constantinople, he grew up in eastern Europe and found his way to the German stage by the circuitous route of the Yiddish theater.

Figure 35. Albert Bassermann as Shylock from *The Merchant of Venice* (Berlin, 1913). Photograph by Hans Ludwig Böhm. Courtesy of the Theaterwissenschaftliche Sammlung of the University of Cologne.

Figure 36. Rudolf Schildkraut as Shylock from *The Merchant of Venice* (Berlin, 1913). Photographer unknown. Courtesy of the Theaterwissenschaftliche Sammlung of the University of Cologne.

Bassermann, whose costume epitomized all the clichés of the Shylock tradition (beard, nose, etc.), played his Shylock with heroic, dignified contours. Schildkraut, by contrast, emphasized the physical in his acting: he sang, ran, hummed. His body, which had an almost geometrical shape because of his orientalized costume, was a major part of his performance. His ring-adorned hand contrasted with the great gap in his teeth and the curious arrangement of his hair. Schildkraut's Shylock evoked no associations with the shtetl; it was more "oriental" in character. Arnold Zweig emphasizes these physical-sensual components in his description:

> Schildkraut's Shylock smells of onions and garlic, and that is at least as good a food and at least as pleasant a smell as that of butchered

swine or kid roasted in its mother's milk . . . And so this Rudolf Schildkraut, plump and wriggling, with all his guttural sounds, has become one of the most powerful fascinations and shocks of the German stage.[51]

Zweig interprets the unmediated sensuality of Schildkraut's Shylock as a postulate of equal rights, casting this in the image of diverse cuisines and Jewish dietary rules. Onions and garlic (metonyms of Jewish cuisine) are as savory and pleasant as "kid roasted in its mother's milk," which is unkosher according to Jewish law. Fundamentally—so Zweig postulates—the two have equal justification.

An especially impressive document pertaining to the reception of *The Merchant of Venice* is a review by Siegfried Jacobsohn (1881–1926) that compares both actors. Jacobsohn, whose very name can be interpreted as a metonym of Jewish acculturation, came from a Jewish family, but, like Reinhardt, rarely made public mention of it. He describes the different court scenes as follows:

> Then comes the catastrophe. Shylock must even be baptized. Bassermann stretches to full height; Schildkraut mutters in horror: Shema Yisrael! What would not be possible for Bassermann, because nobody dares to get too close to him, happens to Schildkraut: an anti-Semite grabs him by the throat and shakes him. Bassermann leaves the room with the stride of one who is never vanquished; Schildkraut staggers off annihilated. Bassermann's trial? *Mea res*—so much so that the blood rises to my head. Schildkraut's? What a spectacle! But alas, only a spectacle, which never warms my artistic interest. With Bassermann the piece is tragic, great, broken, unjust, and unbearable. With Schildkraut it is comic with a touch of sadness, aesthetically pleasing but rather slight.[52]

The vote for Bassermann is unambiguous. True, Jacobsohn regards Schildkraut's Shylock as more authentic, a figure who in a moment of the greatest consternation takes refuge in the Shema Yisrael, the most important prayer in Judaism. But it is precisely this authenticity that fails to satisfy Jacobsohn's explicitly aesthetic criteria. Bassermann's tragic heroism, on the other hand, becomes "his thing" (*mea res*)—to the point of physical reaction.

At first glance this seems to be the expression of an assimilated point of view, for which an ethnic reading of Shylock, as represented by Schildkraut, offers no possibility of identification and is also of secondary interest. But it is more likely Bassermann's idealization, his aesthetic alteration of the role, that captivates Jacobsohn's imagination. For Jacobsohn, *The Merchant of Venice* has become a universal parable that no longer presses for a specifically Jewish interpretation of Shylock, but rather accentuates the universally human.

On second glance, however, Jacobsohn's critique turns out to be a clouded utopia, for, whether he likes it or not, the play forces him too to reflect on the question of ethnic difference and its social significance.

> Bassermann relaxed his rigidity only once, laughed—to our ear in an ominously diabolic manner, to the Christian ear in a way that was innocuously hilarious—when that fearful condition suddenly occurred to him. Schildkraut didn't emphasize the scene at all, just as generally he places more trust in strong material than in his own commentaries, highlights, and nuances.[53]

With one false note, or perhaps just an unsuccessful one, Bassermann's performance slides for a moment into something grotesquely diabolic and so manifests those stereotyped dimensions of the character that so easily become anti-Semitic caricature. The casualness of the parenthetical comment with which Jacobsohn thematizes the dividing line in the audience that suddenly flashes into view may indicate that in 1913 the ideal of a liberal bourgeois society—for which Shylock was merely a character type, but by no means had to be taken as direct commentary on the question of Jewish participation—was still strong enough to overlook such slip-ups.

It would certainly be too simple to attempt to link these productions directly to Reinhardt's personal relationship to his Jewishness. But the mere juxtaposition of two such different interpretations says much about the way he understood himself aesthetically and culturally. It is hardly possible to think of his theater without the freedom that allowed him to give shape to Christian legends, Greek myths, and Jewish characters and to populate his stages with them. This freedom, of which Reinhardt made almost profligate use in the most various ways, corresponds to a growing countercurrent that sought to deny this maneuvering space by emphasizing differences.

It tells us much about Reinhardt's time that his opponents thought they could vilify him because of his Jewishness. If we reread the brief passage from the letter to Rudolf Kommer, used as the epigraph for this chapter, in this context, we begin to sense what a painful experience it must have been for him that his grandmother—representing the most private and intimate aspect of his life—became such a political issue.

Conclusion

◆

The Glorious Heyday and Obscure Demise of Reinhardtian Theater as a Historical Lesson

I mentioned mistrust of the Reinhardt myth at the beginning of this book, and now at the end of my deliberations I want to speak of that myth again, for it is obvious that the course of Max Reinhardt's life lends itself easily to glorification. The "self-made youth from Mosaic Vienna," as his son Gottfried described him, goes out into the world to meet with the loftiest triumphs and honors, becoming a director of theaters and the owner of a palace, only to lose almost everything in the end. Even this tragic outcome can be harmonized in a final melancholy chord.

But glorification closes off the object of its consideration from the outside world. The cyclic form of the Reinhardt myth (which ultimately returns to its point of origin) distorts our view of the interplay of individual talent and historical context. To introduce a critical accent here is not at all to reduce personal life achievement to the product of its historical conditions. It can, however, deliver us from the comfort of historical distance, for the mere admiration of a great name is, historiographically, the smaller coin. Behind the veneration lies a historical (self-)understanding that interprets its object in a purely "decorative" manner: the object may fill the picture of the past, but without entering into any relationship with the present. Yet if historiography is to be more than a mere aid to conversation, it behooves us to reveal the traces that lead to our own time.

From this perspective, I want to use the remaining pages of this book to examine both the emergence and the "failure" of Max Reinhardt and his theater as a historical lesson—a sort of didactic play—that reveals central features of historical development. By "lesson" I mean not to suggest some kind of ex cathedra proclamation of historical truth, but to capture in miniature those social energies that shape historical processes. The "manageability" of the limited object serves as a corrective to all too hasty generalizations.

This historical lesson requires a recognition at the outset that the foundation of the German Empire in 1871 did indeed, as a political act, create a single legal, economic, and governmental sphere, but its intellectual and cultural center remained peculiarly undefined and, consequently, contested. The imperial Hohenzollern dynasty that crowned Prussia's hegemonic ambitions needed to insist so much on historical heritage and tradition, and make theater of them in multiple ways, precisely because it was deficient in both.[1]

Social and economic changes came up against a political system that was oriented toward the absolutism of the seventeenth and eighteenth centuries in terms of its ideas, symbols, and forms of political activity, and that never understood that its citizens had long since lost any inclination to see themselves as mere humble subjects.

Such tensions were especially obvious in the domain of theater. With the new free trade laws and theatrical boom that resulted from them, the Königliches Schauspielhaus (Royal Playhouse) in Berlin—a prestigious theater up to that time—lost much of its significance. This was not merely due to the court's dependence in matters of taste;[2] it was also the result of an established organizational structure that guaranteed that the theater would be managed by veteran officers and bureaucrats instead of theater professionals.[3] These "cavalier intendants"[4] were able to satisfy Wilhelm II's artistic needs, but, with the pressure of competition from the free theaters, this only widened the gap between the court and the rising bourgeoisie, which identified early on more with the houses established in the 1880s (Deutsches Theater, Lessing-Theater, Berliner Theater) than with the court theaters.

Maximilian Harden, who in his 1888 polemic *Berlin als Theaterhauptstadt (Berlin as Theater Capital)* was already critical of the state of the court theaters, declared: "The fact that the Deutsches Theater so quickly acquired an attention-commanding and even tone-setting position in the entire Reich was due not least to the incompetence of the court theater."[5] This tension makes clear that, although the empire itself was a conservative and in certain respects authoritarian regime, the very exclusion of the bourgeoisie channeled numerous energies into the sphere of culture, where the disparity with the representative cultural institutions of the court was palpable. Where political participation was possible only within narrow bounds, there developed—more or less tolerated or hindered by officials—a blooming and multifaceted cultural landscape that reached full development after 1918 under the auspices of the Weimar Republic. As Peter Gay states in his study *Weimar Culture: The Outsider as Insider* (1968): "In a less ominous sense, the modern movement was ripe as well . . . There can be no doubt: the Weimar style was born before the Weimar Republic."[6]

Gay's observation reminds us that historical currents stretching back in time prove how complex and contradictory the process of forming historiographic concepts has to be, or better: how questionable the clarity suggested by many such concepts actually is. Where the "history of events" recognizes caesuras and sharp contours, the culture-historical perspective looks at things in terms of modifications and intensifications. But such caesural classifications are also very widespread in theater and art history. Thus the term "avant-garde," which is still frequently used as an orienting formula, implies a categorical break, a sharp division between yesterday and tomorrow, which on second glance proves to be a matter of a purely programmatic agenda.[7]

Reinhardt's ventures in particular show that such a classification falls short. His theater was certainly innovative and surprising, but it neither appeared with that revolutionary aplomb that rejects everything that has gone before, nor claimed to be a radically new departure. Mediation of the new and a sense of indebtedness to the past were much more the hallmark of his undertakings.

And this is where the secret of his success and his specific cultural position reveal themselves. His was a bourgeois theater that took the changes that had taken place in the bourgeois milieu as its motor force and elixir of life. The "shooting star" saw this bourgeois culture in a way that was not limited by either a need to protect vested rights or a consciousness of tradition. Even the parvenuship for which he was so often reproached allowed Max Reinhardt to transfer ancient Greek plays to the circus arena and stage Ibsen with the eyes of a painter. He was, as both an individual person and a man of the theater, so much the product of social modernization and mobility that he—more enduringly, more luxuriously, and more successfully than others—was able to create a theater that met the aesthetic, but also the cultural and social, needs of his time.

Karl Strecker cites this as one of Reinhardt's strengths in his polemic *Der Niedergang Berlins als Theaterstadt* (1911; *The Demise of Berlin as a Theater City*), which draws a stereotyped caricature of the bourgeois milieu: "Reinhardt has—and only the bitterest of his enemies would contest this—stopped the crisis [of theater], has got part of Berlin's cultivated strata back to attending the theater again. He can mesmerize the hurried metropolitan citizen for five long hours of an evening with a performance of Shakespeare."[8] But Max Reinhardt was not only a border crosser in the social sense; he also seemed to stand between periods of time. He belonged to the nineteenth century to the same degree that his aesthetic pointed ahead to the twentieth. His artistic roots, as well as his social and cultural self-understanding, were deeply influenced by the experience of the new bourgeois lifestyle and the promise it contained. His career from actor to theatrarch was a bourgeois career in a twofold sense: in the first place, because it depended on the bourgeois idea that personal achievement rather than birth should determine one's social position,[9] and in the second place, because—as we have seen in the chapter on the organization and financial structure of the Reinhardtian theaters—his brand of theater would not have been possible without the cultural and financial investment of broad bourgeois circles. Here we catch sight of that liberal, bourgeois Berlin that the aristocratic cliques of imperial Germany merely tolerated but never accepted as a political or social partner. It hardly seems a coincidence from today's perspective that many of those involved in his undertaking belonged to the circle of those beneficiaries of modernization whose success corresponded in a peculiar way to their limited political opportunities.[10]

Max Reinhardt's theater was in no way directed only at the "new" upper level of society that was often stigmatized as the cultureless "plutocracy."[11] It was oriented to the broad "neo-bourgeois" milieu. Reinhardt's production style fulfilled an important integrative function: it made the bourgeois cultural canon accessible—and "consumable"—to those who were not classically schooled. Concomitantly, Reinhardt's theaters soon became a fixed point of reference for the bourgeois way of life, because their character and aesthetic style made participation in public life possible on various levels.

But at its core, this theatrical undertaking—following the avowed agenda of its guiding spirit—aimed at something more than just the Berlin public. Reinhardt kept broadening his field of influence until the general outlines of a metropolitan culture came into view. The dialectical tension this created for him with respect to Berlin can be seen from a London entry in Harry Graf Kessler's diary dated January 2, 1912:

> Reinhardt is delighted with his reception here and seems to feel all the more bitter about his treatment by the Berlin press. Here, he says, people approach one another with equanimity and courtesy; with us, anyone who has something new to offer is treated at first like a criminal; he has to justify his boldness before the public prosecutor, the reviewer, and the tribunal of the audience. As a consequence, in Germany the artist loses any unselfconsciousness he might have, because he knows that any idea that delights him in solitude will be rudely abused and belittled as soon as it comes to public view. He's tired, he says, and longs to live at ease in London. Although he admitted that he could grow only in Berlin, because that's a soil something new can grow in. In Paris and Vienna they've already had everything; and in London, where there might also be fruitful soil, the language would be an insurmountable barrier.[12]

These lines not only document Reinhardt's occasional bitterness about the behavior of the German press;[13] they also open up an interesting panorama of European metropolises. It is striking how Max Reinhardt dismisses Paris and Vienna, the two symbols of European urbanity par excellence, because there could no longer be anything "new" there. By contrast, Berlin and London figure as areas of potential growth.

This assessment bound Reinhardt to the very "parvenupolis" by which he felt so unjustly treated. The tension shows us that he was in a profound sense the product of the prevailing conditions in Berlin. In the context of dramatically changing social structures, areas of great opportunity (*Spielräume*) opened up for those who came across them, partly because official cultural policy was so deficient in the way it reacted to the needs of the growing metropolis.

Arthur Eloesser (1870–1938) gives us a very vivid summation of the conditions in Berlin:

> This new Berlin, a young and clumsy giant, a gourmand of quantities with a marvelous stomach and outstanding tools for wolfing things down and digesting them, harbors the youthful ambition of rejecting nothing and trying everything, while at its own peril, it spares jabbering importers and middlemen the thoughtful selection they would have to make elsewhere for a more decided and discriminant taste.[14]

Only an artist who was not afraid of opulence and sensation could handle this gigantic appetite. Thus it may have been to Reinhardt's advantage that as a "parvenu" he had no phobias about popular culture. The insouciance he showed in associating theater with other urban institutions of spectacle and entertainment defined the cultural position of his whole enterprise.

Reinhardt himself understood the experience of modernized city life as the implicit condition of his art. The theater for him, as he explained in his famous speech "Rede über den Schauspieler" (1928; "On Actors"), was an antithesis to the demands of day-to-day city life. "Bourgeois life is narrowly limited and poor in emotional content. It has made nothing but virtues of its poverty and squeezes out a living among them."[15] The actor's job is diametrically opposed to this: "But the art of acting is also a liberation from the conventional pretences of everyday life; for the actor's job is not to dissimulate, but to reveal."[16]

This "universal" idea of theater, which places itself in an inverse relation to the conditions of modern life, is also distinguished by the fact that it is inherently open to different cultural contexts and no longer depends on the framework of the nation.[17] Its sensuousness places it in opposition to the conventional idea of a literary theater. Reinhardt's theater does not wish to be a "moral institution" at any cost; it offers a fundamental aesthetic experience that it explicitly wants the audience to understand as a response to a desideratum of modernized society.

This testimonial to the historical experience of modernization constituted the nucleus of metropolitan culture at the turn of the century, as Peter Gay observes:

> For the outsiders of the Empire, as, later, for the insiders of the Republic, the most insistent questions revolved around the need for man's renewal, questions made most urgent and practically insoluble by the disappearance of God, the threat of the machine, the incurable stupidity of the upper classes, and the helpless philistinism of the

> bourgeoisie . . . But it was precisely this—the commonplace quality of cosmopolitanism in the Empire—that later gave the Weimar style its toughness of fiber; in its unselfconscious internationalism it shared the vitality of other cultural movements in European history.[18]

Gay's description underscores an important point, which makes a decisive contribution to the understanding of metropolitan culture: it was historically situated in the context of an ever more aggressively vocal nationalism in a time of maximal military and cultural armament against "others" both external and internal. This tension—and the lesson of Reinhardt's theatrical enterprise shows this very clearly—was typical of the Wilhelminian empire. To describe this epoch as monolithically nationalistic may be correct with respect to the "managerial staff," but it underestimates the complex interplay that was taking place within society.

Fritz Stern has observed that this very tension characterized the crucial balance of power within German society:

> To understand the German past is to remember the promise that pre-Hitler Germany represented, and never fully actualized. The achievements in science and in industry, in art, architecture, and academic scholarship, were truly prodigious and a warrant for hope. But it was never a quiet, balanced country: even before the Great War and most especially after it, Germany was restless, fearful, aggressive and divided . . . Till Hitler, it was a country of immense contradictions with a recurrent lure of power, with many Germans having dreams of great national and spiritual unity and denying at the same time the inevitability of social and political conflicts, thus turning them into principled, mortal enmity.[19]

For Stern, this internal conflict between the adherents of a comprehensive modernization and those who in their anxiety saw all change as loss is what was responsible for the enthusiasm—hardly comprehensible from today's perspective—that accompanied the outbreak of the First World War: "Only a nation so internally divided could have welcomed the outbreak of war in 1914 with the extravagant hope that war would unify its people through sacrifice. Instead, the long war . . . bred an atmosphere of suspicion and distrust that, upon Germany's defeat, erupted into both actual and latent civil war."[20]

The political and cultural freedoms of the Weimar Republic were endangered from the start, according to such a point of view. But the argument should not be misinterpreted as nostalgia for the empire—on the contrary, it only underscores the political potential of the ideal of metropolitan culture in light of such tensions. In the context of an officially prescribed nationalism that expressed itself with an increasingly aggressive rhetoric, the project of an international culture centering on the developing metropolis takes on additional political significance. Already in 1888, Maximilian Harden had turned against the nationalistic discourse and warned that, after two decades of political consolidation, even the good patriot might be allowed to think that he was not just a German citizen but also a human being who had his part to play in the great humanistic work of cultural humanity.[21]

Harden's more wishful than factual consolidation was never really there in the sense of an inner balance. Instead, there was a steady sharpening of the opposition between nationalistic feeling, which increasingly demanded the concept of *Volk*, and the growing praxis of international exchange. The latter contained an implicit response to the official political discourse—although an actual political, programmatic confrontation between these two antithetical worldviews came about only during the Weimar Republic. Here, in many cases, cultural engagement was transformed into political partisanship. The in-between sphere of aesthetic and cultural discourse, where political content was more subliminal than overt, was absorbed by the political forum. If we want an explicit sign of this development, Siegfried Jacobsohn comes to mind: after the First World War he programmatically changed the the name of his journal from *Die Schaubühne (Stage)* to *Die Weltbühne (World Stage)*.

If we look at theater history from this perspective, it seems no mere coincidence that Max Reinhardt no longer played the same role in Berlin's theatrical world in the 1920s that he had played up to 1918. It fell to Leopold Jessner (1878–1945) to make the stage a central forum of social discourse by converting the former court theater into a state theater of the Weimar Republic.[22]

For Reinhardt, the huge, sensational successes that had made his theater the talk of the town now occurred more seldom—his project of developing a metropolitan culture out of bourgeois theater seemed to have less of a place in the atmosphere of increasing political tensions.

His forced departure from Germany in 1933 and the various stops on his way to exile in the United States mark the last phases of a till then unparalleled career. The cultural project practiced by Reinhardt found no permanent place in either Germany or Austria. Quite the contrary, civil (or bourgeois) society (*Bürgergesellschaft*) was replaced by the ideal of the national community (*Volksgemeinschaft*). From the political point of view, Reinhardt's project of a "theater that gives people joy again"[23] may seem to have been too weak, bordering on naivete. But it was not meant as a theater that would take on the task of strengthening people's political convictions. Instead, it was the living embodiment of the idea of a liberal society and sought to provide an opulent aesthetic experience of its merits. The fact that the idea never fulfilled its promise was due not to the individual failure of its protagonists, but to the historical impossibility of creating the transition to a modernized society. Thus the history of Max Reinhardt and his theater points beyond the biography of a great director to the history of his audience.

Epilogue: "Yeah, He's Still Here"

This is what the cemetery custodian said after a quick look in his register to see whether Max Reinhardt's grave was still in Hastings-on-Hudson, a village twenty miles north of New York City. The trip to the last resting place of this seemingly so restless artist leads from downtown New York to a small town near the East Coast of the United States—from the pulsing metropolis to the unsettlingly peaceful countryside.

The cemetery itself, maintained by the liberal Jewish Stephen Wise Free Synagogue, is in a small wooded area outside of town. Reinhardt lies in good company: Marc Chagall, George and Ira Gershwin, Lee Strasberg, and a number of other famous New York names can be found in the surrounding graves, which are not really graves, but small mausoleums elaborately constructed with costly materials.

Figure 37. The community mausoleum in Hastings-on-Hudson, where Max Reinhardt is buried. Photograph by Peter W. Marx, 2006.

Conclusion

Max Reinhardt has found his final home in a mausoleum belonging to the congregation, a plain structure with two slim Doric columns. There is no nameplate or plaque mentioning him on the outside. Only within hangs a small brass plate—water-stained and distinctly smaller than those on the neighboring graves—that bears, in unadorned lettering, the name "Max Reinhardt."

To the question of whether visitors often ask after the grave, the custodian answers, with an embarrassed smile, that the grave is very old by now, but when the weather is good, sometimes . . .

The seclusion of the grave, which in fact was intended as a makeshift solution, is moving, because it recalls the remoteness of Reinhardt's death in New York in 1943. After long years of exile, which offered few opportunities for work, Max Reinhardt died there two years before the end of the war. He did not live to experience the end of National Socialism or the horror of knowing the magnitude of the Holocaust. His son Gottfried Reinhardt writes of this:

> He was laid to rest in a Jewish cemetery near Hastings-on-Hudson. A receiving vault is what the people at the cemetery called the tight, eerie stone structure his coffin was lifted into. "Receiving," meaning temporary, fit into our plans perfectly, as it was to have been a provisory arrangement—our intention being to maintain it only so long as the war lasted and until the situation in Europe cleared sufficiently for us to decide on the place of his final interment. The war has long since ended and the situation in Europe has become as "clear" as it will ever be, but not so far as Max Reinhardt is concerned. At least not sufficiently so to justify his remains being returned there. The decision to do so—with which I was faced a number of times—was all the more difficult as he had stated emphatically that he never wanted to go back to Germany or Austria. While I have little doubt that, with changing circumstances, he, like so many other émigrés, would have changed his mind, I didn't feel it was my right arbitrarily to act in contradiction to his wishes.[24]

The "provisory arrangement" of his last resting place, as Gottfried Reinhardt calls it, is also the outward expression of the fact that Max Reinhardt's world has been irretrievably destroyed and lost:

> My own private conviction is that the timely death which has kept Max Reinhardt from returning to a world that is neither inwardly nor outwardly his amounts to a great and deserved stroke of fortune. It is one of my nightmares to imagine what or who would have been there to greet him amid all the honors on his return home. For he was not a person who would have used the wrong done to him as a form of blackmail, nor was he capable of canceling the debt owed to him.[25]

A visitor from Germany coming to the grave today cannot help thinking of another cemetery that is almost the foil to this one. The Dorotheenstädtischer Friedhof in Berlin, especially since the 1950s, has become something of a "celebrity graveyard," where many artists and intellectuals like Bertolt Brecht, Hans Eisler, Hans Mayer, Heiner Müller, and Heinrich Mann (who died shortly before his planned return to Germany) are buried. In its tasteful simplicity, the cemetery is the equivalent of the Panthéon in Paris: here, the intellectual history of Germany that was not compromised by National Socialism has a place.

One's first impulse is to wish Max Reinhardt were included in this latter circle—so important a pillar of this non-nationalistic culture of Germany does he seem to be. But on second thought, his absence is even more expressive. The actual seclusion of his grave, thousands of miles from Berlin, underscores the fact that his project, the world of metropolitan culture he inhabited, could find no place in Berlin—a missed opportunity that might have altered not just the history of Germany, but possibly also our picture of the world, which seems smaller in the era of "globalization," but also more endangered.

On the way back to the metropolis, all that remains as admonition is the adage of Solomon from the book of Proverbs (10:7) that stands engraved on the pediment of the mausoleum housing Reinhardt's urn: "The Memory of the Righteous Is a Benediction."

NOTES

Introduction

Epigraphs: Frank 1929, 13; Frank 1946, 235. Goldmann 1910, 39.
1. Herald 1915, 9.
2. Herrmann 1914, 5.
3. In this regard, see Fischer-Lichte 1999c.
4. See Balme and Davis 2015; and Davis and Balme 2016.
5. See Münz 1979.
6. Münz 1998, 198–201.
7. Baumbach 2002, 1.
8. Kotte 2002, 2.
9. See Kotte 2005, 15–90.
10. Bayerdörfer 1990, 50–51.
11. Bayerdörfer 1990, 51. [Translator's comment: August Wilhelm Iffland (1759–1814) was an important actor, director, and dramatic author of his time.]
12. Bayerdörfer 1990, 51–52.
13. Thus, for example, Hans-Thies Lehmann in his influential book *Postdramatisches Theater* (1999) implicitly took the idea of the avant-garde, which he discusses in a thoroughgoing critical manner, as his point of departure by distinguishing between pre-, post-, and dramatic theater. See also Hoffmann 2001 on this concept.
14. Elsaesser 2002a, 26.
15. Elsaesser 2002a, 94.
16. Geertz 1973, 21.
17. Balme 1994, 52.
18. Geertz 1973, 25.
19. Geertz 1973, 28.
20. Anderson 1983, 2–3.
21. See Hobsbawm 1983.
22. Winkler 2000, 244–45.
23. For the population figures, see Zimmermann 2000, 16, 25.
24. Brauneck 1999, 625.
25. See especially Epstein 1911 and Epstein 1914.
26. Kocka 1987, 44.
27. Hein and Schulz 1996, 13.
28. On the concept of the metropolis, see also Zimmermann 2000, 32–38.
29. A good example of this type of ensemble were the "girl troupes," such as the Ziegfeld Follies and the Tiller Girls, which became firm fixtures of the international "revue culture."
30. Martersteig 1904, 631.

31. For an expanded documentation of these laments, see Marx and Watzka 2009, 9–15.
32. For an overview of virtuoso theater, see Stettner 1998 and Brandstetter 2002.
33. For the court theaters' loss of significance, see also Daniel 1995, 359–97.
34. Frenzel 1980, 56.
35. Between 1874 and 1890, the Meiningen troupe gave around 2,590 performances in 38 cities.
36. For L'Arronge, see Raeck 1928.
37. Reinhardt 1989, 70.
38. Jacobsohn 1910b, viii.

Chapter 1

1. Reinhardt 1989, 73; Esslin 1977, 9.
2. Reinhardt 1989, 76; Esslin 1977, 9–10.
3. See the detailed description in Bernauer 1955, 96–147.
4. See Brauneck 1999, 611, for information.
5. See Jelavich 1993, 26–27.
6. This type of shadow theater was later introduced into Germany; see Kluncker 1978.
7. See Jansen 1990, 161–63.
8. See Bayerdörfer 2000, 74–76; and Chrisholm 2000, 21–22.
9. Bierbaum 1897, 359.
10. See Aschheim 2000 for an introduction to this topic.
11. See Chrisholm 2000, 23.
12. See Mommsen 1987 for an introduction to the subject.
13. See Kühn 1984, 14–15.
14. Bierbaum 1897, 358.
15. The entry in *Kluges etymologisches Wörterbuch* reads: "*Tingeltangel* . . . 'cheap entertainment music; place where this is offered' (<19th c). Onomatopoetic term for brass music with cymbals and sleighbells, first attested in Berlin, where the word indicated dubious music halls (*cafés chantants*)"; Seebold 1995, 825.
16. Jansen 1990, 61; see also Jelavich 1993, 21, where the film *The Blue Angel* is mentioned.
17. Jansen 1990, 157.
18. Avenarius 1910, 99–100.
19. Jansen 1990, 164.
20. Wolzogen 1970, 122.
21. See Jelavich 1993, 53–55.
22. Jelavich 1993, 41; see also Chrisholm 2000, 26–27.
23. Chrisholm 2000, 28.
24. Frenzel 1903, 287.
25. For her performance style, see Bayerdörfer 2000, 80–81.
26. Jelavich 1993, 104.
27. G. Reinhardt 1973, 241.
28. Other "financiers" involved were Emmy Loewenfeld and the actress Louise Dumont (1862–1932); see Huesmann 1983, 12.

29. See Sprengel 1991b, 9.

30. Max Epstein gives a detailed report on this failed theater; see Epstein 1996, 44–47. The case is noteworthy because it allows us to see how risky and difficult it was to found an "art theater." And we may further see by comparison how cautious Reinhardt's progress through cabaret was; it was a place for him to test new forms, and the colorful nature of the program served to mitigate the risk.

31. Sprengel 1991b, 45.

32. See Sprengel 1991b, 63–70.

33. Quoted in Sprengel 1991b, 81–82.

34. Sprengel 1991b, 85.

35. Sprengel 1991b, 95.

36. Reinhardt 1989, 81.

37. Chrisholm 2000, 29–30, points to the fact that both figures appeared initially in the satirical journal *Simplicissimus*.

38. Quoted from Sprengel 1991b, 62.

39. See Jelavich 1993, 73.

40. Quoted from Sprengel 1991b, 124.

41. Sprengel 1991b, 32–33.

42. Jelavich 1993, 78.

43. On this, see, for example, Völmecke 1997, 25–30.

44. The Darmstadt Mathildenhöhe was an epitome of Jugendstil, of which Behrens was one of the most famous representatives. See Hofer 2001 for an introduction.

45. For the physical layout, see Zielske 1971, 247–50.

46. The masks were made by the Swiss artist Arnold Böcklin; see Jelavich 1993, 69.

47. Huesmann 1983, 13.

48. See Carlson 1989, 110–27.

49. Jelavich 1993, 10.

50. See Hahn 1995; and Völmecke 1997.

51. Reinhardt 1989, 88.

52. Thus, Heinrich Huesmann in his listing cites plays by Oscar Wilde (*Salome*, *Bunburry*), August Strindberg (*Intoxication*), and Frank Wedekind (*Earth Spirit*); see Huesmann 1983, Numbers 162–73.

53. Reinhardt 1989, 73.

Chapter 2

Epigraphs: Goldmann 1908, 232; Heilborn 1986, 569.

1. Originally built for lighter theatrical fare, the Theater am Schiffbauerdamm soon became one of the iconic places for modern German theater. Not only through Reinhardt, but also through the 1928 premiere of Brecht and Weill's *Threepenny Opera* and the fact that the building has been the home of Brecht's Berliner Ensemble since 1954, it holds a special place in Berlin's and Germany's theater history. See Funk and Jansen 1992 for information on the building.

2. See Winterstein 1947, 170.

3. Heilborn 1986, 569.

4. Anonymous 1986, 570.

5. Düsel 1986a, 567.

6. See Stümcke 1986a, 574.
7. Winterstein 1947, 172–73.
8. The revolving stage itself was the contribution of theater technician Karl Lautenschläger (1843–1906), who first introduced it in 1896.
9. Stümcke 1986a, 574–75.
10. Goldmann 1908, 232.
11. See Zabludowski 1930, 48, for a detailed description of the use of the revolving stage.
12. This turns up as a constant refrain regardless of the overall judgment on the staging; see Heilborn 1986, 570; Müller-Fürer 1986, 572; and Meyerfeld 1905, 307.
13. Düsel 1986a, 568.
14. Prellwitz 1905, 150.
15. Meyerfeld 1905, 307. The reference to Arnold Böcklin is interesting because Böcklin's aesthetic often depicts mythical subjects with an explicitly erotic charge. Böcklin's influence on Reinhardt is even more evident in some of his films, particularly *Isle of the Blessed*; see pp. 113–15 in this book.
16. Harden 1905, 194.
17. Harden 1905, 195.
18. See Fischer-Lichte 2005b, 1–14; and Niemann 1993 and 1995.
19. The American scholar Marvin Carlson has described this phenomenon as "haunting"; see Carlson 2003.
20. Goldmann 1908, 232.
21. Anonymous 1986, 570–71.
22. Düsel 1908, 568.
23. Müller-Fürer 1986, 571.
24. Goldmann 1908, 232–33.
25. Heilborn 1986, 569.
26. See Huesmann 1983, 18–19.
27. Kafitz 1989, 310–11.
28. Kafitz 1989, 312.
29. Kafitz 1989, 313.
30. Jaron, Möhrmann, and Müller 1986, 76.
31. "Freie Bühne" is a literal translation of Théâtre Libre, the name of a theater troupe founded in Paris in 1887 by André Antoine to foster Naturalism on stage. The influence of this concept emphasizes to what extent Naturalism was a genuinely international movement.
32. Landau 1986, 78.
33. Landau 1986, 77.
34. Landau 1986, 78–79.
35. See Midböer 1978 for a detailed account of this collaboration, as well as the basic features of the production.
36. Arthur Kahane in a letter to Munch; cited from Midböe 1978, 25.
37. Reinhardt 1989, 111.
38. Reinhardt 1910, 110.
39. Reinhardt 1910, 110.
40. Niessen 1958, 18.
41. Herald 1915, 121.

42. Fischer-Lichte 2005b, 53, refers to Gernot Böhme (Böhme 1995) for a definition of atmosphere, but puts special emphasis on the connection between actors and audience; see also Fischer-Lichte 2005b, 54–55.
43. See Ackerman 2001, 133–34.
44. Jacobsohn 1910b, 29–30.
45. Stümcke 1986b, 618.
46. See Midböer 1978, 17.
47. See Midböer 1978, 49–50.
48. See also Kayssler 1927 on Sorma in this production.
49. Jacobsohn 1910b, 31.
50. Jacobsohn 1910b, 30.
51. Stümcke 1986b, 617.
52. See Bernau 2005 for detailed information.
53. G.L. 1986, 615.
54. Midböer 1978, 22.
55. Harden 1907, 112 .
56. Kerr 1917, 166.
57. Durieux 1971, 102.
58. See Hahn 1999 on the demise of this culture.
59. Harden 1907, 13–14.
60. Kessler's diary for November 20, 1906: see Kessler 2005, 208. Although the entry concerns Wedekind's *Spring's Awakening*, his impression of the rooms can be taken more generally.
61. Reinhardt 1989, 80.
62. Streisand 2001, 306.
63. Herald 1915, 121.
64. See Sauter 1995.
65. See Szondi 1963.
66. Thus Freud and Schnitzler had a lively exchange with each other: see Hausner 1970, as well as Urban 1974.
67. Perlmann 1987, 36.
68. Höcker 1906/7, 587.
69. Düsel 1986b, 613.

Chapter 3

1. See Marx 2006.
2. On the Salzburg Festival, see Steinberg 2000, as well as Schuler 2006.
3. Fischer-Lichte 2005a, 13.
4. Tönnies 1963, 14; Tönnies 1957, 42.
5. Tönnies 1963, 40; Tönnies 1957, 65–66.
6. Tönnies 1963, 53; Tönnies 1957, 77.
7. Simmel 1903, 187; Simmel 1950, 409.
8. Simmel 1903, 188; Simmel 1950, 410.
9. Simmel 1903, 189; Simmel 1950, 411. [Translator's note: Wolff translates "ravishments" (*Vergewaltigungen*) as "overwhelming power."]
10. Berking 1984, 66.
11. Simmel 1903, 197; Simmel 1950, 417.
12. Simmel 1903, 200; Simmel 1950, 419.

13. Müller 1992, 46.
14. See Le Bon 1896, 26.
15. Le Bon 1896, 35–36.
16. See Le Bon 1896, 36.
17. Le Bon 1896, 32.
18. Geiger 1967, 168.
19. Geiger 1967, 38.
20. Geiger 1967, 169.
21. See p. xvi of this book.
22. So the art historian Hans Belting defines the concept of the "imaginary": Belting 2001, 74.
23. Fritzsche 1998, 1.
24. Fritzsche 1998, 128.
25. See Epstein 1914, 27.
26. Lethen 1986, 202–3.
27. Martersteig 1904, 697.
28. See Jansen 1987, 18–19.
29. Frenzel 1891, 447.
30. See Freydank 1995, 23.
31. Schmitt 1904, 15.
32. It is notable in this connection that Georg Simmel ascribes a crucial significance to public clocks in the life of the metropolis, since they synchronize the various life rhythms it contains. A similar effect can be ascribed to the theater, for its conditions of production established an independent rhythm that both artists and audience had to observe. By creating a public space of encounter and experience, the theater was able to become an important catalyst of urban life and its imagination.
33. Kracauer 1977, 51; Kracauer 1995, 76.
34. Kracauer 1977, 54; Kracauer 1995, 79.
35. Kracauer specifically designates this as the fundamental assumption of his historiographic argument: "The position that an epoch occupies in the historical process can be determined more strikingly from an analysis of its inconspicuous surface-level expressions than from that epoch's judgments about itself." Kracauer 1977, 50; Kracauer 1995, 75.
36. Giese 1925, 141.
37. See Kretschmer 1999 for an introduction to the topic.
38. Delbrück 1892b, 352. Barbara Kirshenblatt-Gimblett has noted that even the Paris Exposition of 1878 had 13 million visitors. See Kirshenblatt-Gimblett 1998, 81. But the increased rate of attendance alone shows the growing importance of the world expositions.
39. See Kunczik 1997, 192–95.
40. Thanks to Christopher B. Balme for alerting me to this work.
41. Paquet 1908, 35.
42. Delbrück 1892b, 352.
43. Delbrück 1892b, 352.
44. Delbrück 1892b, 353.
45. Kirshenblatt-Gimblett 1998, 79.
46. Dahn 1890, 3.

47. The transitions to the National Socialist *Thing-Spiel* are fluid here: see Niven 2000, as well as Fischer-Lichte 2005b, 122–58.
48. See Sprengel 1989 for details.
49. Sprengel 1989, 88.
50. See Sprengel 1989, 96 and 105–7.
51. Fischer-Lichte 2005b, 26 (brackets added).
52. Paquet 1908, 35.
53. Paquet 1908, 36–37.
54. Architekten-Verein 1896, 244.
55. Ancient Pergamum was excavated in the years 1878–86 by the German archaeologist Carl Humann (1839–1896), on commission from the Berlin museums. The central find, the so-called Pergamum Altar, was exhibited between 1897 and 1899 in a specially built museum in Berlin.
56. See Huesmann 1983, 21.
57. See Bose and Brinkmann 1978, 138; and Otte 2006.
58. See, for example, Architekten-Verein 1896, 514.
59. See Schmitt 1904 for a detailed account.
60. Schmitt 1904, 15. Unfortunately, we have to note that more meticulous research of the circus remains a great desideratum.
61. Schmitt 1904, 82–91.
62. See Maertens 1889a and 1889b; Seeling 1889a and 1889b; and Sturmhoefel 1889a.
63. Sturmhoefel 1889b, 1.
64. See Sturmhoefel 1889b, 8.
65. See Sturmhoefel 1889b, 2.
66. See Sturmhoefel 1889b, 112–14.
67. See Huesmann 1983, 24, on this.
68. See Düsel 1911, 453.
69. See Düsel 1910/11, 935, as well as Gürtler 1911, 81.
70. See Braulich 1969, 161.
71. See Weiglin 1919/20, 658.
72. Poelzig as cited in Bernauer 1990, 127.
73. Poelzig 1920, 121.
74. Düsel 1919/20, 637.
75. Weiglin 1919/20, 659.
76. Scheffler 1970, 138.
77. Scheffler 1970, 136.
78. Scheffler 1970, 138.
79. Düsel 1919/20, 637.
80. Baumgarten 1920, 45. Racial slur spelled out in the original.
81. Baumgarten 1920, 45.
82. This, however, represents a diminution in comparison with the original Zirkus Schumann, with its 5,125 seats.
83. See, for example, Wilamowitz-Moellendorf 1928, 254–55.
84. See Flashar 1991, 110–18. Brauchlich claims that Max Reinhardt took part in these projects as an actor, but there is no documentation for this—just the circumstantial evidence that Oberländer and Reinhardt later collaborated. See Brauchlich 1969, 36–37.

85. Flashar 1991, 118.
86. See Winterstein 1947, 241–42.
87. See especially Conrad 1911, 321–22.
88. Düsel 1910/11, 782–83.
89. Kienzl 1910, 164.
90. Conrad 1910a, 533.
91. Kienzl 1910, 164.
92. Hofmannsthal 1983, 133.
93. Höcker 1910/11, 233.
94. Conrad 1910a, 535.
95. Engel 1986, 403.
96. Düsel 1910/11, 611.
97. Frenzel 1911, 462.
98. Düsel 1910/11, 611.
99. Engel 1986, 402.
100. Fischer-Lichte 2005b, 52.
101. Fischer-Lichte 2005b, 58. Fischer-Lichte borrows the idea of a "theatrical community" from Warstat 2005.
102. Fischer-Lichte 2005b, 64.
103. Hildebrandt 1920, 103.
104. Neuweiler 1919, 12.
105. Neuweiler 1919, 43.
106. Pinthus 1920, 44–45.
107. Friedrich Düsel places this observation at the beginning of his discussion of the Grosses Schauspielhaus: "The fibers of our nerves have become too coarsened through the shocks of the five wartime years for even a building of these proportions and these crowds to be able to shake us, anymore"; Düsel 1919/20, 637.
108. Already in the days of the Weimar Republic, Erwin Piscator had become the epitome of a political director. Piscator was poised not only to give politically inspired interpretations of plays, but to create a new kind of theater that was partly aimed at mobilizing its audience—without being merely agitprop. He is most famous for his cooperation with the playwright Ernst Toller (1893–1939) and their attempt to create a socialist revue.
109. Jacobsohn 1920, 118.
110. Kienzl 1911b, 305.
111. On Bonn, see Müller 2004.
112. Kienzl 1911a, 126.
113. Düsel 1911, 607.
114. See Fischer-Lichte 2005b, 49–50.
115. Kienzl 1911a, 127.
116. Baumgarten 1920, 13.
117. Baumgarten 1920, 14.
118. Jacobsohn 1910a, 1178.

Chapter 4

1. Reinhardt 1989, 76.
2. Jacobsohn 1911, 285.

3. Jacobsohn 1911, 287.

4. Lately, these questions of mobility have attracted increased scholarly attention. Christopher Balme's research group on "global theater history" in Munich is exemplary for this new approach; see Balme 2015 and Leonhardt 2015.

5. See Kreuder 2005 for an introduction to the subject.

6. See Fischer-Lichte 1999b, 9–20.

7. See Marx 2003b for an introduction to the subject.

8. See Kitching 2000 for an introduction.

9. See Watzka 2012.

10. See also Ackman and Silver 2005.

11. See Winterstein 1947, 242–43.

12. Stanislawski 1951, 213; see also 213–17.

13. We have only to think of such diverse actors and actresses as Marlon Brando (1924–2004), James Dean (1931–1955), Marilyn Monroe (1926–1962), and Sidney Poitier (1927–2022).

14. See Marakowa 1995.

15. This intensive exchange underwent a renaissance in the 1920s, when many Russian avant-garde artists came to Berlin to show their productions. Of course, these encounters occurred under very different auspices, since the the Russian, or rather Soviet, theater was now understood as an expression of post-bourgeois society.

16. See Fischer-Lichte 1991.

17. See Rydell and Kroes 2005.

18. Epstein 1918, 182.

19. Herald 1915, 234.

20. Braulich 1969, 220.

21. See Grohmann 1935.

22. See Balme 2005.

23. Epstein 1918, 190.

24. An example of this is Jacobsohn's warning: "Either Reinhardt renounces Mammon in favor of Art. That won't be easy for him. Or he rakes in the money from the Russians, the Americans, and the Hottentots till he has enough to suit him and thumbs his nose at Berlin"; Jacobsohn 1911, 287.

25. See Sefanek 1969 for a portrayal of these efforts.

26. B. 1911, 247.

27. See Stefanek 1969, 376.

28. Tree was known for fidelity of detail and opulent productions. It is characteristic that Reinhardt's *Midsummer Night's Dream* was constantly compared with Tree's works.

29. Palmer 1912a, 9.

30. See also the description of Carter 1914, 223–40.

31. See Stefanek 1969, 378.

32. See Huesmann 1983, 25; and Carter 1914, 240.

33. In Vollmoeller's script it reads: "The crowd's enthusiasm turns into a wild orgasm. They all try to press forward to the beautiful woman to touch her body . . . A free-for-all ensues." Vollmoeller 1914, 17–18.

34. Vollmoeller 1914, 18.

35. See Elb 1913/14, 423.

36. Vollmoeller 1914, 10.
37. Stern 1955, 68. See also Stefanek 1969, 383.
38. Stern 1955, 64.
39. See Prossnitz 1986, 75.
40. H. W. M. 1911b, 549. See also Anonymous 1912.
41. Palmer 1912a, 10.
42. See Stern 1955, 66–67.
43. H. W. M. 1911b, 549.
44. See Fischer-Lichte 2005b, 90–96.
45. Anonymous 1911b, 91.
46. Palmer 1912b, 75.
47. The reviewer in the *Times* noted that, in contrast to a traditional pageant, this production had no clearly prescribed perspective, but demonstrated instead a diversity of points of view. See Anonymous 1911a, as well as Fischer-Lichte 1991.
48. Stefanek 1969, 384. That the individual tableaux riveted the attention of the audience—in part, to the detriment of the arc of dramatic tension—can be inferred from the fact that the audience didn't realize that the plot was divided into scenes of frame narrative and internal dreaming: "Nothing could persuade an audience that dreams were in question at all; for what they have seen is too massively, almost oppressively, full of concrete life, and life of a period when it was more full, perhaps, of colour, contrast, and vigour than at any other times." Anonymous 1911a. Apparently the tableaux developed such a dynamic of their own and such charm that they could no longer be integrated into the overarching plot.
49. Anonymous 1911a.
50. For many representatives, this "absence" of history was not a "lack" but a programmatic refusal and rejection of the past and its traditions. As their name already indicates, the Italian Futurists, for example, even fantasized about burning down museums and libraries to liberate the present from the oppression of the past.
51. Reinhardt 1989, 178.
52. See Anonymous 1911 for the German-language coverage, and both Anonymous 1912 and Watson 1912, for example, for detailed reportage on *The Miracle* in London.
53. See Fuhrich-Leisler and Prossnitz 1976, 15.
54. See Kommer 1924a.
55. See Collins 2002.
56. Reinhardt 1989, 192.
57. Reinhardt 1989, 191–92.
58. See Watson 1912.
59. See Collins 2002.
60. In this context, Clemens Zimmermann has noted that the metropolises of the early twentieth century were not just important places of social life; they also, very quickly, acquired a paradigmatic character; see Zimmermann 2000, 33–34.
61. See especially Anonymous 1924b.
62. Stefanek 1969, 383.
63. Corbin 1924, 17.

Notes to Pages 104–115

64. See Anonymous 1924c.
65. Monahan 1924, X4.
66. Corbin 1924.
67. See Anonymous 1924a, 210.
68. As cited by Fuhrich-Leisler and Prossnitz 1976, 60.
69. Monahan 1924, X4.
70. Corbin 1924.
71. See Metcalf 1924.
72. See DeWF 1924, 77.
73. Monahan 1924, X4.
74. See Hersey 1926.
75. See Braulich 1969, 222.
76. Braulich 1969, 222.
77. Reinhardt showed, among other works, Shakespeare's *Midsummer Night's Dream*, Büchner's *Danton's Death*, and Hofmannsthal's *Everyman*.
78. Kommer 1924b.

Chapter 5

1. Reinhardt 1989, 442.
2. See Kügelgen 1983.
3. Herbert Birett notes that the film was initially dismissed in the criticism as "uncinematic" and was subsequently revised—with the addition of close-ups, among other things. The revision, however, did not lead to any lasting success. See Birett 1991, 628.
4. Klaus Kreimeier summarizes Davidsohn's career as follows in his groundbreaking study *Die Ufa-Story* (1992): "An important trailblazer of UFA was Paul Davidsohn, the German film entrepreneur who resolutely entered into a pact with finance capital: 1906 the founder of Allgemeine Kinematographische Gesellschaft in Frankfurt am Main, from which emerged the first German-owned chain of movie theaters in Germany; 1908 owner of the largest German film palace, the Union Theater (UT) in the Berlin Alexanderplatz; 1909 general director of the Projektions-AG Union (PAGU) . . . 1912 the Union—the German film industry's first corporation—doubled its original share capital of 500,000 gold marks, moved its seat to Berlin, set up its production shops in Tempelhof, and got into the loan business. The Tempelhofer Filmfabrik . . . becomes part of the UFA empire five years later, and the East Prussian merchant's son Paul Davidsohn, who started out as a traveling curtain salesman and got interested in show business while attending a "magic theater" in Paris, will sit in its central administration." Kreimeier 1992, 26.
5. See Rebhan 1983, 45.
6. See Cor 1959 on Kahane.
7. Here as well as in his 1905 *A Midsummer Night's Dream*, Reinhardt's work reverberates from the works of the then very popular Swiss painter Arnold Böcklin (1827–1901). Mythological themes were a trademark of Böcklin's paintings, often in an eroticized manner.
8. Cited from Rebhan 1983, 49.
9. Schwarzschild 1913, 827.
10. For an extensive discussion of the film, see Volz 2017.

11. This criticsm led, among other things, to the film's being banned in Munich, and in Berlin only adults were permitted to see it. See Birett 1980, 333 and 541.
12. Berthold and Vogt 1983, 61.
13. See Greve 1983.
14. See Elsaesser 2002a, 129–30.
15. Elsaesser 2002a, 129.
16. Elsaesser 2002b, 28.
17. This account by Ulrich Rauscher may serve as the paradigm for this negative assessment: "The cinema of today is dreadful. It is beneath any other form of public entertainment. Even the most tedious variety show offers, amid the drivel of its chansonettes, a trapeze or acrobatic act that, thanks to some very well-developed physical skills, has something to do with beauty and disciplined strength." Rauscher 1913, 1.
18. This is deducible from the fact that the first public film showing in Germany took place in 1895 at the Berlin Wintergarten Variété (see Kreimeier 1992, 15), a very elegant establishment, which through its price structure cultivated the so-called "better audiences." On the Wintergarten, see Ret 1996.
19. Müller 1994, 34–35.
20. Müller 1994, 126.
21. Elsaesser 2002b, 36.
22. This corresponds to the "cinema of attractions" described by Tom Gunning; see Gunning 1990.
23. Elsaesser 2002a, 80.
24. See Bolter and Grusin 1999, 55–56.
25. Kreimeier 1992, 15.
26. See Vardac 1949, 153–54.
27. Vardac 1949, 156.
28. Vardac 1949, 159.
29. See Vardac 1949, 216.
30. See Brewster and Jacobs 1997, 7.
31. See Brewster and Jacobs 1997, 140.
32. Brewster and Jacobs 1997, 158.
33. Freksa 1912/13, 223.
34. Düsel 1910, 253. See also Bie 1910 for a similar reaction.
35. Harden 1910, 284.
36. Herald 1925, 8.
37. Fuhrich-Leisler and Prosnitz 1976, 132.
38. See Eisner 1973.

Chapter 6

1. See Atze 1998.
2. See Kvam 1988.
3. Reinhardt 1989, 277.
4. Adorno describes the connection between art and economy as a dialectical one without giving up the idea of the freedom of art: "Art was only ever able to exist as a separate sphere in its bourgeois form. Even its freedom, as negation of the social utility which is establishing itself through the market, is essentially conditioned by the commodity economy . . . The principle of idealist aesthetics,

purposiveness without purpose, reverses the schema socially adopted by bourgeois art: purposelessness for purposes dictated by the market." Adorno 1993, 9; Horkheimer and Adorno 2002, 127–28.

5. Horkheimer and Adorno 1994, 145; Horkheimer and Adorno 2002, 109.
6. Simmel 2001, 531; Simmel 1978, 469.
7. Simmel 2001, 1; Simmel 1978, 59.
8. Simmel 2001, 31; Simmel 1978, 80.
9. See, for example, Bourdieu and Wacquant 1996, 128.
10. Bourdieu 1995, 31; Bourdieu 1985, 736.
11. Epstein 1914, 5.
12. Here it would also be good to acknowledge the question of actors' training, which, starting from an obscure system of private lessons and personal patronage, gradually became institutionalized and increasingly took place in professional acting schools. It was one of the special features of Reinhardt's apparatus that he himself founded an acting school—today's Hochschule für Schauspielkunst "Ernst Busch" (Ernst Busch College of Acting) in Berlin. See Egbert 1987. This professionalization was also a result of the theater boom.
13. On this subject, see also Watzka 2006.
14. As early as 1841, the Deutsches Bühnenverein (German Stage Association) was founded as a professional organization for directors of theaters, followed by the 1871 founding of the Genossenschaft der Deutschen Bühnenangehörigen, or GDBA (German Stage Workers Cooperative): both are still in existence today.
15. See Greisenegger-Georgila 1994, 16–19; and Ibscher 1972.
16. Its complement is horizontal integration: a firm's increased engagement on the same production level by buying up competitors or starting new enterprises.
17. Epstein 1911, 68–70.
18. Stange 1996, 75.
19. Epstein 1911, 129.
20. Epstein 1911, 130.
21. Epstein 1911, 84.
22. Epstein 1911, 134.
23. Epstein 1911, 162–63.
24. Epstein 1911, 165.
25. *FAZ (Frankfurter Allgemeine Zeitung)*, no. 153 (July 5, 2003), 35.
26. In this connection, Cornelia Dümcke has made us aware of a remarkable shift: "In the 1911/1912 season, what German theaters made on admission tickets still amounted to about 63 percent of operating expenses. Presently, it is only 10 percent . . . By contrast, state subventions have risen from a 27 percent share of operating costs at the beginning of this century to a rate of over 85 percent in direct public subsidies during the last season." Dümcke 1994, 70.
27. Epstein 1911, 80.
28. Epstein 1911, 170.
29. Kahane 1930a, 29–30.
30. See Lederer 1953, 946.
31. See G. Reinhardt 1973, 239. [Translator's note: "The Unseemly Old Lady" ("Die unwürdige Greisin") is the title of a short story in Brecht's *Tales from the Calendar*, trans. Yvonne Kapp (London: Methuen, 1961), which has nothing biographically to do with Emmy Loewenfeld.]

32. Reissmann 1996, 160.
33. G. Reinhardt 1973, 239.
34. See also Balme 2005, 44.
35. Epstein 1918, 1.1
36. See Hahn 1996.
37. As early as 1965, W. J. Baumol and W. G. Bowen showed that the criterion of efficiency—usually a key marker in increasing profit from a sector—is almost irrelevant to the field of performing arts because there are some fixtures, think of time and space, that cannot be cut or expanded; see Baumol and Bowen 1965.
38. See Reissmann 1996, 161.
39. See Huesmann 1983, number 712.
40. Rudin 1978, 129–30.
41. Kortner 1991, 195.
42. See Engeli 1979, 51.
43. Kleinsteuber and Thomass 1996, 129.
44. See Müller 1997, 111–16.
45. See Huesmann 1983, 30.
46. Balme 2005, 48–49.
47. See p. 55 of this book.
48. See Müller 1997, 97–98.
49. Epstein 1918, 266.
50. Epstein 1918, 103.
51. See Epstein 1918, 264–65.
52. Balme 2005, 45.
53. On Kessler, see also Easton 2002.
54. Epstein 1918, 182.
55. Epstein 1918, 172.

Chapter 7

Epigraph: Reinhardt 1989, 335, in a letter to Rudolf K. Kommer of May 5, 1942. The mentioned "palace" refers to Leopoldskron. See also Hofinger 2005 for the events surrounding Leopoldskron. [Translator's note: The significance of the "G-" is obscure—possibly an Austrian expletive. Quotation marks in the original.]

1. The adoption of stage names developed into something approaching an obligatory practice in the nineteenth century, to which figures like Adolphe L'Arronge (Aronsohn) and Otto Brahm (Abrahamson) had also submitted. In this connection, Hans-Peter Bayerdörfer has suggested that literature, not theater, was the "paradigm of participation in the majority culture, equality in relation to it, and independence"; Bayerdörfer 1995, 29.

2. Ironically enough, it was Werner Krauss (1884–1959) who proposed this "honor" to Reinhardt; Krauss was the actor who later so ingloriously appeared in Veit Harlan's film *Jud Süss* (1940); see Reinhardt 1989, 273.

3. Scholem 1995a, 10; Scholem 2012, 63.

4. Volkov 2001b, 30–31.

5. Cultural studies has developed an understanding of ethnicity that unambiguously distinguishes the concept from all biological definitions, such as those that lie at the root of the concept of race. Thus Mario Erdheim's definition: "Ethnicity has nothing to do with race because cultural characteristics can no more be

inherited than the symbols that are connected with them. They must instead be learned, although the learning process is largely unconscious and takes place more through actions than by reflection." Erdheim 1993, 165. See also Sollors 1989.

6. Erdman 1997, 6.

7. Charlotte Engel Reimers, in her statistical survey *Die deutschen Bühnen und ihre Angehörigen* (1911; *German Theaters and Their People*), has been able to show that very few people engaged in theater came from an educated bourgeois background. Reinhardt's career can therefore be regarded as typical in terms of his social background. See Engel Reimers 1911.

8. See Rathenau 2002, 17.

9. Kessler 2005, 549.

10. See Easton 2002 for a biography of Kessler.

11. Volkov 2000a, 23.

12. See, for example, Gilman 1998 or Klein 1999 on these features.

13. See the apologetic references in Kalser 1927 or Jessner 1979.

14. Epstein 1918, 122.

15. Epstein 1918, 123.

16. Epstein 1918, 125.

17. Epstein 1918, 124.

18. See Wagner 2000, 160–61, for example.

19. See Nietzsche 1966, 235.

20. Epstein 1918, 125.

21. Epstein 1918, 209.

22. The diagnosis of a specifically Jewish "self-hatred" has occurred since the nineteenth century in the most various contexts and manifestations. Surely the best-known example is Theodor Lessing's book: *Der jüdischer Selbsthass* (1910).

23. Bergmann 1906, 14.

24. Bergmann 1906, 16.

25. Bergmann 1906, 37.

26. Bergmann 1906, 38.

27. Bergmann 1906, 38.

28. Dinter 1916, 10.

29. Dinter 1916, 17.

30. Dinter 1916, 16.

31. Dinter 1916, 21.

32. Dinter 1916, 22.

33. This novel, which was first published as an independent text in 1911, was largely incorporated into *Wilhelm Meister's Apprenticeship* (1795/96). The conspicuousness of the fact that both novels were published in the same year indicates how much Freksa used Goethe's novel as a backdrop. [Translator's note: English translation by John R. Russell (Columbia, SC: Camden House, 1995).]

34. Unfortunately, we cannot reconstruct the novel's contemporary reception (it was barely reviewed), nor is it easy to draw conclusions about Freksa's motive for this public break with Reinhardt. Gottfried Reinhardt mentions the novel and decodes some of Freksa's allusions; see G. Reinhardt 1973, 238–39; and G. Reinhardt 1979, 273–74. All in all, there are many references that can no longer be deciphered today.

35. Freksa 1913, v. 1, 112.
36. Freksa 1913, v. 1, 11.
37. Freksa 1913, v. 2, 50.
38. Freksa 1913, v. 1, 9.
39. Freksa 1913, v. 2, 12.
40. The narrator "exposes" this too at the very beginning of the novel: "Under the impression of this space, the visitor's facial features betrayed the timid reserve the low-born always feel in more elegant surroundings. His eyes surveyed the unfamiliar objects, trying to calculate the exact value of everything there"; Freksa 1913, v. 1, 13.
41. Freksa 1913, v. 1, 168.
42. Freksa 1913, v. 2, 51.
43. Freksa 1913, v. 2, 259–60.
44. This is a reference to Schloss Leopoldskron near Salzburg, which Reinhardt bought in 1918.
45. This was a rather common topic in Weimar Germany; it can be found in the ecstatic reception of Josephine Baker on her German tour—she was perceived as a revolutionary novelty—as well as in Ernst Krenek's most successful opera, *Jonny spielt auf* (1927; *Johnny Strikes Up the Band*).
46. Frank 1929, 18; Frank 1946, 237.
47. Frank 1929, 65–66; Frank 1946, 253–54.
48. Frank 1929, 85; Frank 1946, 260.
49. See Frank 1929, 79; Frank 1946, 258–59.
50. The central scene for this aspect of the play is a monologue in which Roter Itzig demands equal rights.
51. Zweig 1928, 179.
52. Jacobsohn 1913/14, 102.
53. Jacobsohn 1913/14, 101.

Conclusion

1. See Hobsbawm 1983.
2. Maximilian Harden is mocking in this regard: "A repertoire like that of the Schauspielhaus simply means artistic bankruptcy, a complete relinquishment of any leading position in the life of German theater"; Harden 1888, 14.
3. By contrast, the Burgtheater in Vienna during the nineteenth century was led by a series of directors with considerable theatrical experience, such as Joseph Schreyvogel (1768–1832), Heinrich Laube (1806–84), Franz Dingelstedt (1814–81), and Paul Schlenther (1854–1916).
4. See Harden 1888, 14–15. See also Koch 1957 and Reichel 1962 for an overview with respect to the two last court intendants.
5. Harden 1888, 36.
6. Gay 2001, 5.
7. See the critical remarks of Appadurai 1996, 9.
8. Strecker 1911, 42.
9. See also Hettling and Hoffmann 1991 on this bourgeois orientation of values.
10. Fritz Stern describes the career of Walther Rathenau, also one of Reinhardt's benefactors, in this atmosphere of tension; see Stern 1999b, 165–96.

11. Maximilian Harden's description is typical of this characterization, which is popularly connected with Berlin: "In general the plutocracy dominates our theaters; that feared pack of premiere hounds who seem to hold the destiny of any serious work of art in their hands, are almost without exception more familiar with the scenery of the stock exchange than with that of the stage." Harden 1888, 6.

12. Kessler's diary, January 2, 1912; Kessler 2005, 771–72.
13. See the critical remarks of Strecker 1911, 43–48.
14. Eloesser 1910, 699.
15. Reinhardt 1989, 434.
16. Reinhardt 1989, 436.
17. The extent to which Reinhardt understood the vital "play instinct" in the actor as a *condition humana* is evident in the fact that for him childhood was the crucial paradigm of theatrical play, and beyond this he describes mimetic play as a phylogenetic stage; see Reinhardt 1989, 435–36.
18. Gay 2001, 7–8.
19. Stern 1999a, 4.
20. Stern 1999b, 6–7.
21. Harden 1888, 9.
22. See Heilmann 2005.
23. Reinhardt 1989, 73.
24. G. Reinhardt 1973, 394; G. Reinhardt 1979, 393.
25. G. Reinhardt 1973, 398.

WORKS CITED

Reviews

Reviews of Ghosts (1889)

Harden, Maximilian. 1986. *Die Gegenwart* 18:40 (1889). In *Berlin—Theater der Jahrhundertwende: Bühnengeschichte der Reichshauptstadt im Spiegel der Kritik (1889–1914)*, ed. Norbert Jaron, Renate Möhrmann, and Hedwig Müller, 82–83. Tübingen: Niemeyer.

Hart, Heinrich. 1986. *Tägliche Rundschau*, October 1, 1889. In *Berlin—Theater der Jahrhundertwende: Bühnengeschichte der Reichshauptstadt im Spiegel der Kritik (1889–1914)*, ed. Norbert Jaron, Renate Möhrmann, and Hedwig Müller, 81–82. Tübingen: Niemeyer.

Landau, Isidor. 1986. *Berliner Börsen-Courier*, September 29, 1889. In *Berlin—Theater der Jahrhundertwende: Bühnengeschichte der Reichshauptstadt im Spiegel der Kritik (1889–1914)*, ed. Norbert Jaron, Renate Möhrmann, and Hedwig Müller, 77–80. Tübingen: Niemeyer.

Schönhoff, Leopold. 1986. *Frankfurter Zeitung*, September 30, 1889. In *Berlin—Theater der Jahrhundertwende: Bühnengeschichte der Reichshauptstadt im Spiegel der Kritik (1889–1914)*, ed. Norbert Jaron, Renate Möhrmann, and Hedwig Müller, 80–81. Tübingen: Niemeyer.

Reviews of A Midsummer Night's Dream (1905)

Anonymous. 1986. *Neue Freie Presse*, February 3, 1905. In *Berlin—Theater der Jahrhundertwende: Bühnengeschichte der Reichshauptstadt im Spiegel der Kritik (1889–1914)*, ed. Norbert Jaron, Renate Möhrmann, and Hedwig Müller, 570–71. Tübingen: Niemeyer.

Düsel, Friedrich. 1986a. *Deutsche Zeitung*, February 2, 1905. In *Berlin—Theater der Jahrhundertwende: Bühnengeschichte der Reichshauptstadt im Spiegel der Kritik (1889–1914)*, ed. Norbert Jaron, Renate Möhrmann, and Hedwig Müller, 567–68. Tübingen: Niemeyer.

Frenzel, Karl. 1905. "Die Berliner Theater." *Deutsche Rundschau* 123: 296–309.

Harden, Maximilian. 1905. "Theater." *Die Zukunft* 52: 186–96.

Hart, Julius. 1986. *Der Tag*, February 2, 1905. In *Berlin—Theater der Jahrhundertwende: Bühnengeschichte der Reichshauptstadt im Spiegel der Kritik (1889–1914)*, ed. Norbert Jaron, Renate Möhrmann, and Hedwig Müller, 572–73. Tübingen: Niemeyer.

Heilborn, Ernst. 1986. *Frankfurter Zeitung*, February 4, 1905. In *Berlin—Theater der Jahrhundertwende: Bühnengeschichte der Reichshauptstadt im Spiegel der*

Kritik (1889–1914), ed. Norbert Jaron, Renate Möhrmann, and Hedwig Müller, 569–70. Tübingen: Niemeyer.
Meyerfeld, Max. 1905. "Berliner Theaterschau." *Shakespeare-Jahrbuch* 41: 302–7.
Müller-Fürer, Theodor. 1986. *Neue Preussische Zeitung*, February 1, 1905. In *Berlin—Theater der Jahrhundertwende: Bühnengeschichte der Reichshauptstadt im Spiegel der Kritik (1889–1914)*, ed. Norbert Jaron, Renate Möhrmann, and Hedwig Müller, 571–72. Tübingen: Niemeyer.
Prellwitz, Gertrud. 1905. "Theater-Korrespondenz." *Preussische Jahrbücher* 120: 149–55.
Stümcke, Heinrich. 1986a. *Bühne und Welt*, October 7, 1905. In *Berlin—Theater der Jahrhundertwende: Bühnengeschichte der Reichshauptstadt im Spiegel der Kritik (1889–1914)*, ed. Norbert Jaron, Renate Möhrmann, and Hedwig Müller, 574–75. Tübingen: Niemeyer.

Reviews of Ghosts (1906)

Düsel, Friedrich. 1986b. *Deutsche Zeitung*, November 11, 1906. In *Berlin—Theater der Jahrhundertwende: Bühnengeschichte der Reichshauptstadt im Spiegel der Kritik (1889–1914)*, ed. Norbert Jaron, Renate Möhrmann, and Hedwig Müller, 613–15. Tübingen: Niemeyer.
Engel, Fritz. 1986. *Berliner Tageblatt*, November 10, 1906. In *Berlin—Theater der Jahrhundertwende: Bühnengeschichte der Reichshauptstadt im Spiegel der Kritik (1889–1914)*, ed. Norbert Jaron, Renate Möhrmann, and Hedwig Müller, 611–13. Tübingen: Niemeyer.
Harden, Maximilian. 1907. "Theater." *Die Zukunft* 58: 105–14.
Höcker, Paul Oskar. 1906/7. "Die Berliner Bühnen." *Velhagen & Klasings Monatshefte* 1: 586–96.
Kerr, Alfred. 1917. "Gespenster." In *Das Mimenreich: Lenker, Schauspieler, Tänzer, Dramaturgen*, ed. Alfred Kerr, 166–70. Berlin.
L., G. 1986. *Norddeutsche Allgemeine Zeitung*, November 11, 1906. In *Berlin—Theater der Jahrhundertwende: Bühnengeschichte der Reichshauptstadt im Spiegel der Kritik (1889–1914)*, ed. Norbert Jaron, Renate Möhrmann, and Hedwig Müller, 615–16. Tübingen: Niemeyer.
Stümcke, Heinrich. 1986b. *Bühne und Welt*, May 9, 1906. In *Berlin—Theater der Jahrhundertwende: Bühnengeschichte der Reichshauptstadt im Spiegel der Kritik (1889–1914)*, ed. Norbert Jaron, Renate Möhrmann, and Hedwig Müller, 616–18. Tübingen: Niemeyer.

Reviews of Oedipus the King (1910)

Anonymous. 1911. "Die Eroberung des Zirkus für die Bühne." *Rundschau zweier Welten* 3: 142–43.
Conrad, Hermann. 1910a. "Theater-Korrespondenz: König Oedipus von Sophokles im Zirkus Schumann." *Preussische Jahrbücher* 142: 527–36.
Düsel, Friedrich. 1910/11a. "Dramatische Rundschau." *Westermanns Monatshefte* 55, no. 109: 604–11.
———. 1910/11b. "Dramatische Rundschau." *Westermanns Monatshefte* 55, no. 109: 784–88.

Works Cited

———. 1911a. "Dramatische Rundschau." *Westermanns Monatshefte* 55, no. 110: 603–10.
———. 1911b. "Zur Eröffnung der Berliner Theatersaison." *Der Kunstwart* 25, no. 1: 41–45.
Feuchtwanger, Lion. 1910. "Sophokles und Hofmannsthal." *Die Schaubühne* 6, no. 46: 1171–76.
Frenzel, Karl. 1911. "Die Berliner Theater." *Deutsche Rundschau* 147: 461–72.
Höcker, Paul Oskar. 1910/11. "Die Berliner Bühnen." *Velhagen & Klasings Monatshefte* 25, no. 2: 226–33.
Jacobsohn, Siegfried. 1910a. "Reinhardt und Oedipus." *Die Schaubühne* 6, no. 46: 1176–78.
Kienzl, Hermann. 1910. "Von den Berliner Theatern 1910/11." *Bühne und Welt* 13: 162–66.
Schaumberg, Georg. 1910/11. "Von den Münchener Theatern 1910/11." *Bühne und Welt* 13: 78–79.
Seaman, Owen. 1912a. "At the Play: Oedipus Rex." *Punch* 142: 68–69.

Reviews of Oresteia (1910)

Conrad, Hermann. 1910b. "Theater-Korrespondenz: Die Orestie des Aeschylus." *Preussische Jahrbücher* 146: 321–34.
Kaltschmidt, Karl. 1911. "Die 'Orestie' als Reinhardt-Schau in München." *Der Kunstwart* 25, no. 1: 45–47.

Reviews of Sumurûn (1911)

B. 1911. "'Sumurun' at the Coliseum." *Spectator* 106, no. 4312: 247–48.
Bie, Oskar. 1911. "Sumurun." *Die neue Rundschau* 21: 874–75.
Düsel, Friedrich. 1910. "Berliner Theater. (Sumurun)." *Der Kunstwart* 23, no. 16: 253–55.
Harden, Maximilian. 1910. "Pantomimus." *Die Zukunft* 71: 273–84.
Jacobsohn, Siegfried. 2005a. "Sumurûn." 1910. In *Schrei nach dem Zensor: Schriften 1909–1915*, ed. Siegfried Jacobsohn, 50–53. Göttingen: Wallstein. (Vol. 2 of Siegfried Jacobsohn, *Gesammelte Schriften*, 1900–1926.)
M., H. W. 1911a. "The Wordless Play." *Nation* 10, no. 3: 128.
Seaman, Owen. 1911. "At the Play: Sumurun." *Punch* 141: 264.
Stümcke, Heinrich. 1910. "Von den Berliner Theatern 1909/10." XIV. In *Bühne und Welt* 12 (1910): 674–77.

Reviews of The Miracle (from 1911)

Anonymous. 1911a. "'The Miracle' at Olympia: Professor Reinhardt's Great Spectacle." *Times*, no. 39777 (December 25, 1911), 8.
Anonymous. 1911b. "Reinhardt and His 'New Art.'" *Nation* 10, no. 2: 90–91.
Anonymous. 1912. "Reinhardt's New Spectacle: 'The Miracle' Said to Be the Most Profoundly Moving Thing Ever Seen in London." *New York Times*, January 14, 1912.

Avenarius, Ferdinand. 1913. "Reinhardts Mirakel." *Der Kunstwart* 27, no. 2: 160–61.
Bier, Marcus J. 1983. "Das Mirakel—auf dem Weg zum neuen Medium." In *Max Reinhardts Theater im Film: Materialien*, ed. Margot Berthold, 20–42. Munich: Münchner Filmzentrum.
Düsel, Friedrich. 1914. "Ein paar nachträgliche Worte über Halbes 'Freiheit' und Vollmöllers 'Mirakel.'" *Der Kunstwart* 27, no. 17: 324–26.
Elb, Richard. 1913/14. "Mirakuli—Mirakula!" *Bühne und Welt* 16: 422–23.
Jacobsohn, Siegfried. 2005b. "Mirakel" (1914). In *Schrei nach dem Zensor: Schriften 1909–1915*, ed. Siegfried Jacobsohn, 396–98. Göttingen: Wallstein. (Vol. 2 of Siegfried Jacobsohn, *Gesammelte Schriften, 1900–1926*.)
Ludwig, Emil. 1912. "Reinhardts Mirakel in London." *Die Schaubühne* 8: 13–15.
M., H. Wb. 1911. "Signs of Change." *Nation* 10, no. 13: 548–49.
Merbach, Paul Alfred. 1913/14. "Berliner Theater, XIII." *Bühne und Welt* 16: 343–45.
Palmer, John. 1912a. "The Miracle." *The Saturday Review* 113, no. 2932: 9–10.
———. 1912b. "Footlights and the Super-Doll." *The Saturday Review* 113, no. 2934: 74–76.
Seaman, Owen. 1912b. "At the Play: The Miracle." *Punch* 142: 32.
Watson, Malcolm. 1912. "Reinhardt's Stupendous Miracle About to Go On." *New York Times*, January 31, 1912.

Reviews of The Miracle (U.S. from 1924)

Anonymous. 1924a. "The Miracle." *Outlook*, February 6, 1924, 209–11.
Anonymous 1924b. "The Miracle Statistically." *New York Times*, February 3, 1924.
Anonymous. 1924c. "A Pantomime Wonder of the Stage World." *Current Opinion*, March 1, 1924, 330.
Corbin, John. 1924. "'The Miracle,' Fine Spectacle, Shown." *New York Times*, January 16, 1924, 17.
DeWF, H. 1924. "The Miracle." *Independent*, February 2, 1924, 77.
Hersey, Eleanor. 1926. "The Miracle." *Overland Monthly and Out West Magazine*, no. 11: 351.
McClung, Lawson. 1924. "The Meaning of the Piper." *New York Times*, February 17, 1924.
Metcalfe. 1924. "Again 'The Miracle.'" *Wall Street Journal*.
Monahan, Michael. 1924. "The Miracle." *New York Times*, February 17, 1924.
Speakman, Harold. 1924. "The Miracle." *Methodist Review* 4: 601–6.

Reviews of Oresteia (1919/20)

Düsel, Friedrich. 1919/20. "Dramatische Rundschau." *Westermanns Monatshefte* 64, no. 127: 637–44.
Stümcke, Heinrich. 1911/12. "Von den Berliner Theatern 1911/12." *Bühne und Welt* 14: 28–31.
Weiglin, Paul. 1919/20. "Von deutschen Bühnen: Max Reinhardts Grosses Schauspielhaus." *Velhagen & Klasings Monatshefte* 34: 658–63.

Scholarly Literature

Ackerman, Alan L. 2001. "Visualizing Hamlet's Ghost: The Spirit of Modern Subjectivity." *Theatre Journal* 53, no. 1: 119–44.
Adams, Bluford. 1997. *E Pluribus Barnum: The Great Showman & U.S. Popular Culture*. Minneapolis: University of Minesota Press.
Adorno, Theodor W. 1993. *Ästhetische Theorie* (1970). Frankfurt am Main: Suhrkamp.
———. 1997a. "Résumé über Kulturindustrie" (1963). In *Kulturkritik und Gesellschaft*, ed. Theodor W. Adorno, vol. 1: 337–45. Frankfurt am Main: Suhrkamp. (Adorno, *Gesammelte Schriften* 10.1.)
———. 1997b. *Aesthetic Theory*. Edited and translated by Robert Hullot-Kentor. Minneapolis: University of Minnesota Press.
Alberti, Conrad. 1887. *Ohne Schminke: Wahrheiten über das moderne Theater*. Dresden: E. Pierson.
Anderson, Benedict. 1983. *Imagined Communities: Reflections on the Origin and Spread of Nationalism*. London: Verso.
Anonymous. 1911. "Reinhardt als Retter des deutschen Theaters in den Vereinigten Staaten." *Rundschau zweier Welten* 5, no. 9: 469–72.
Appadurai, Arjun. 1996. *Modernity at Large: Cultural Dimensions of Globalization*. Minneapolis: University of Minnesota Press.
Architekten-Verein zu Berlin. 1896. *Berlin und seine Bauten*, vols. 2 and 3: *Hochbauten*. Berlin: Wilhelm Ernst & Sohn.
Aschheim, Steven E. 2000. *Nietzsche und die Deutschen: Karriere eines Kults* (1992). Stuttgart: J. B. Metzler.
Atze, Marcel. 1998. "'Sehr geehrter Herr Minister!' oder Nachrichten von Reinhardt-Editoren und ihren Sünden: Zugleich ein Stück Theatergeschichte des Dritten Reichs." In *Max Reinhardt: Manuskripte, Briefe, Dokumente: Katalog der Sammlung Dr. Jürgen Stein*, ed. Hugo Wetscherek, 180–94. Vienna: Inlibris.
Avenarius, Ferdinand. 1910. "Bunte Bühne." *Der Kunstwart* 24, no. 2: 98–101.
Balme, Christopher B. 1994. "Kulturanthropologie und Theatergeschichtsschreibung: Methoden und Perspektiven." In *Arbeitsfelder der Theaterwissenschaft*, ed. Erika Fischer-Lichte, Wolfgang Greisenegger, and Hans-Thies Lehmann, 45–57. Tübingen: Narr.
———. 2005. "Die Marke Reinhardt: Theater als modernes Wirtschaftsunternehmen." In *Max Reinhardt und das Deutsche Theater: Texte und Bilder aus Anlass des 100-jährigen Jubiläums seiner Direktion*, ed. Roland Koberg, Bernd Stegemann, and Henrike Thomsen, 41–49. Berlin: Henschel.
———. 2015. "The Bandmann Circuit: Theatrical Networks in the First Age of Globalization." *Theatre Research International* 40, no. 1: 19–36.
Balme, Christopher B., and Tracy Davis. 2015. "A Cultural History of Theatre: A Prospectus." *Theatre Survey* 56, no. 3: 402–21. doi: 10.1017/S0040557415000320.
Baumbach, Gerda. 2002. "Vom Verschwinden und von der Beharrlichkeit der Comödie." In *Theaterkunst & Heilkunst. Studien zu Theater und Anthropologie*, ed. Gerda Baumbach, 1–38. Cologne: Böhlau.

Baumgarten, Franz Ferdinand. 1920. *Zirkus Reinhardt*. Potsdam: Hans Heinrich Tillgner.
Baumol, W. J., and W. G. Bowen. 1965. "On the Performing Arts: The Anatomy of Their Economic Problem." *American Economic Review* 55: 495–502.
Baur, Detlev. 1999. *Der Chor im Theater des 20. Jahrhunderts: Typologie des theatralen Mittels Chor*. Tübingen: Niemeyer.
Bayerdörfer, Hans-Peter. 1978. "Überbrettl und Überdrama: Zum Verhältnis von literarischem Kabarett und Experimentierbühne." In *Literatur und Theater im Wilhelminischen Zeitalter*, ed. Hans-Peter Bayerdörfer, Karl-Otto Conrady, and Helmut Schanze, 292–325. Tübingen: Niemeyer.
———. 1990. "Probleme der Theatergeschichtsschreibung." In *Theaterwissenschaft heute*, ed. Renate Möhrmann, 41–63. Berlin: Reimer.
———. 1995. "Jüdisches Theater der Zwischenkriegszeit—östliche Wurzeln, westliche Ziele? Umrisse einer Kontroverse." In *Theater der Region—Theater Europas: Kongress der Gesellschaft für Theaterwissenschaft*, ed. Andreas Kotte, 25–45. Basel: Theaterkultur.
———. 1997. "'Geborene Schauspieler'—Das jüdische Theater des Ostens und die Theaterdebatte im deutschen Judentum." In *Jüdische Selbstwahrnehmung*, ed. Hans Otto Horch and Charlotte Wardi, 195–215. Tübingen: Niemeyer.
———. 2000. "Unscheinbare Bühne—Unerhörte Stimme: Diseusen der Weimarer Republik und die Reform im Theater." In *Literarisches und politisches Kabarett von 1901 bis 1999*, ed. Sigrid Bauschinger, 71–93. Tübingen: Francke.
Beer-Hofmann, Richard. 1994. "Der Graf von Charolais" (1904). In *Der Graf von Charolais und andere dramatische Entwürfe*, ed. Richard Beer-Hofmann, 5–235. Paderborn: Igel. (Beer-Hofmann, *Werke*, vol. 4.)
Belting, Hans. 2001. *Bild-Anthropologie: Entwürfe einer Bildwissenschaft*. Munich: Wilhelm Fink.
Bergmann, Ernst. 1906. *Der Fall Reinhardt oder Der künstlerische Bankerott des Deutschen Theaters zu Berlin: Eine kritische Studie*. Berlin: Dr. E. Bergmann.
Berking, Helmuth. 1984. *Masse und Geist: Studien zur Soziologie in der Weimarer Republik*. Berlin: WAV.
Bernau, Nikolaus. 2005. "Wo hing Munchs 'Lebens-Fries' Zu dem Bau der Kammerspiele und ihrem berühmtesten Schmuckstück." In *Max Reinhardt und das Deutsche Theater. Texte und Bilder aus Anlass des 100-jährigen Jubiläums seiner Direktion*, ed. Roland Koberg, Bernd Stegemann, and Henrike Thomsen, 65–77. Berlin: Henschel.
Bernauer, Markus. 1990. *Die Ästhetik der Masse*. Basel: Wiese.
Bernauer, Rudolf. 1955. *Das Theater meines Lebens: Erinnerungen*. Berlin: Lothar Blanvalet.
Berthold, Margot, and Uwe Vogt. 1983. "Venetianische Nacht—'Traum, Erlebnis, wer weiss?'" In *Max Reinhardts Theater im Film: Materialie*, ed. Margot Berthold, 54–64. Munich: Münchner Filmzentrum.
Bie, Oskar. 1910. "Akrobatik." *Die neue Rundschau* 21: 571–75.
Bier, Marcus J. 1983. "Das Mirakel—auf dem Weg zum neuen Medium." In *Max Reinhardts Theater im Film: Materialien*, ed. Margot Berthold, 20–42. Munich: Münchner Filmzentrum.
Bierbaum, Otto Julius. 1897. *Stilpe: Ein Roman aus der Froschperspektive*. Berlin: Schuster & Loeffler.

Works Cited

Bilsky, Emily D. 1999a. "Images of Identity and Urban Life: Jewish Artists in Turn-of-the-Century Berlin." In *Berlin Metropolis: Jews and the New Culture, 1890–1918*, ed. Emily D. Bilsky, 102–45. Berkeley: University of California Press.

———. 1999b. Introduction to *Berlin Metropolis: Jews and the New Culture, 1890–1918*, ed. Emily D. Bilsky, 2–13. Berkeley: University of California Press.

Bilsky, Emily D., and Emily Braun. 2005. "The Power of Conversation: Jewish Women and Their Salons." In *Jewish Women and Their Salons: The Power of Conversation*, ed. Emily D. Bilsky and Emily Braun, 1–147. New Haven, CT: Yale University Press.

Birett, Herbert. 1980. *Verzeichnis in Deutschland gelaufener Filme: Entscheidungen der Filmzensur, 1911–1920 Berlin, Hamburg, München, Stuttgart*. Munich: K. G. Saur.

———. 1991. *Das Filmangebot in Deutschland 1895–1911*. Munich: Filmbuchverlag Winterberg.

Boeser, Knut, and Renata Vatková, eds. 1984. *Max Reinhardt in Berlin*. Berlin: Edition Hentrich.

Böhme, Gernot. 1995. *Atmosphäre: Essays zur neuen Ästhetik*. Frankfurt am Main: Suhrkamp.

Bolter, Jay David, and Richard Grusin. 1999. *Remediation: Understanding New Media*. Cambridge: MIT Press.

Bose, Günter, and Erich Brinkmann. 1978. *Circus: Geschichte und Ästhetik einer niederen Kunst*. Berlin: Wagenbach.

Bourdieu, Pierre. 1984. *Die feinen Unterschiede: Kritik der gesellschaftlichen Urteilskraft* (1979). Frankfurt am Main: Suhrkamp.

———. 1985. "The Social Space and the Genesis of Groups." Translated by Richard Nice. *Theory and Society* 14, no. 6: 723–44.

———. 1987. *Sozialer Sinn: Kritik der theoretischen Vernunft*. Frankfurt am Main: Suhrkamp.

———. 1995. "Sozialer Raum und 'Klassen'" (1984). In *Sozialer Raum und "Klassen": Leçon sur la leçon: Zwei Vorlesungen*, ed. Pierre Bourdieu, 7–46. Frankfurt am Main: Suhrkamp.

Bourdieu, Pierre, and Loïc J. D. Wacquant. 1996. "Die Ziele der reflexiven Soziologie: Chicago-Seminar, Winter 1987" (1992). In *Reflexive Anthropologie*, ed. Pierre Bourdieu and Loïc J. D. Wacquant, 95–249. Frankfurt am Main: Suhrkamp.

Brand, Henri. 1992. "Massenkultur versus Angestelltenkultur: Siegfried Kracauers Auseinandersetzung mit Phänomenen der modernen Kultur in der Weimarer Republik." In *Zwischen Angstmetapher und Terminus: Theorien der Massenkultur seit Nietzsche*, ed. Norbert Krenzlin, 73–101. Berlin: Akademie-Verlag.

Brandlmeier, Thomas. 2002. "Frühe deutsche Filmkomödie 1895–1917." In *Kino der Kaiserzeit: Zwischen Tradition und Moderne*, ed. Thomas Elsaesser and Michael Wedel, 62–79. Munich: Text + Kritik.

Brandstetter, Gabriele. 2002. "Die Szene des Virtuosen: Zu einem Topos von Theatralität." *Hofmannsthal-Jahrbuch* 10: 213–43.

Braulich, Heinrich. 1969. *Max Reinhardt: Theater zwischen Traum und Wirklichkeit*. Berlin: Henschel.

Brauneck, Manfred. 1999. *Die Welt als Bühne: Geschichte des europäischen Theaters*, vol. 3. Stuttgart: J. B. Metzler.

Brewster, Ben, and Lea Jacobs. 1997. *Theatre to Cinema: Stage Pictorialism and the Early Feature Film.* Oxford: Oxford University Press.

Brokoph-Mauch, Gudrun. 1989. "Max Reinhardt am Broadway." In *Deutschsprachige Exilliteratur seit 1933*, vol. 2: *New York*, ed. John M. Spalek and Joseph Strelka, 1580–91. Bern: Francke Verlag.

Carlson, Marvin. 1972. *The German Stage in the Nineteenth Century.* Metuchen, NJ: Scarecrow.

———. 1989. *Places of Performance: The Semiotics of Theatre Architecture.* Ithaca, NY: Cornell University Press.

———. 2003. *The Haunted Stage: The Theatre as Memory Machine* (2001). Ann Arbor: University of Michigan Press.

Carter, Huntly. 1914. *The Theatre of Max Reinhardt.* London: Frank and Cecil Palmer.

Chrisholm, David. 2000. "Die Anfänge des literarischen Kabaretts in Berlin." In *Literarisches und politisches Kabarett von 1901 bis 1999*, ed. Sigrid Bauschinger, 21–37. Tübingen: Francke.

Collins, Theresa M. 2002. *Otto Kahn: Art, Money, & Modern Time.* Chapel Hill: University of North Carolina Press.

Conquergood, Dwight. 1991. "Rethinking Ethnography: Towards a Critical Cultural Politics." *Communication Monographs* 58: 179–94.

Cor, Etta. 1959. "Max Reinhardts erster Dramaturg: Zur Position des Dramaturgen am bürgerlichen Theater." *Theater der Zeit* 14, no. 3: 30–35.

Dahn, Felix. 1890. *Moltke: Festspiel zur Feier des neunzigsten Geburtstags des Feldmarschalls Grafen Helmuth Moltke.* Leipzig: Breitkopf & Härtel.

Daniel, Ute. 1995. *Hoftheater: Zur Geschichte des Theaters und der Höfe im 18. und 19. Jahrhundert.* Stuttgart: Klett-Cotta.

Davis, Tracy C. 2000. *The Economics of the British Stage, 1800–1914.* Cambridge: Cambridge University Press.

Davis, Tracy C., and Christopher B. Balme. 2016. "A Cultural History of Theatre: A Desideratum." *Theatre Survey* 57, no. 3: 459–70. doi: 10.1017/S0040557416000491.

Delbrück, Hans. 1892a. "Die Berliner Weltausstellung." *Preussische Jahrbücher* 70: 229–36.

———. 1892b. "Die Krisis des deutschen Weltausstellungsplans." *Preussische Jahrbücher* 70: 350–59.

Delius, Annette. 1976. *Intimes Theater: Untersuchungen zur Programmatik und Dramaturgie einer bevorzugten Theaterform der Jahrhundertwende.* Kronberg: Victor.

Dinter, Artur. 1916. *Weltkrieg und Schaubühne.* Munich: J. F. Lehmann.

Dreifuss, Alfred. 1987. *Deutsches Theater Berlin: Schumannstr. 13a. Fünf Kapitel aus der Geschichte einer Schauspielbühne.* Berlin: Henschel.

Dümcke, Cornelia. 1994. "Zu aktuellen Theaterentwicklungen aus ökonomischer Sicht." In *Das Theater und sein Preis: Beiträge zur Theaterreform*, ed. Sebastian Popp and Bernd Wagner, 67–77. Frankfurt am Main: Hessische Gesellschaft für Demokratie und Ökologie.

Durieux, Tilla. 1971. *Meine ersten neunzig Jahre: Erinnerungen.* Munich: Herbig.

Düsel, Friedrich. 1910/11c. "Dramatische Rundschau." *Westermanns Monatshefte* 55, no. 109: 935–45.

———. 1911c. "Zögern und Zagen, Verpfuschen und Verkennen: Berliner Theater." *Der Kunstwart* 24, no. 13: 36–37.
———. 1911d. "Dramatische Rundschau." *Westermanns Monatshefte* 55, no. 110: 445–54.
———. 1911e. "Dramatische Rundschau." *Westermanns Monatshefte* 56, no. 111: 451–62.
Easton, Laird M. 2002. *The Red Count: The Life and Times of Harry Kessler.* Berkeley: University of California Press.
Ebert, Gerhard. 1987. *Schauspieler werden in Berlin: Von Max Reinhardts Schauspielschule zur Hochschule für Schauspielkunst Ernst Busch.* Berlin: Berlin-Information.
Eisner, Lotte H. 1973. *The Haunted Screen: Expressionism in the German Cinema and the Influence of Max Reinhardt* (1952). London: Secker and Warburg.
Eloesser, Arthur. 1910. "Berliner Theatersaison." *Die neue Rundschau* 21: 699–708.
Elsaesser, Thomas. 2000. *Weimar Cinema and After: Germany's Historical Imaginary.* London: Routledge.
———. 2002a. *Filmgeschichte und frühes Kino: Archäologie eines Medienwandels.* Munich: Text + Kritik.
———. 2002b. "Kino der Kaiserzeit: Eine Einleitung." In *Kino der Kaiserzeit: Zwischen Tradition und Moderne,* ed. Thomas Elsaesser and Michael Wedel, 11–42. Munich: Text + Kritik.
Engel Reimers, Charlotte. 1911. *Die deutschen Bühnen und ihre Angehörigen: Eine Untersuchung über ihre wirtschaftliche Lage.* Leipzig: Duncker & Humblot.
Engeli, Christian. 1979. "Max Reinhardt gegen Berlin: Ein Steuerstreit aus den Zwanziger Jahren." *Der Bär von Berlin: Jahrbuch des Vereins für die Geschichte Berlins* 28: 33–62.
Epstein, Max. 1911. *Das Theater als Geschäft.* Berlin-Charlottenburg: Axel Juncker.
———. 1914. *Theater und Volkswirtschaft.* Berlin: Leonhard Simion.
———. 1918. *Max Reinhardt.* Berlin: Winckelmann Söhne.
———. 1996. *Das Theater als Geschäft* (1911). Berlin: Fannei & Walz.
Erdheim, Mario. 1993. "Das Eigene und das Fremde: Über ethnische Identität." In *Fremdenangst und Fremdenwirklichkeit,* ed. Mechthild M. Jansen and Ulrike Prokop, 163–82. Frankfurt am Main: Stroemfeld.
Erdman, Harley. 1997. *Staging the Jew: The Performance of an American Ethnicity, 1860–1920.* New Brunswick, NJ: Rutgers University Press.
Esslin, Martin. 1977. "Max Reinhardt: 'High Priest of Theatricality.'" *Drama Review* 21, no. 2: 3–24.
Eysoldt, Gertrud. 2002. "Max Reinhardt und seine Familie" (1946). *Sinn und Form* 54, no. 1: 62–67.
Feinberg, Anat. 2003. "Leopold Jessner: German Theatre and Jewish Identity. *Leo Baeck-Institute Yearbook* 48: 111–33.
Fetting, Hugo, ed. 1989. *Max Reinhardt: Leben für das Theater: Schriften und Selbstzeugnisse.* Berlin: Argon.
Fiebach, Joachim. 1991. *Von Craig bis Brecht: Studien zu Künstlertheorien des 20. Jahrhunderts* (1975). Berlin: Henschel.

Fiedler, Leonhard M. 1975. *Max Reinhardt*. Reinbek: Rowohlt.
———. 1979. "Max Reinhardt im Exil." In *Theater im Exil 1933–1945: Ein Symposion der Akademie der Künste*, ed. Lothar Schirmer, 262–71. Berlin: Akademie der Künste.
———. 1986. "Reinhardt, Shakespeare and the 'Dreams.'" In *Max Reinhardt: The Oxford Symposium*, ed. Margaret Jacobs and John Warren, 79–95. Oxford: Oxford Polytechnic.
———. 1991a. "'Bleiben *doch* die ewgen Juden . . .' Max Reinhardts Exil." In *Exiltheater und Exildramatik 1933–1945*, ed. Edita Koch and Frithjof Trapp. Maintal: E. Koch.
———. 1991b. "Die Überwindung des Naturalismus auf der Bühne: Das Theater Max Reinhardts." In *Drama und Theater der Jahrhundertwende*, ed. Dieter Kafitz, 69–85. Tübingen: Francke.
Fischer-Lichte, Erika. 1991. "Die Entdeckung des Zuschauers: Paradigmenwechsel auf dem Theater des 20. Jahrhunderts." *Zeitschrift für Literaturwissenschaft und Linguistik* 21, no. 81: 13–36.
———. 1993. *Kurze Geschichte des deutschen Theaters*. Tübingen: Francke.
———. 1998. "Berliner Theater im 20. Jahrhundert." In *Berliner Theater im 20. Jahrhundert*, ed. Erika Fischer-Lichte, Doris Kolesch, and Christel Weiler, 9–42. Berlin: Fannei & Walz.
———. 1999a. "Between Text and Cultural Performance: Staging Greek Tragedies in Germany." *Theatre Survey* 40: 1–29.
———. 1999b. *Das eigene und das fremde Theater*. Tübingen: A. Francke.
———. 1999c. "From Text to Performance: The Rise of Theatre Studies as an Academic Discipline in Germany." *Theatre Research International* 24: 168–78.
———. 2004. *Ästhetik des Performativen*. Frankfurt am Main: Suhrkamp.
———. 2005a. "Sinne und Sensationen: Wie Max Reinhardt Theater neu erfand." In *Max Reinhardt und das Deutsche Theater: Texte und Bilder aus Anlass des 100-jährigen Jubiläums seiner Direktion*, ed. Roland Koberg, Bernd Stegemann, and Henrike Thomsen, 13–27. Berlin: Henschel.
———. 2005b. *Theatre, Sacrifice, Ritual: Exploring Forms of Political Theatre*. London: Routledge.
Flashar, Hellmut. 1991. *Inszenierungen der Antike: Das griechische Drama auf der Bühne der Neuzeit 1585–1990*. Munich: C. H. Beck.
Fleischmann, Benno. 1948. *Max Reinhardt: Die Wiederentdeckung des Barocktheaters*. Vienna: Paul Neff.
Frank, Bruno. 1929. *Der Magier: Novelle*. Berlin: Ernst Rowohlt.
———. 1946. *"The Magician" and Other Stories*. New York: Viking.
Freksa, Friedrich. 1912/13. "Persönliche Pantomimenerfahrungen." *Velhagen & Klasings Monatshefte* 27, no. 3: 223–28.
———. 1913. *Erwin Bernsteins theatralische Sendung: Ein Berliner Theaterroman*. 2 vols. Munich: Georg Müller.
Frenzel, Karl. 1891. "Die Berliner Theater." *Deutsche Rundschau* 67: 447–61.
———. 1903. "Die Berliner Theater." *Deutsche Rundschau* 115: 287–303.
———. 1980. "Zwei Shakespeare Vorstellungen in Meiningen" (1870). In *Die Meininger: Texte zur Rezeption*, ed. John Osborne, 50–56. Tübingen: Max Niemeyer.
Freydank, Ruth. 1988. *Theater in Berlin*. Berlin: Argon.

———. 1995. "Berliner Geschäftstheater." In *Unterhaltungstheater in Deutschland: Geschichte—Ästhetik—Ökonomie*, ed. Wolfgang Jansen, 19–28. Berlin: Weidler.
Fritzsche, Peter. 1998. *Reading Berlin 1900* (1996). Cambridge, MA: Harvard University Press.
Fuchs, Georg. 1909. *Die Revolution des Theaters: Ergebnisse aus dem Münchener Künstlertheater*. Munich: Georg Müller.
Fuhrich, Edda, Ulrike Dembski, and Angela Eder, eds. 2004. *Ambivalenzen: Max Reinhardt und Österreich*. Vienna: Christian Brandstätter.
Fuhrich-Leisler, Edda, and Gisela Prossnitz. 1976. *Max Reinhardt in Amerika*. Salzburg: Otto Müller.
Funke, Christoph, and Wolfgang Jansen. 1992. *Theater am Schiffbauerdamm: Die Geschichte einer Berliner Bühne*. Berlin: C. H. Links.
Gay, Peter. 2001. *Weimar Culture: The Outsider as Insider* (1968). New York: W. W. Norton.
Geertz, Clifford. 1973. *The Interpretation of Cultures*. New York: Basic Books.
———. 1997. "Dichte Beschreibung: Bemerkungen zu einer deutenden Theorie von Kultur" (1973). In *Dichte Beschreibung: Beiträge zum Verstehen kultureller Systeme*, ed. Clifford Geertz, 7–43. Frankfurt am Main: Suhrkamp
Geiger, Theodor. 1967. *Die Masse und ihre Aktion: Ein Beitrag zur Soziologie der Revolutionen* (1926). Stuttgart: Ferdinand Enke.
Geyer, Emil. 1905. "Reinhardts Dekorationen." *Die Schaubühne* 1: 353–57.
Giese, Fritz. 1925. *Girlkultur: Vergleiche zwischen amerikanischem und europäischem Rhythmus und Lebensgefühl*. Munich: Delphin.
Gilman, Sander L. 1991. *The Jew's Body*. New York: Routledge.
———. 1998. "'Die Rasse ist nicht schön'—'Nein, wir Juden sind keine hübsche Rasse': Der schöne und der hässliche Jude." In *"Der Schejne Jid": Das Bild des "jüdischen Körpers" in Mythos und Ritual*, ed. Sander L. Gilman and Robert Jütte, 57–74. Vienna: Picus.
Goldmann, Paul. 1908. *Vom Rückgang der deutschen Bühne: Polemische Aufsätze über Berliner Theater-Aufführungen*. Frankfurt am Main: Rütten & Loening.
———. 1910. *Literatenstücke und Ausstattungsregie: Polemische Aufsätze über Berliner Theater-Aufführungen*. Frankfurt am Main: Rütten & Loening.
Greiner, Bernhard. 1996. "'Damenopfer' für das Theater: Hofmannsthals und Reinhardts Begegnung in der Arbeit an *Elektra*." In *Von Franzos zu Canetti: Jüdische Autoren aus Österreich, Neue Studien*, ed. Mark H. Gelber, Hans Otto Horch, and Sigurd Paul Scheichl, 253–71. Tübingen: Max Niemeyer.
Greisenegger-Georgila, Vana. 1994. *Theater von der Stange: Wiener Ausstattungskunst in der zweiten Hälfte des 19. Jahrhunderts*. Vienna: Böhlau.
Greve, Jochen. 1983. "Ein Sommernachtstraum—'Eine herbstliche Schönheit.'" In *Max Reinhardts Theater im Film: Materialien*, ed. Margot Berthold, 69–84. Munich: Münchner Filmzentrum.
Grimm, Jürgen. 1982. *Das avantgardistische Theater Frankreichs: 1895–1930*. Munich: C. H. Beck.
Grohmann, Walter. 1935. *Das Münchner Künstlertheater in der Bewegung der Szenenund Theaterreformen*. Berlin: Gesellschaft für Theatergeschichte.

Grossmann, Stefan. 1920a. "Gesellschaftsabend bei Reinhardt." *Das Tage-Buch* 1, no. 7: 265–67.
———. 1920b. "Reinhardt, UFA und Berlin." *Das Tage-Buch* 1, no. 32: 1049–53.
———. 1920c. "Zweifel am Zirkustheater: Zur Hamlet-Aufführung im Grossen Schauspielhaus." *Vossische Zeitung*, vol. 18 (January 1920).
Gunning, Tom. 1990. "The Cinema of Attractions: Early Film, Its Spectator, and the Avant-Garde" (1986). In *Early Cinema: Space, Frame, Narrative*, ed. Thomas Elsaesser, 56–62. London: BFI.
Gürtler, Franz. 1911. "Deutsches Theater und 'Deutsches Theater.'" *Der Kunstwart* 24, no. 8: 81–86.
Haenni, Sabine. 2003 "'A Community of Consumers': Legitimate Hybridity, German American Theatre, and the American Public." *Theatre Research International* 28, no. 3: 267–88.
Hahm, Thomas. 1970. "Das Gastspiel des Meininger Hoftheaters im Urteil der Zeitgenossen unter besonderer Berücksichtigung der Gastspiele in Berlin und Wien." Dissertation. Cologne.
Hahn, Barbara. 1999. "Encounters at the Margins: Jewish Salons around 1900." In *Berlin Metropolis: Jews and the New Culture, 1890–1918*, ed. Emily Bilsky, 56–62. Berkeley: University of California Press.
———. 2005. "A Dream of Living Together: Jewish Women in Berlin around 1800." In *Jewish Women and Their Salons: The Power of Conversation*, ed. Emily D. Bilsky and Emily Braun, 149–57. New Haven, CT: Yale University Press.
Hahn, Ines. 1996. "Das Metropol-Theater: Theater als sichere Geldanlage." In *Theater als Geschäft: Berlin und seine Privattheater um die Jahrhundertwende*, ed. Ruth Freydank, 89–103. Berlin: Edition Hentrich.
Hake, Sabine. 1992. *Passions and Deceptions: The Early Films of Ernst Lubitsch*. Princeton, NJ: Princeton University Press.
Halbert, A. 1906. "Der Jude Max Reinhardt: Eine Studie zur Rassentheorie." *Allgemeine Zeitung des Judentums*, no. 23: 271.
Hampicke, Evelyn, and Christian Dirks. 2004. "Paul Davidsohn: Die Erfindung des Generaldirektors." In *Pioniere in Celluloid: Juden in der frühen Filmwelt*, ed. Irene Stratenwerth and Hermann Simon, 49–55. Berlin: Henschel.
Harden, Maximilian. 1888. *Berlin als Theaterhauptstadt*. Berlin: F. & P. Lehmann.
———. 1911. "Theater." (Faust II). *Die Zukunft* 75: 151–68.
Hart, Heinrich, and Julius Hart. 1882. "Das 'Deutsche Theater' des Herrn L'Arronge." *Kritische Waffengänge* 4: 1–69.
Hausner, Henry H. 1970. "Die Beziehungen zwischen Arthur Schnitzler und Sigmund Freud." *Modern Austrian Literature: Journal of the International Arthur Schnitzler Research Association* 3, no. 2: 48–61.
Heilmann, Matthias. 2005. *Leopold Jessner—Intendant der Republik: Der Weg eines deutsch-jüdischen Regisseurs aus Ostpreussen*. Tübingen: Max Niemeyer.
Hein, Dieter, and Andreas Schulz. 1996. Introduction to *Bürgerkultur im 19. Jahrhundert: Bildung, Kunst und Lebenswelt*, ed. Dieter Hein and Andeas Schulz, 9–16. Munich: C. H. Beck.
Herald, Heinz. 1915. *Max Reinhardt: Ein Versuch über das Wesen der modernen Regie*. Berlin: Felix Lehmann.
———. 1925. "I.P.G." (Internationale Pantomimen-Gesellschaft). In *Pantomimen-Gesellschaft, Internationale*, ed. *Die Pantomime*, 9–19. Berlin.

———. 1930. "Die Jahre 1924–1930: Dokumentierung von Reinhardts Persönlichkeit." In *Max Reinhardt: 25 Jahre Deutsches Theater, Ein Tafelwerk*, ed. Hans Rothe, 59–68. Munich: R. Piper.
Herrmann, Max. 1914. *Forschungen zur deutschen Theatergeschichte des Mittelalters und der Renaissance*. Berlin: Weidmann.
Herterich, Fritz. 1937. *Theater und Volkswirtschaft*. Munich: Duncker & Humblot.
Hettling, Manfred, and Stefan-Ludwig Hofmann. 1997. "Der bürgerliche Wertehimmel: Zum Problem individueller Lebensführung im 19. Jahrhundert." *Geschichte und Gesellschaft* 23: 333–59.
Hildebrand, Petra S. 2000. "Theateragenten im deutschsprachigen Raum des 19. Jahrhunderts—ein erster Blick auf ihre Engagementsvermittlungen an deutschsprachigen Bühnen im Ausland." In *Die Geschichte des deutschsprachigen Theaters im Ausland: Von Afrika bis Wisconsin—Anfänge und Entwicklungen*, ed. Laurence Kitching, 167–76. Frankfurt am Main: Peter Lang.
Hildebrandt, Hans. 1920. "Die Wiedererweckung des griechischen Dramas." In *Das Große Schauspielhaus: Zur Eröffnung herausgegeben vom Deutschen Theater zu Berlin*, ed. Heinz Herald, 89–104. Berlin: Verlag der Bücher des Deutschen Theaters.
Hobsbawm, Eric. 1983. "Mass-Producing Traditions: Europe, 1870–1914." In *The Invention of Tradition*, ed. Eric Hobsbawm and Terence Ranger, 263–307. Cambridge: Cambridge University Press.
Hofer, Sigrid. 2001. "Die Ästhetisierung des Alltags: Architektur für die Reform des Lebens von Peter Behrens bis Paul Schultze-Naumburg." In *Die Lebensreform: Entwürfe zur Neugestaltung von Leben und Kunst um 1900*, vol. 1, ed. Kai Buchholz, 271–77. Darmstadt: Haeusser Media.
Hoffmann, Eric Alexander. 2001. "Historische Avantgarde: Versuch einer Bestimmung und Vorstudien zu einer Geschichte und Theorie des modernen Theaters." *Forum Modernes Theater* 16, no. 2: 135–50.
Hofinger, Johannes. 2005. *Die Akte Leopoldskron: Max Reinhardt—Das Schloss—Arisierung und Restitution*. Salzburg: Pustet.
Hofmannsthal, Hugo von. 1925. "Über die Pantomime." In *Pantomimen-Gesellschaft, Internationale*, ed. *Die Pantomime*, 5–8. Berlin.
———. 1983. "König Ödipus" (1910). In *Hugo von Hofmannsthal: Sämtliche Werke VIII, Dramen 6*, ed. Wolfgang Nehring and Klaus E. Bohnenkamp, 129–84. Frankfurt am Main: S. Fischer.
Horch, Franz. 1930. "Die Spielpläne Max Reinhardts." In *Max Reinhardt: 25 Jahre Deutsches Theater, Ein Tafelwerk*, ed. Hans Rothe, 72–74. Munich: R. Piper.
Horkheimer, Max, and Theodor W. Adorno. 1994. *Dialektik der Aufklärung: Philosophische Fragmente* (1944). Frankfurt am Main: Fischer.
———. 2002. *Dialectic of Enlightenment*. Edited by Gunzelin Schmid Noerr, translated by Edmund Jephcott. Palo Alto, CA: Stanford University Press.
Huesmann, Heinrich. 1983. *Welttheater Reinhardt: Bauten, Spielstätten, Inszenierungen*. Munich: Prestel.
Ibscher, Edith. 1972. *Theaterateliers des Deutschen Sprachraums im 19. und 20. Jarhundert*. Frankfurt am Main.

Ihering, Herbert. 1929. *Reinhardt, Jessner, Piscator oder Klassikertod?* Berlin: Rowohlt.
Jacobsohn, Siegfried. 1910b. *Max Reinhardt*. Berlin: Erich Reiss.
———. 1911. "Reinhardts Zukunft." *Die Schaubühne* 7: 285–87.
———. 1913/14. *Das Jahr der Bühne*, vol. 3. Berlin: Oesterhold & Co.
———. 1920. "Hamlet im Zirkus." *Die Weltbühne* 16: 117–20.
———. 2005c. "Das Theater der Reichshauptstadt" (1904). In *Das Theater der Reichshauptstadt. Schriften 1900–1909*, ed. Siegfried Jacobsohn, 11–102. Göttingen: Wallstein. (Vol. 1 of Siegfried Jacobsohn, *Gesammelte Schriften, 1900–1926*.)
Jansen, Wolfgang. 1987. *Glanzrevuen der zwanziger Jahre*. Berlin: Edition Hentrich.
———. 1990. *Das Varieté: Die glanzvolle Geschichte einer unterhaltenden Kunst*. Berlin: Edition Hentrich.
Jaron, Norbert, Renate Möhrmann, and Hedwig Müller, eds. 1986. *Berlin—Theater der Jahrhundertwende: Bühnengeschichte der Reichshauptstadt im Spiegel der Kritik (1889–1914)*. Tübingen: Max Niemeyer.
Jelavich, Peter. 1993. *Berlin Cabaret*. Cambridge, MA: Harvard University Press.
———. 1999. "Performing High and Low: Jews in Modern Theater, Cabaret, Revue, and Film." In *Berlin Metropolis: Jews and the New Culture, 1890–191*, ed. Emily D. Bilsky, 208–35. Berkeley: University of California Press.
Jessner, Leopold. 1979. "Das 'verjudete' Theater" (1922). In *Leopold Jessner, Schriften: Theater der Zwanziger Jahre*, ed. Hugo Fetting. Berlin: Henschel.
Kafitz, Dieter. 1989. *Grundzüge einer Geschichte des deutschen Dramas von Lessing bis zum Naturalismus*. Frankfurt am Main: Athenäum.
Kahane, Arthur. 1911. "Der Regisseur Reinhardt." *Die Zukunft* 76: 377–84.
———. 1930a. "Die Jahre 1905–1924." In *Max Reinhardt: 25 Jahre Deutsches Theater, Ein Tafelwerk*, ed. Hans Rothe, 15–58. Munich: R. Piper & Co.
———. 1930b. *Theater: Aus dem Tagebuch des Theatermannes*. Berlin: Wegweiser.
Kalser, Erwin. 1927. "Über die Juden und das Theater." *Jahrbuch für jüdische Geschichte und Literatur* 28: 63–83.
Kayssler, Friedrich. 1927. "Mit der Sorma bei Reinhardt." In *Agnes Sorma: Ein Gedenkbuch*, ed. Julius Bab, 88–91. Heidelberg: Niels Kampmann.
Kessler, Harry Graf. 2005. *Das Tagebuch: 1880–1937, Vierter Band: 1906–1914*. Stuttgart: Cotta.
Kienzl, Hermann. 1911a. "Von den Berliner Theatern 1910/11: XIV." *Bühne und Welt* 13: 126–29.
———. 1911b. "Von den Berliner Theatern 1910/11: XVIII." *Bühne und Welt* 13: 304–6.
Kindermann, Heinz. 1969. *Max Reinhardts Weltwirkung: Ursachen, Erscheinungsformen und Grenzen*.
Kirshenblatt-Gimblett, Barbara. 1998. *Destination Culture: Tourism, Museums, and Heritage*. Berkeley: University of California Press.
Kitching, Laurence. 2000. "Wandering the Globe: German-Language Theatre abroad from Africa to Wisconsin." In *Die Geschichte des deutschsprachigen Theater im Ausland: Von Afrika bis Wisconsin—Anfänge und Entwicklungen*, ed. Lauence Kitching, xiii–xvii. Frankfurt am Main: Peter Lang.

Klein, Peter K. 1999. "'Jud, dir guckt der Spitzbub aus dem Gesicht!' Traditionen antisemitischer Bildstereotypen oder die Physiognomie des 'Juden' als Konstrukt." In *Abgestempelt—judenfeindliche Postkarten: Auf der Grundlage der Sammlung Wolfgang Haney*, ed. Helmut Gold and Georg Heuberger, 43–78. Heidelberg: Umschau Braus.

Kleinsteuber, Hans J., and Barbara Thomass. 1996. "Konkurrenz versus Konzentration: Unternehmensverflechtungen im globalen Medienmarkt." In *Internationale Kommunikation: Eine Einführung*, ed. Miriam Meckel and Markus Kriener, 125–44. Opladen: Westdeutscher Verlag.

Kluncker, Karlhans. 1978. "Die Schwabinger Schattenspiele." In *Literatur und Theater im Wilhelminischen Zeitalter*, ed. Hans-Peter Bayerdörfer, Karl-Otto Conrady, and Helmut Schanze, 326–45. Tübingen: Niemeyer.

Koch, Marianne. 1957. "Das Königliche Schauspielhaus in Berlin unter Bolko Graf von Hochberg: Eine Untersuchung mit besonderer Berücksichtigung zeitgenössischer Theaterkritik." Dissertation. Berlin.

Kocka, Jürgen. 1987. "Bürgertum und Bürgerlichkeit als Probleme der deutschen Geschichte vom späten 18. bis zum frühen 20. Jahrhundert." In *Bürger und Bürgerlichkeit im 19. Jahrhundert*, ed. Jürgen Kocka, 21–63. Göttingen: Vandenhoeck & Ruprecht.

———. 2001. *Das lange 19. Jahrhundert: Arbeit, Nation und bürgerliche Gesellschaft*. Stuttgart: Klett-Cotta.

Kohlmayer, Rainer. 1996. *Oscar Wilde in Deutschland und Österreich: Untersuchungen zur Rezeption der Komödien und zur Theorie der Bühnenübersetzung*. Tübingen: Niemeyer.

Koljasin, Wladimir. 1995. "Gastspiele russischer Theater in Berlin in den zwanziger und dreissiger Jahren. Von Ost nach West, von Tairow zu Meyerhold." In *Berlin—Moskau / Moskau—Berlin 1900–1950*, ed. Irina Antonowa and Jörn Merkert, 173–77. Munich: Prestel.

Kommer, Rudolf. 1924a. "Archbishop Firmian, Max Reinhardt, and Morris Gest: Five Summer Days in Salzburg." In *The Miracle*, ed. Morris Gest. New York: Oliver M. Sayler.

———. 1924b. "The Genesis of 'The Miracle.'" In *The Miracle*, ed. Morris Gest. New York: Oliver M. Sayler.

Kortner, Fritz. 1991. *Aller Tage Abend* (1959). Berlin: Alexander.

Kothes, Franz-Peter. 1977. *Die theatralische Revue in Berlin und Wien 1900–1938: Typen, Inhalte, Funktionen*. Wilhelmshaven: Henschel.

Kotte, Andreas. 2002. "Theatralität konstituiert Gesellschaft, Gesellschaft Theater: Was kann Theaterhistoriographie leisten?" In *Theaterwissenschaftliche Beiträge* (Theater der Zeit—Insert), 2–9.

———. 2005. *Theaterwissenschaft: Eine Einführung*. Cologne: Böhlau.

Kracauer, Siegfried. 1977. "Das Ornament der Masse" (1927). In *Das Ornament der Masse: Essays*, ed. Siegfried Kracauer, 50–63. Frankfurt am Main: Suhrkamp.

———. 1995. *The Mass Ornament: Weimar Essays*. Translated by Thomas Levin. Cambridge, MA: Harvard University Press.

Kreimeier, Klaus. 1992. *Die Ufa-Story: Geschichte eines Filmkonzerns*. Munich: Carl Hanser.

Kretschmer, Winfried. 1999. *Geschichte der Weltausstellungen*. Frankfurt am Main: Campus.

Kreuder, Friedemann. 2005. "Schauspieler." In *Metzler Lexikon Theatertheorie*, ed. Erika Fischer-Lichte, Doris Kolesch, and Matthias Warstat, 283–86. Stuttgart: J. B. Metzler,
Kuchenbuch, Thomas. 1992. *Die Welt um 1900: Unterhaltungs- und Technikkultur.* Stuttgart: J. B. Metzler.
Kügelgen, Henning von. 1983. "Sumurun—Malheur oder Missverständnis?" In *Max Reinhardts Theater im Film: Materialien*, ed. Margot Berthold, 9–19. Munich: Münchner Filmzentrum.
Kühn, Volker. 1984. *Das Kabarett der frühen Jahre: Ein freches Musenkind macht erste Schritte.* Berlin: Quadriga.
Kunczik, Michael. 1997. *Geschichte der Öffentlichkeitsarbeit in Deutschland.* Cologne: Böhlau.
Kvam, Wayne. 1988. "The Nazification of Max Reinhardt's Deutsches Theater Berlin." *Theatre Journal* 40, no. 3: 357–74.
Le Bon, Gustave. 1896. *The Crowd, a Study of the Popular Mind.* Translator anonymous. London: T. Fisher Unwin.
———. 1973. *Psychologie der Massen* (1895). Stuttgart: Alfred Kröner.
Lederer, Moritz. 1953. "Max Reinhardt und sein Bruder." *Deutsche Rundschau* 79: 943–49.
———. 1958. "Baumeister des deutschen Theaters: II, Edmund—Max Reinhardts Bruder." *Deutsche Rundschau* 11: 1158–62.
Lehmann, Hans-Thies. 1999. *Postdramatisches Theater.* Frankfurt am Main: Verlag der Autoren.
Leonhardt, Nic. 2015. "'From the Land of the White Elephant through the Gay Cities of Europe and America': Re-routing the World Tour of the Boosra Mahin Siamese Theatre Troupe (1900)." *Theatre Research International* 40, no. 2: 140–55.
Lessing, Theodor. 1984. *Der jüdische Selbsthass: Mit einem Essay von Boris Groys* (1930). Munich: Matthes & Seitz.
Lethen, Helmut. 1986. "Chicago und Moskau: Berlins moderne Kultur der 20er Jahre zwischen Inflation und Weltwirtschaftskrise." In *Die Metropole: Industriekultur in Berlin im 20. Jahrhundert*, ed. Jochen Boberg and Tilman Fichter, 190–213. Munich: C. H. Beck.
Linsemann, Paul. 1897. *Die Theaterstadt Berlin: Eine kritische Umschau.* Berlin: Richard Taendler.
Löden, Brigitte. 1976. *Max Reinhardts Massenregie auf der Guckkastenbühne von 1905 bis 1910: Ein Versuch zu Darstellungsmittel und Regieintention.* Frankfurt am Main: Peter Lang.
Maertens. 1889a. "Zur Lösung der Volkstheaterfrage." *Deutsche Bauzeitung* 23, no. 36: 214–16.
———. 1889b. "Zur Lösung der Volkstheaterfrage." *Deutsche Bauzeitung* 23, no. 42: 251.
Makarowa, Galina. 1995. "Das Moskauer und das Berliner Theater zu Beginn des 20. Jahrhunderts." In *Berlin—Moskau / Moskau—Berlin 1900–1950*, ed. Irina Antonowa and Jörn Merkert, 43–45. Munich: Prestel.
Martersteig, Max. 1904. *Das deutsche Theater im neunzehnten Jahrhundert: Eine kulturgeschichtliche Darstellung.* Leipzig: Breikopf & Härtel.

Marx, Peter W. 2003a. "Berlin." In *The Oxford Encyclopedia of Theatre & Performance*, vol. 1, ed. Dennis Kennedy, 140–42. London: Oxford University Press.

———. 2003b." Festivals of Theatre." In *The Oxford Encyclopedia of Theatre & Performance*, vol. 1, ed. Dennis Kennedy, 455–56. London: Oxford University Press.

———. 2005. "Die drei Gesichter Shylocks: Zu Max Reinhardts Projekt eines metropolitanen, liberalen Theaters vor dem Hintergrund seiner jüdischen Herkunft." In *Max Reinhardt und das Deutsche Theater: Texte und Bilder aus Anlass des 100-jährigen Jubiläums seiner Direktion*, ed. Roland Koberg, Bernd Stegemann, and Henrike Thomsen, 51–59. Berlin: Henschel.

———. 2006. "Consuming the Canon: Theatre, Commodification, and Social Mobility in Late Nineteenth-Century German Theatre." *Theatre Research International* 31, no. 2: 129–44.

———. 2007. "Ein richtiger Wald, ein wirklicher Traum: Max Reinhardts *Sommernachtstraum* 1905." *Forum Modernes Theater* 22, no. 1: 17–31.

Marx, Peter W., and Stefanie Watzka., eds. 2009. *Berlin auf dem Weg zur Theaterhauptstadt: Theaterstreitschriften zwischen 1869 und 1914*. Tübingen: Francke Verlag.

McMullen, Sally. 1986. "Sense and Sensuality: Max Reinhardt's Earliest Productions." In *Max Reinhardt: The Oxford Symposium*, ed. Margaret Jacobs and John Warren, 16–33. Oxford: Oxford Polytechnic.

Mell, Max. 1972. "Die Josefstadt." In *Max Reinhardts Theater in der Josefstadt: Eines der schönsten Theater der Welt*, ed. Fritz Klingenbeck, 7–9. Salzburg: Residenz.

Mendes-Flohr, Paul. 1999. "The Berlin Jew as Cosmopolitan." In *Berlin Metropolis: Jews and the New Culture, 1890–1918*, ed. Emily D. Bilsky, 14–31. Berkeley: University of California Press.

Midböe, Hans. 1978. "Max Reinhardts Inszenierung von Ibsens 'Gespenstern' in den Kammerspielen des Deutschen Theaters Berlin 1906: Ausstattung Edvard Munch." *Maske und Kothurn* 24: 17–76.

Mommsen, Hans. 1987. "Die Auflösung des Bürgertums seit dem späten 19. Jahrhundert." In *Bürger und Bürgerlichkeit im 19. Jahrhundert*, ed. Jürgen Kocka, 288–315. Göttingen: Vandenhoeck & Ruprecht.

Mühl-Benninghaus, Wolfgang. 2002. "*Don Juan heiratet* und *Der Andere*: Zwei frühe filmische Theateradaptionen." In *Kino der Kaiserzeit: Zwischen Tradition und Moderne*, ed. Thomas Elsaesser and Michael Wedel, 336–47. Munich: Text + Kritik.

———. 2004. *Vom Augusterlebnis bis zur UFA-Gründung: Der deutsche Film im 1. Weltkrieg*. Berlin: Avinus.

Müller, Brigitte. 2004. *Ferdinand Bonn—Frauenheld, Lebemann und Weltverbesserer: Frauen, Adel und Volk im Leben und Werk von Ferdinand Bonn*. Marburg: Tectum.

Müller, Corinna. 1994. *Frühe deutsche Kinematographie: Formale, wirtschaftliche und kulturelle Entwicklungen*. Stuttgart: Metzler.

Müller, Gisela. 1992. "Der Massencharakter des Lebens und das ratlose Ich: Eine Lesart zu Georg Simmels Moderne-Bild." In *Zwischen Angstmetapher und*

Terminus: Theorien der Massenkultur seit Nietzsche, ed. Norbert Krenzlin, 43–72. Berlin: Akademie-Verlag.
Müller, Meike Elisabeth. 1997. "'Reklamowicz-Klimbimsky': Historische Befunde zur Öffentlichkeitsarbeit für Theater in Deutschland: Die Theaterstadt Berlin und Max Reinhardt." Master's thesis. Mainz.
Münz, Rudolf. 1979. *Das "andere" Theater: Studien über ein deutschsprachiges teatro dell'arte der Lessingzeit*. Berlin: Henschel.
———. 1998. "'Ein Kadaver, den es noch zu töten gilt': Das Leipziger Theatralitätskonzept als methodisches Prinzip der Historiographie älteren Theaters" (1994). In *Theatralität und Theater: Zur Historiographie von Theatralitätsgefügen*, ed. Rudolf Münz, 82–103. Berlin: Schwarzkopf & Schwarzkopf.
Neuweiler, Arnold. 1919. *Massenregie: Eine Studie über die Schauspielchöre, ihre Wirkung und ihre Behandlung*. Bremen: Werbezentrale Lloyd.
Newman, Lindsay. 1986. "Reinhardt and Craig?" In *Max Reinhardt. The Oxford Symposium*, ed. Margaret Jacobs and John Warren, 6–15. Oxford: Oxford Polytechnic.
Niemann, Carsten. 1993. "Die Schauspielerlin Gertrude Eysoldt als Darstellerin der Salome, Lulu, Nastja, Elektra und des Puck im Berliner Max-Reinhardt-Ensemble." Dissertation. Frankfurt am Main.
———. 1995. *"Das Herz meiner Künstlerschaft ist Mut": Die Max-Reinhardt-Schauspielerin Gertrud Eysoldt*. Hanover: Theatermuseum und -archiv der Niedersächsen Staatstheater.
Niessen, Carl. 1958. *Max Reinhardt und seine Bühnenbildner*. Cologne: Greven & Bechtold.
Nietzsche, Friedrich. 1966. *Werke in drei Bänden*, vol. 2. Munich: Carl Hanser.
Niven, William. 2000. "The Birth of Nazi Drama? *Thing* Plays." In *Theatre under the Nazis*, ed. John London, 54–95. Manchester: Manchester University Press.
Ockman, Carol, and Kenneth E. Silver. 2005. "Introduction: The Mythic Sarah Bernhardt." In *Sarah Bernhardt: The Art of High Drama*, ed. Carol Ockman and Kenneth E. Silver, 1–17. New Haven, CT: Yale University Press.
Otte, Marline. 2006. *Jewish Identities in German Popular Entertainment, 1890–1933*. Cambridge: Cambridge University Press.
Paquet, Alfons. 1908. *Das Ausstellungsproblem in der Volkswirtschaft*. Jena: Gustav Fischer.
Parish, Fraeda. 1977. "Max Reinhardt's American Tour 1927–28: A Legacy Understood or Misunderstood?" *Modern Austrian Literature* 10: 55–67.
Perlmann, Michaela L. 1987. *Arthur Schnitzler*. Stuttgart: Metzler.
Pinthus, Kurt. 1920. "Möglichkeiten zukünftigen Volkstheaters." In *Das Grosse Schauspielhaus: Zur Eröffnung herausgegeben vom Deutschen Theater zu Berlin*, ed. Heinz Herald, 37–54. Berlin: Bücher des Deutschen Theaters.
Poelzig, Hans. 1920. "Bau des Grossen Schauspielhauses." In *Das Grosse Schauspielhaus: Zur Eröffnung herausgegeben vom Deutschen Theater zu Berlin*, ed. Heinz Herald, 117–22. Berlin: Bücher des Deutschen Theaters.
Prölß, Robert. 1899. "Das Meiningersche Hoftheater und die Entwicklung und kulturhistorische Bedeutung seiner Gastspiele." *Bühne und Welt* 1: 673–78.
Prossnitz, Gisela. 1986. "Bühnenformen und Spielstätten bei Reinhardt." In *Max Reinhardt: The Oxford Symposium*, ed. Margaret Jacobs and John Warren, 67–78. Oxford: Oxford Polytechnic.

Raeck, Kurt. 1928. *Das Deutsche Theater zu Berlin unter der Direktion Adolph L'Arronge: Beiträge zu seiner Geschichte und Charakteristik*. Berlin: Verlag des Vereins für die Geschichte Berlins.
Rathenau, Walther. 2002. *Die schönste Stadt der Welt* (1902). Berlin: Philo.
Rauscher, Ulrich. 1913. "Die Kino-Ballade." *Der Kunstwart* 26, no. 13: 1–6.
Rebhan, Angelika. 1983. "Insel der Seligen—Ein heiteres Flimmerspiel." In *Max Reinhardts Theater im Film: Materialien*, ed. Margot Berthold, 45–53. Munich: Münchner Filmzentrum.
Reichel, Hans-Günther. 1962. "Das Königliche Schauspielhaus unter Georg Graf von Hülsen-Haeseler (1903–1918): Mit besonderer Berücksichtigung der zeitgenössischen Tagespresse." Dissertation. Berlin.
Reicke, Georg. 1912. "Die Grossstadt." *Die neue Rundschau* 23: 202–23.
Reinhardt, Gottfried. 1973. *Der Liebhaber: Erinnerungen seines Sohnes an Max Reinhardt*. Munich: Droemer/Knaur.
———. 1979. *The Genius: A Memoir of Max Reinhardt*. New York: Knopf.
Reinhardt, Max. 1989. *Leben für das Theater: Schriften und Selbstzeugnisse*. Edited by Hugo Fetting. Berlin: Argon.
Reissmann, Bärbel. 1996. "Max Reinhardt: Ein erfolgreiches Theaterexperiment." In *Theater als Geschäft: Berlin und seine Privattheater um die Jahrhundertwende*, ed. Ruth Freydank, 157–71. Berlin: Edition Hentrich.
Ret, Angelika. 1996. "Der Wintergarten: Weltstadtvarieté im Central-Hotel." In *Theater als Geschäft: Berlin und seine Privattheater um die Jahrhundertwende*, ed. Ruth Freydank, 51–64. Berlin: Edition Hentrich.
Rokem, Freddie. 2000. *Performing History: Theatrical Representations of the Past in Contemporary Theatre*. Iowa City: University of Iowa Press.
Rorrison, Hugh. 1986. "Reinhardt and Ernst Stern." In *Max Reinhardt: The Oxford Symposium*, ed. Margaret Jacobs and John Warren, 55–66. Oxford: Oxford Polytechnic.
Rossbach, Nikola, ed. 2005. *Ibsen-Parodien in der frühen Moderne*. Munich: Martin Meidenbauer.
Rothe, Hans. 1930. "Kurze Chronik." In *Max Reinhardt: 25 Jahre Deutsches Theater, Ein Tafelwerk*, ed. Hans Rothe, 69–71. Munich: R. Piper & Co.
Rudin, Alexander. 1978. "Max Reinhardts dritte und vierte Besetzung: Zum künstlerischen Betrieb der Reinhardt-Bühnen in Berlin." *Kleine Schriften der Gesellschaft für Theatergeschichte* 29/30: 113–24.
Rydell, Robert W., and Rob Kroes. 2005 *Buffalo Bill in Bologna: The Americanization of the World, 1869–1922*. Chicago: University of Chicago Press.
Sauer, Klaus, amd German Werth. 1971. *Lorbeer und Palme: Patriotismus in deutschen Festspielen*. Munich: Deutscher Taschenbuch.
Sauter, Willmar. 1995. "Eine verschrumpfte Avantgarde: Das Intima Teatern des August Strindberg." In *Theater Avantgarde: Wahrnehmung, Körper, Sprache*, ed. Erika Fischer-Lichte.Tübingen: Francke.
Schaper, Rüdiger. 2000. *Moissi: Triest, Berlin, New York: Eine Schauspielerlegende*. Berlin: Argon.
Scheffler, Karl. 1970. "Das Grosse Schauspielhaus" (1920). In *Hans Poelzig: Gesammelte Schriften und Werke*, ed. Julius Posener, 136–40. Berlin: Gebr. Mann Verlag.

Schmitt, Eduard. 1904. *Entwerfen, Anlage und Einrichtung der Gebäude. 6. Halbband Gebäude für Erziehung, Wissenschaft und Kunst. 6. Heft: Zirkus- und Hippodromgebäude.* Stuttgart: Arnold Bergsträsser Verlagsbuchhandlung.

Scholem, Gershom. 1995a. "Wider den Mythos vom deutsch-jüdischen Gespräch" (1964). In *Judaica 2*, ed. Gershom Scholem, 7–11. Frankfurt am Main: Suhrkamp.

———. 1995b. "Noch einmal: Das deutsch-jüdische Gespräch" (1965). In *Judaica 2*, ed. Gershom Scholem, 12–19. Frankfurt am Main: Suhrkamp.

———. 2012. "Against the Myth of German-Jewish Dialogue." In Gershom Scholem, *On Jews and Judaism in Crisis: Selected Essays*, ed. and trans. Werner J. Dannhauser. New York: Schocken Books.

Schuler, Constanze. 2006. "Rauminszenierungen zwischen Festspiel und Ritual: Die Salzburger Kollegienkirche als Aufführungsort der Festspiele." Dissertation. Mainz.

Schulz, Andreas. 2005. *Lebenswelt und Kultur des Bürgertums im 19. und 20. Jahrhundert.* Munich: Oldenbourg. (*Enzyklopädie deutscher Geschichte*, 75.)

Schumacher, Fritz. 1919. "Probleme der Grossstadt." *Deutsche Rundschau* 45: 66–81, 262–85, 416–29.

Schwarzschild, Leopold. 1913. "Professor-Max-Reinhardt-Film." *März* 7, no. 4: 826–27.

Seebold, Elmar. 1995. *Kluge: Etymologisches Wörterbuch der deutschen Sprache.* Berlin: Walter de Gruyter.

Seeling, H. 1889a. "Ein Beitrag zur Lösung der Volkstheaterfrage." *Deutsche Bauzeitung* 23: 115–17, 127–30, 139–42.

———. 1889b. "Noch einmal der neueste 'Beitrag zur Lösung der Volkstheaterfrage.'" *Deutsche Bauzeitung* 23, no. 30: 174–75.

Senelick, Laurence, ed. 1989. *Cabaret Performance, Volume I: Europe 1890–1920, Songs, Sketches, Monologues, Memoirs.* New York: PAJ.

Shaffer, Elinor. 1986. "Christian Morgenstern and Max Reinhardt: The Early Years of Cabaret." In *Max Reinhardt: The Oxford Symposium*, ed. Margaret Jacobs and John Warren, 124–41. Oxford: Oxford Polytechnic.

Simmel, Georg. 1903. "Die Grossstädte und das Geistesleben." In *Die Grossstadt: Vorträge und Aufsätze zur Städtausstellung*, ed. Karl Bücher et al., 185–206. Dresden: Zahn & Jaensch.

———. 1950. *The Sociology of George Simmel.* Translated by Kurt H. Wolff. Glencoe, IL: Free Press.

———. 1978. *The Philosophy of Money.* Translated by Tom Bottomore and David Frisby. London: Routledge & Kegan Paul.

———. 2001. *Philosophie des Geldes* (1920). Cologne: Parkland.

Sollors, Werner. 1989. "The Invention of Ethnicity." In *The Invention of Ethnicity*, ed. Werner Sollors, ix–xx. New York: Oxford University Press.

Spaich, Herbert. 1992. *Ernst Lubitsch und seine Filme.* Munich: W. Heyne.

Speirs, Ronald. 1986. "Reinhardt and Brecht." In *Max Reinhardt: The Oxford Symposium*, ed. Margaret Jacobs and John Warren, 169–82. Oxford: Oxford Polytechnic.

Sprengel, Peter. 1989. "Festspiel Gerhart Hauptmann—Spielleitung Max Reinhardt" (1913). *IASL* 14: 74–107.

———. 1991a. *Die inszenierte Nation: Deutsche Festspiele 1813–1913.* Tübingen: Francke.

———, ed. 1991b. *Schall und Rauch: Erlaubtes und Verbotenes: Spieltexte des ersten Max-Reinhardt-Kabaretts (Berlin 1901/02)*. Berlin: Nicolai.
Sprengel, Peter, and Gregor Streim. 1998. *Berliner und Wiener Moderne: Vermittlungen und Abgrenzungen in Literatur, Theater, Publizistik*. Vienna: Böhlau.
Stadler, Edmund. 1963. "Reinhardt und Shakespeare, 1904–1914." *Shakespeare-Jahrbuch* 99: 95–109.
Stange, Heike. 1996. "Berliner Ausstattungsfirmen: Eine selbständige Branche für die Theater." In *Theater als Geschäft: Berlin und seine Privattheater um die Jahrhundertwende*, ed. Ruth Freydank, 65–77. Berlin: Edition Hentrich.
Stanislawski, Konstantin S. 1951. *Mein Leben in der Kunst*. Berlin: Henschel.
Stefanek, Paul. 1969. "Max Reinhardts frühe englische Inszenierungen." *Maske und Kothurn* 15: 374–91.
———. 1970. "Max Reinhardt in England: Die Inszenierungen der dreissiger Jahre." *Maske und Kothurn* 16: 180–93.
———. 1986. "Karl Kraus versus Reinhardt oder: Kraus als Schauspieler unter Reinhardt?" In *Max Reinhardt: The Oxford Symposium*, ed. Margaret Jacobs and John Warren, 112–23. Oxford: Oxford Polytechnic.
Steinberg, Michael P. 2000. *Ursprung und Ideologie der Salzburger Festspiele 1890–1938*. Salzburg: Pustet.
Stern, Ernst. 1955. *Bühnenbildner bei Max Reinhardt*. Berlin: Henschel.
Stern, Fritz. 1999a. *Dreams and Delusions: The Drama of German History (1987)*. New Haven, CT: Yale University Press.
———. 1999b. *Einstein's German World*. Princeton, NJ: Princeton University Press.
Stettner, Anna. 1998. "Wer ist ein Virtuose in der Schauspielkunst? Das Phänomen des Virtuosentums im deutschen Sprechtheater des 19. Jahrhunderts." Dissertation. Munich.
Stoddart, Helen. 2000. *Rings of Desire: Circus History and Representation*. Manchester: Manchester University Press.
Stoklaska, Juliane. 1980. "Wechselwirkung Regisseur—Bühnenbildner: Max Reinhardt–Oskar Strand." *Maske und Kothurn* 26: 286–92.
Strecker, Karl. 1911. *Der Niedergang Berlins als Theaterstadt*. Berlin: C. A. Schwentschke & Sohn.
Streisand, Marianne. 2001. *Intimität: Begriffsgeschichte und Entdeckung der "Intimität" auf dem Theater um 1900*. Munich: Fink.
Stümcke, Heinrich. 1911a. "Theaterbilanz." *Bühne und Welt* 13: 363–67.
———. 1911b. "Von den Berliner Theatern 1910/11." *Bühne und Welt* 13: 126–29.
———. 1911c. "Von den Berliner Theatern 1910/11." *Bühne und Welt* 13: 304–6.
Sturmhoefel, A. 1889a. "Ein Beitrag zur Lösung der Volkstheaterfrage: Richtigstellung der Besprechung des Hrn. Seeling." *Deutsche Bauzeitung* 23: 166–68.
———. 1889b. *Scene der Alten und Bühne der Neuzeit: Ein Beitrag zur Lösung der Volkstheaterfrage, zugleich ein Versuch zur Raumgestaltung grosser Zuschauerräume; aus den bisher üblichen Theaterformen entwickelt*. Berlin: Ernst & Korn.
Styan, J. L. 1982. *Max Reinhardt*. Cambridge: Cambridge University Press.
Szondi, Peter. 1963. *Theorie de modernen Dramas (1880–1950) (1959)*. Frankfurt am Main: Suhrkamp.

Thomsen, Christian. 1986. "Max Reinhardt and Frank Wedekind." In *Max Reinhardt: The Oxford Symposium*, ed. Margaret Jacobs and John Warren, 157–68. Oxford: Oxford Polytechnic.
Throsby, David. 1999. "Cultural Capital." *Journal of Cultural Economics* 23: 3–12.
Tönnies, Ferdinand. 1957. *Community and Society*. Translated by Charles P. Loomis. East Lansing: Michigan State University Press.
———. 1963. *Gemeinschaft und Gesellschaft: Grundbegriffe der reinen Soziologie*. Darmstadt: Wissenschaftliche Buchgesellschaft.
Urban, Bernd. 1974. "Arthur Schnitzler und Sigmund Freud: Aus den Anfängen des Doppelgängers: Zur Differenzierung dichterischer Intuition und Umgebung der frühen Hysterieforschung." *Germanisch-Romanische Monatsschrift* 24: 193–23.
Vardac, A. Nicholas. 1949. *Stage to Screen: Theatrical Origin of Early Film: David Garrick to D. W. Griffith*. New York: Da Capo.
Vögele, Walther. 1983. "Sumurun von Ernst Lubitsch und Max Reinhardts Einfluss auf den deutschen Stummfilm." In *Max Reinhardts Theater im Film: Materialien*, ed. Margot Berthold, 65–68. Munich: Münchner Filmzentrum.
Volkov, Shulamit. 2000a. "Antisemitismus als kultureller Code" (1978). In *Antisemitismus als kultureller Code: Zehn Essays*, ed. Shulamit Volkov, 13–36. Munich: C. H. Beck.
———. 2000b. "Antisemitismus als Problem jüdisch-nationalen Denkens und jüdischer Geschichtsschreibung" (1979). In *Antisemitismus als kultureller Code: Zehn Essays*, ed. Shulamit Volkov, 88–110. Munich: C. H. Beck.
———. 2001a. "Antisemitismus und Antifeminismus: Soziale Norm und kultureller Code" (1993). In *Das jüdische Projekt der Moderne: Zehn Essays*, ed. Shulamit Volkov, 62–81. Munich: C. H. Beck.
———. 2001b. "Minderheiten und der Nationalstaat: Eine postmoderne Perspektive" (1999). In *Das jüdische Projekt der Moderne: Zehn Essays*, ed. Shulamit Volkov, 13–31. Munich: C. H. Beck.
Vollmoeller, Karl. 1914. *Das Mirakel*. (*Das Wunder*). Berlin: Ed. Bote & G. Bock.
———. 1920. "Zur Entwicklungsgeschichte des grossen Hauses." In *Das Grosse Schauspielhaus: Zur Eröffnung herausgegeben vom Deutschen Theater zu Berlin*, ed. Heinz Herald, 15–21. Berlin: Bücher des Deutschen Theaters.
Völmecke, Jens-Uwe. 1997. *Die Berliner Jahresrevuen 1903–1913 und ihre Weiterführung in den Revue-Operetten des Ersten Weltkrieges*. Cologne: TUV Rheinland.
Volz, Dorothea. 2017. *SchauSpielPlatz Venedig: Theatrale Rezeption und performative Aneignung eines kulturellen Imaginären um 1900*. Bielefeld: Edition Kulturwissenschaft, transcript.
Wagner, Richard. 2000. "Das Judentum in der Musik" (1869). In *Richard Wagners "Das Judentum in der Musik": Eine kritische Dokumentation als Beitrag zur Geschichte des Antisemitismus*, ed. Jens Malte Fischer, 139–96. Frankfurt am Main: Insel.
Ward, Philip. 2002. *Hofmannsthal and Greek Myth: Expression and Performance*. Oxford: Peter Lang.
Warren, John. 1983. "Max Reinhardt and the Viennese Theatre of the Interwar Years." *Maske und Kothurn* 29: 123–36.

Warstat, Matthias. 2005. *Theatrale Gemeinschaften: Zur Festkultur der Arbeiterbewegung 1918–33*. Tübingen: A. Francke.
Watzka, Stefanie. 2006. "(Verborgene) Vermittler als 'Geburtshelfer' des modernen Theaters. Ansätze zu einer Historie der Theateragenten und -verleger." Master's thesis. Mainz.
———. 2012. *Die "Persona" der Virtuosin Eleonora Duse im Kulturwandel Berlins in den 1890er Jahren: "Italienischer Typus" oder "Heimathloser Zugvogel"?* Mainzer Studien zu Drama und Theater 45. Tübingen: A. Francke.
Wilamowitz-Moellendorff, Ulrich von. 1928. *Erinnerungen. 1848–1914*. Leipzig: K. F. Koehler.
Williams, Rhys. 1986. "Reinhardt and Sternheim." In *Max Reinhardt: The Oxford Symposium*, ed. Margaret Jacobs and John Warren, 96–111. Oxford: Oxford Polytechnic.
Winkler, Heinrich August. 2000. *Deutsche Geschichte vom Ende des Alten Reiches bis zum Untergang der Weimarer Republik*. Bonn: Bundeszentrale für politische Bildung.
Winterstein, Eduard von. 1947. *Mein Leben und meine Zeit: Ein halbes Jahrhundert deutscher Theatergeschichte*. Berlin: Oswald Arnold.
Witte, Karsten. 2002. "Der Zuschauer als Komplize: Ernst Lubitsch und *Schuhpalast Pinkus*." In *Kino der Kaiserzeit: Zwischen Tradition und Moderne*, ed. Thomas Elsaesser and Michael Wedel, 284–90. Munich: Text + Kritik.
Wolzogen, Ernst von. 1970. "Das Überbrettl" (1900/01). In *Manifeste und Dokumente zur deutschen Literatur 1890–1910*, ed. Erich Ruprecht and Dieter Bändsch, 120–27. Stuttgart: Metzler.
Wörner, Martin. 1999. *Vergnügen und Belehrung: Volkskultur auf den Weltausstellungen 1851–1900*. Münster: Waxmann.
Zabludowski, Nina. 1930. "Ein Max-Reinhardt-Jubiläum: Reinhardts 'Sommernachtstraum' vom 31. Januar 1905 und die Neuinszenierungen von 1907, 1909, 1913, 1921 und 1925." *Die Scene* 20: 47–63.
Zeydel, Edwin Hermann. 1915. "The German Theatre in New York City, with Special Consideration of the Years 1878–1914." *Deutsch-Amerikanische Geschichtsblätter* 15: 255–309.
Zickel, Reinhold. 1913. *Das Wunder, wie es Max Reinhardt vollbringt: Von einem unfreiwilligen Zuschauer erlebt*. Frankfurt am Main: Knauer.
———. 1914. *Grundsätzliches über das Verhältnis von Kunst und Moral: Nebst einem Wort über die Polemik der Volksstimme gegen meine Schrift "Das Wunder, wie es Max Reinhardt vollbringt."* Frankfurt am Main: Knauer.
Zielske, Harald. 1971. *Deutsche Theaterbauten bis zum Zweiten Weltkrieg: Typologischhistorische Dokumentation einer Baugattung*. Berlin: Selbstverlag der Gesellschaft für Theatergeschichte.
Zimmermann, Clemens. 2000. *Die Zeit der Metropolen: Urbanisierung und Grossstadtentwicklung* (1996). Frankfurt am Main: Fischer.
Zweig, Arnold. 1928. *Juden auf der deutschen Bühne*. Berlin: Der Heine Bund.

INDEX

Page locators in *italics* indicate illustrations.

Actors Studio (New York), 88
actor training/salary, 88, 136–37, 189n12
Adler, Gusti, 127
Adorno, Theodor W., 130
advertising, 19, *134*, 135, 137, 146–47
Akademische Verein für Kunst und Literatur, 72
Alberti, Conrad, xx–xxi
allegorical figures, 14–16, 61–62, *63*, 104
America vs. Europe, 58, 102–3, 108, 159–61
Anderson, Benedict, xvi, 55
anti-Semitism, 152–58, *153*, 161–62, 165–66
Antoine, André, 180n31
Apollo Theater (Düsseldorf), 67
Architects Association of Berlin, 64–65
arena productions. *See* festival theater
Aristotelian poetics, 33
Arminius, 60
Arnold, Victor, *17*
art theaters, 2, 12, 22, 88–89, 103, 108
Asch, Sholem, 162
association theaters, xxii, 135
atmosphere: Grosses Schauspielhaus, 69–71, *70*, 74–79, 102; Kammerspiele, 42–44, 50; *The Miracle*, 97, 103–7; Reinhardt's work of, 36–38, 63, 127, 156
audience/stage boundary, 42–44, 61, 67, 75, 77–78, 80, 96–97, 103, 105–6
avant-garde, xii, xviii, 1, 14, 45, 169, 185n15
Avenarius, Ferdinand, 7

Bailey, James, 89
Baker, Josephine, 192n45
Ballet Russe, 103

Balme, Christopher B., ix, xiv, 145–47, 185n4
Barbarossa, Friedrich, 60
Barnay, Ludwig, xix
Barnum, P. T., 82, 89
Bassermann, Albert, 141, 162, *163*, 164–66
Bauhaus, 69
Baumbach, Gerda, x
Baumgarten, Franz Ferdinand, 71, 82
Baumol, W. J., 190n37
Bayerdörfer, Hans-Peter, xi–xiii, 190n1
Bayreuth festival, 60
Beer-Hofmann, Richard, 162
Behrens, Peter, 20, 69
Belasco, David, 101–3, 108–9
Belting, Hans, 55
Bergmann, Ernst, 155–56, 158
Berlin: Jewish figures in, 153–56, *153*; metropolis of, 20–21, 64–65, 151–52, 158–60, 169–73; public spaces/layout, *xxvi*, 20–21, 64–65, 68–69, 71, 113, 176; theater scene of, xx–xxi, xxiii, 9–10, 55, 168. *See also individual theaters*
Berliner Theater, xix, 137, 168
Bernauer, Rudolph, 2
Bernhardt, Sarah, 87, 112
Berthold, Margot, 116
Bierbaum, Otto Julius, 5–6, 8–9
Bildungsroman, 5, 157, 162
Birett, Herbert, 187n3
Blücher, Gebhard Leberecht von (Marschall Vorwärts), 62, *62*
Blumenthal, Oscar, xix
Böcklin, Arnold, 28, 179n46, 187n7
Böhm, Hans Ludwig, 27
Böhme, Gernot, 181n42
Bolter, Jay David, 124

219

Bonn, Ferdinand, 81–82
Böse Buben, 2
Bourdieu, Pierre, 132
bourgeoisie/bourgeoisness: art/economy connection and, 130, 133; cabaret's opposition to, 4–7, 10, 114; cultural, xix, 4, 6, 56–57, 65, 72–73, 80, 169; in Ibsen's plays, 31–34, *34*; philistinism of, 113–14, 171–72; Reinhardt and, 139, 173; Reinhardt's entrance into, 151–52; salon culture and, 20–21, 41–44, 47–48, 50, 55, 139, 141; theater as site of negotiation of, xviii–xix, 85, 168–71; vs. the masses, 53–54, 78, 80, 83
bourgeois theater: vs. ancient drama, 72–73; cabaret's broadening of, 10–11; vs. circus, 56, 66–67, 82–83; vs. commercial/entertainment forms, 108, 118–19, 162; critics' hopes for, xx–xxi, xxiii; emergence/rise of, ix–x, xix, 133; vs. festival theater, 50, 56, 75, 108; financing of, 90, 138, 169; vs. metropolitan culture, 109, 173; vs. pageants/pantomime, 61, 97–99, 126; post-, 145; "suitable" themes for, 34, *34*; touring performers and, xxi, 86–90
Bowen, W. G., 190n37
Brahm, Otto (Abrahamson): Deutsches Theater directorship, vii, xxii–xxiii, 2, 11, 139, 146, 151, 154; *Ghosts* production, 35, 37–39; stage name, 190n1
Braulich, Heinrich, 68, 89–90, 107–8, 183n84
Brauneck, Manfred, xvii
Brecht, Bertolt, 139, 176, 179n1
Brewster, Ben, 125
Briand, Aristide, *91*
Bruant, Aristide, 4, 7
Büchner, Georg, 44, 187n77
Buntes Theater (Berlin), 5, 7–10, *8*, 19–20, 40
Burgtheater (Vienna), 192n3

cabaret (*Brettl*): film and, 120; prehistories of, 3–11, *3*, *8*, 43; significance to Reinhardt, 2, 11, 14, 16, 22, 179n30; *Überbrettl*, 5, 9, 14, 21. *See also* Schall und Rauch

capitalism, 57, 80, 82, 135–36, 142–43. *See also* economics
caricatures, 34, *34*, 90, *91*, 153–54, *153*
Carl-Schulze-Theater (Hamburg), 136
Carlson, Marvin, 21, 180n19
Carni, Maria, *105*
Cassirer, Paul, 139
casting practices, 38, 141–42, 162–66, *163–64*
censorship, xxii, 15, 18, 188n11
Century Theater (New York), 102–3, 107. *See also* Miracle, The
Chagall, Marc, 174
Chat Noir (Paris), 3–4, *3*
cinema. *See* film
circus: forms of presentation of, 56, 66–67, 82, 97, 124; grounds/structures of, 64–67, *66*, 69, 71, 73–74, 92; mass audiences and, 49–50, 78, 81–83; touring and, 66, 89. *See also* festival theater
Cochran, Charles B., 92
Cody, William Frederick (Buffalo Bill), 89
collective imaginary, 55–61, 64, 80, 97
Comédie-Française, 112
comic songs, 4, 7–9, 16, 19
commedia dell'arte, 86
commercial theater, 4, 7, 22, 130, 133, 156, 162
community vs. society, 51–54, 64, 78–79, 155–56, 173
Comstock, Ray, 104
conférencier, 4, 14
Conrad, Hermann, 74–75
Corbin, John, 106
cosmopolitanism, xvi, 21, 55, 60, 106–7, 171–73
costumes: historical, xxi, 9; *The Miracle*, 93, 98, 104, *105*, 107; *Oedipus the King*, 74, 76, 79; outsourced, 135; Puck, 28; Shylock, 163–64, *164*. *See also* scenography
Count of Charolais, The (Beer-Hofmann), 162
court theaters, xvii, xix, xxi, 82, 86–87, 90, 133, 168, 173. *See also* Meiningen Ensemble
Craig, Edward Gordon, 99
Creditors (Strindberg), 44

Index

crowds. *See* masses
cultural studies, viii–ix, xiv–xv, 124, 130, 149–51, 168
culture industry, 22, 130

Dahn, Felix, 60
danse macabre, 93, 104
Danton's Death (Büchner), 187n77
Davidsohn, Paul, 112–13, 116, 119–20
Davis, Tracy C., ix
Dawison, Bogumil, 101
Dean, James, 185n13
dehumanization of actor, 97–99
Delbrück, Hans, 59
Der Burggraf (Lauff), 18
"Der Laufgraf" (Morgenstern), 18
Dernburg, Hermann, 95
Der Roland von Berlin, 10
Déry, Juliane, 44
"Descent to Hell of the 43rd Supercabaretist, The" (Reinhardt), 14–16
Deutsches Theater (Berlin): bourgeois culture and, xix, 50, 168; Brahm/L'Arronge/others at, vii, xxii–xxiii, 11–12, 30, 35, 38; economics of, 136–37, 141–43, 145; productions at, 18, 112, 115, 141–43; Reinhardt's directorship of, 30, 38–39, 41, 73, 83, 129, 139, 146, 153; space/location of, xxvi, 68, 71; Stanislavski and, 88–89. *See also* Kammerspiele
Die Brille, 11
Die Elf Scharfrichter, 7
Dietrich, Mary, 114
Dingelstedt, Franz, 192n3
Dinter, Artur, 156–58
Doll's House, A (Ibsen), 31–32
Dorotheenstädtischer Friedhof (Berlin), 176
dream worlds/sequences, 23, 26, 30, 93, 104–5, 115, *116*, 117, 161
Dümcke, Cornelia, 189n26
Dumont, Louise, 178n28
Durieux, Tilla, 42, 76
Duse, Eleonora, 87, 103
Düsel, Friedrich: on productions, 25, 27, 73–74, 77, 126; on theater spaces, 47–48, 69–71, 73–74, 77, 82, 184n107

economics: art's connection to, 129–33, 145–48, 154, 156, 169; bourgeois theater and, 90, 138, 169; capital circulation/exchange, 131–32, 145–47; capitalism, 57, 80, 82, 135–36, 142–43; of Deutsches Theater, 136–37, 141–43, 145; economies of scale, 144–45; film industry and, 118–20, 124, 127; free-trade laws, xvii, xix, 87, 133, 168; joint-stock companies, 12, 139, 145; of Kleines Theater, 22, 23, 30, 140; plutocracy, 170; Reinhardt empire's funding/management, 133, 138–39, 145; Reinhardt's strategies of success in, 140–47; subventions, 22, 90, 129, 145, 189n26; theater expenditures/income streams, 10, 41–42, 47, 136–38, 140; theater sector, 133–38, *134*, 140–41; touring and, xxii, 87, 90, 103, 107–8, 127, 143–45; vertical integration, 135–36. *See also* Reinhardt's theatrical empire
education, xviii, 20–21, 59, 67, 72, 88, 119, 132, 151–52
Eiffel Tower, 59
Eisler, Hans, 176
Eisner, Lotte H., 127
Elektra (Hofmannsthal), 28, 73
Eloesser, Arthur, 171
Elsaesser, Thomas, xii–xiii, 118, 120–21
Emberg's Salon (Berlin). *See* Kammerspiele
Endell, August, 8
Engel, Fritz, 77–78, 80
Engel Reimers, Charlotte, 191n7
"ennobling" of taste/arts, 7–8, 11, 19, 113, 118–20
Epstein, Max: on Berlin theaters, 55, 154–55, 157, 179n30; on Reinhardt, 89–90, 146–47, 155; on theater economic sector, 133, 135–40
Erdman, Harley, 151
Erwin Bernstein's Theatrical Calling (Freksa), 157–61
ethnicity. *See* Jewishness
Europe vs. America, 58, 102–3, 108, 159–61
Everyman (Hofmannsthal), viii, 50, 187n77

Ewers, Hanns Heinz, 9
exhibition grounds, 64–65, 89, 92
externalities, 99, 158, 162
Eysoldt, Gertrud, 27–28, 27

Falck, August, 45
Falckenberg, Otto, 7
Felix Bloch Erben, 136
festival theater: vs. bourgeois theater, 50, 56, 75, 108; chorus/Greek forms centered in, 72–80, 74, 76–77, 79; crowd scenes in, 73, 76–78, 80, 96–97, 96, 127; instability of, 81–83, 143; mass theater designs for, 67–72, 68, 70; use of circus spaces for, 65, 67, 71, 73–74, 78, 81–83, 92, 169. *See also* circus; *Miracle, The*
Festspiel. See pageants
film: early conventions, 117, 120–25, 122–23; economies of scale, 144; historical context, xii–xiii, 117–20; movie houses, xvii, xix, 55, 113, 118–20, 124, 187n4; Reinhardt's influence/oeuvre, 111–18, 120, *122–23*, 127–28; theater/pantomime and, 4, 111–13, 118, 120–21, 124–27, 144
Film d'Art, 112
Fischer-Lichte, Erika, 37, 63, 78–80
Fokine, Michel, 103
foreignness, 85, 87, 89, 97, 99–102, 108, 160–61, 170
Forskrevet (Drachmann), 5
Frank, Bruno, vii, 157, 160–61
Frankfurt school, 130
free-trade laws, xvii, xix, 87, 133, 168
Freie Bühne (Berlin), xxii, 33–35, *34*, 38–39
Freksa, Friedrich, 157–61. *See also Sumurûn*
French Revolution, 31
Frenzel, Karl, xxi–xxii, 9, 56, 77
Freud, Sigmund, 45, 105
Fritzsche, Peter, 55–56, 146
Froissart, Jean, 95
Fuchs, Georg, 145

Gay, Peter, 168, 171–72
Geddes, Norman Bel, 103–4
Geertz, Clifford, xiv–xv
Geiger, Theodor, 54

Gemeinschaft/Gesellschaft, 51, 173. *See also* community vs. society
Georg II, Duke, xxi, 36, 87. *See also* Meiningen Ensemble
German film industry, 112–20, 127–28
German history, xvi–xx, 60–62, 68, 87, 144, 167–68, 171–73. *See also* Jewishness; National Socialism; Weimar Republic; Wilhelminian society
German theater history: bourgeoisness and, xviii–xix; cabaret troupes in, 7–11; economic factors in, xvii, xix, 90, 129; national theater called for, 67; nineteenth-century boom in, xx–xxiii, *xxvi*, 134–36, 168; pageants in, 60–61; theater as economic sector, 133–38, *134*; touring performers and, 86–90
German Werkbund, 69
Gershwin, George and Ira, 174
Gest, Morris (Moses Gershonovitch), 102–4, 109
Ghosts (Ibsen): performance genealogy, xxii, 30, 33–35, *34*, 38–39, *46*; plot/text, 31–33, 37; Reinhardt's staging/interpretation, 30, 35–40, 46–47, 141
Giese, Fritz, 57–58
girl troupes, 56–58, 80, 177n29
God of Vengeance (Asch), 162
Goethe, Johann Wolfgang von, ix, 157–58
Goldmann, Max. *See* Reinhardt, Max
Goldmann, Paul, vii, 23, 26, 29, 146
Gorky, Maxim, 22, 23, 88, 140
Gottsched, Johann Christoph, ix
Graetz, Paul, 19
Greek antiquity, x, 20, *20*, 61–62, *63*, 65, 71–74, 77–80, 169. *See also Oedipus the King*
Grosses Schauspielhaus (Berlin): experience/atmosphere, 69–71, *70*, 81, 102; opening, viii, 50, 68, 79, 145; second Schall und Rauch at, 2, 19; space/location, *xxvi*, 68–72, *70*, 184n107. *See also Oedipus the King*; Zirkus Schumann
Grusin, Richard, 124
Guilbert, Yvette, 4
Gunning, Tom, 188n22

Habsburg empire, xvi, 149
Halbe, Max, 44, 46
Hamlet (Shakespeare), 81, 141
Harden, Maximilian: on Berlin/German theater, xxi, 168, 173, 192n2, 193n11; on Reinhardt's work, 28, 41–42, 47, 126, 147
Hardy, James, 139
Harlan, Veit, 190n2
Hart, Heinrich and Julius, xx
Hauptmann, Gerhart, 16–18, 61–62, 62–63, 88
Heilborn, Ernst, 23–25, 29–30
Hein, Dieter, xviii
Held, Berthold, 12, 16, 43, 73, 100
Helmer, Fritz, 81
Herald, Heinz, vii, 36, 38, 44, 89, 97, 126
Herrmann, Max, viii–ix, 63, 109
Herzberg, Walter, *91*
high culture. *See* "serious" theater/art
Hildebrand, Petra, 134
Hildebrandt, Hans, 79
historiography: complex/contradictory processes of, viii, 121, 124–25, 167–69; German-Jewish, 149–51; metropolitan culture and, 99–100, 102, 107, 109, 171–73; theater, viii–xv, 86, 89, 108–9, 112, 130–33
Hitler, Adolf, 172
Hobbes, Thomas, 51–52
Hochschule für Schauspielkunst "Ernst Busch" (Berlin), 189n12
Höcker, Paul Oskar, 46–47
Hofmannsthal, Hugo von, viii, 28, 50, 73, 187n77. *See also Oedipus the King*
Hohenzollern dynasty, xvi, 18, 168
Hollaender, Felix, 146–47
Hollaender, Friedrich, 19
Hollaender, Victor, 125
Hollywood, 117, 128
Holocaust, 150, 175
Horkheimer, Max, 130
Huck, August, 139, 147
Huesmann, Heinrich, 93, 141, 179n52
Hugo Baruch & Co., 135
Humann, Carl, 183n55
Humperdinck, Engelbert, 99, 125

Ibsen, Henrik, 31–34, 40, 42, 169. *See also Ghosts*
Iffland, August Wilhelm, xi
impresarios, 92, 102–4
industrialization, xvii–xviii, 33, 60
interiority, 35–37, 45–47, 162
internationalism: film and, 112–13, 144; of metropolitan culture, xix–xx, 89, 100, 109; touring theater artists and, 86–90, *91*, 103, 108–9, 143–45; of Weimar era, 172–73
International Pantomime Association, 126
Intima Teatern (Stockholm), 45
Intimate Theater (Munich), 46
Isle of the Blessed, 112–17, 180n15
Italian Futurists, 186n50

Jacobs, Lea, 125
Jacobsohn, Siegfried: on Berlin theater/criticism, xxi, xxiii, 30, 81, 173; on Reinhardt's productions, 37–39, 83, 165–66; on Reinhardt's touring, 85–86, 109, 185n24
Jansen, Wolfgang, 6–7
Jaques-Dalcroze, Émile, 58
Jelavich, Peter, 10, 18–19, 21
Jessner, Leopold, 173
Jewishness: ethnicity and, 151, 155, 161, 165–66; in literary portrayals of Reinhardt, 157–62; Reinhardt's personal relationship with, 149–50, 162, 165–66, 174–75; Shylock and, 162–66, *163–64*; Wilhelminian/Weimar era anti-Semitism, 152–58, *153*
Jud Süss, 190n2
Jugendstil, 8, 179n44
Julius Caesar (Shakespeare), xxi–xxii

Kafitz, Dieter, 32–33
Kahane, Arthur, 113, 138
Kahn, Otto H., 101–2
Kammerspiele (Berlin): bourgeois culture and, 41–44, 47, 50, 55, 139; Reinhardt management of, 30, 35, 92, 137; space/location of, 39–44, *40–41*, *43*, 47. *See also* Deutsches Theater; *Ghosts*
Kayssler, Friedrich, 12, *12*, 18, 20

Kerr, Alfred, 42
Kessler, Harry, Graf, 42, 147, 151–52, 170
Kienzl, Hermann, 81
Kindermann and Serenissimus (characters), 16–19, *17*, 22
Kirshenblatt-Gimblett, Barbara, 182n38
Kleines Theater (Berlin): cabaret roots of, 2, 9, 19, 21–22; economic viability, 22, 23, 30, 140; productions in, 22, 23, 73, 88; space/location of, *xxvi*, 23, 39
Kleinsteuber, Hans, 144
Kocka, Jürgen, xviii
Kommer, Rudolf, 109, 166
Königliches Schauspielhaus (Berlin), xx, 20–21, 168
Kortner, Fritz, 142–43
Kotte, Andreas, x
Kracauer, Siegfried, 57, 80
Krauss, Werner, 190n2
Kreimeier, Klaus, 124, 187n4
Krenek, Ernst, 192n45
Krupp Company, 59
Kruse, Max, 5, 40
Kügelgen, Henning von, 112

Laban, Rudolf von, 58
Landau, Isidor, 33–34, 38
L'Arronge, Adolphe (Aronsohn), xix, xxii–xxiii, 30, 35, 38, 190n1
Laube, Heinrich, 192n3
Lauff, Joseph von, 18–19
Lautenschläger, Karl, 180n8
Lebenswelt, xvi–xvii, 29–30, 36, 47, 55, 69
Le Bon, Gustave, 53–54
Lehmann, Hans-Thies, 177n13
Leonce and Lena (Büchner), 44
Lessing, Gotthold Ephraim, ix, 24, 146
Lessing, Theodor, 191n22
Lessing-Theater (Berlin), xix, 136, 168
Linsemann, Paul, xxi
Loewenfeld, Emmy, 139, 178n28
London: metropolis of, 100, 170; *The Miracle* in, 50, 92, *94*, 95–100, *95–96*, 103–5, *105*, 107; other arts/theater in, 56, 58, 135; Reinhardt in, 50, 92–93, *94*, 95–101, 115, 170

Lower Depths, The (Gorky), 22, 23, 88, 140
Lubitsch, Ernst, 120, 127–28

Maeterlinck, Maurice, 12, 93
"Magician, The" (Frank), 157, 160–61
Mann, Heinrich, 176
Martersteig, Max, xx, 56
Martin, Paul, 12
Marx, Karl, 130–32
Massary, Fritzi, 160
masses: audience as, 77–80; circus as place of, 49–50, 64–67, *66*, 78, 81–83, 92; Greek forms/chorus and, 72–80, *74*, 76–77, *79*; *The Miracle* and, 92, *94*, 96–97, *96*; pageants and, 60–64, *62–63*, 68; revues/girl troupes and, 55–58, 72, 80; shape of in Reinhardt's theater, 72, 80–83; theater designs for, 67–72, *68*, *70*; theorized, 50–55; *Volk*/*völkisch* movement, 60, 64, 155–57, 173; world expositions and, 58–60. *See also* festival theater; metropolis
mass ornament, 57, 80
mass theater. *See* festival theater
Mathildenhöhe, 20
"Max der Regisseur" (Reutter), 49
Mayer, Hans, 176
Meery, Hans, 35
Mehring, Walter, 19
Meinhard, Carl, 2
Meiningen Ensemble, xxi–xxii, 33, 36, 87–89
Mendelssohn, Robert von, 139
Menzel, Adolph von, 146
Merchant of Venice, The (Shakespeare), 162–66, *163–64*
"Merry Husband, The" (Bierbaum/Strauss), 8–9
Merry Wives of Windsor, The (Shakespeare), 24
metropolis: Berlin as, 20–21, 64–65, 151–52, 158–60, 169–73; Grosses Schauspielhaus's seeming rejection of, 69–71, *70*, 80; internationalism of, xix, 89, 100, 109; London as, 100, 170; New York as, 102, 106–7, 174; rhythm of, 57–58, 182n32; as site of cultural collapse, 158–60, 162; theater

at center of, 20–21, 30, 50, 55–56, 67–69, 71, 146, 168; theorized, 50–53, 186n60. See also masses
metropolitan culture: impresarios and, 102–3; nationalism and, 171–73; Paris exhibitions and, 4–5; Reinhardt and, xix–xx, xxiv, *xxv*, 109, 127, 169–71, 173, 176; relationship to history, 99–100, 102, 107, 109, 171–73
Metropol-Theater (Berlin), 21, 139
middle class. See bourgeoisie/bourgeoisness
Midsummer Night's Dream, A (Shakespeare): atmosphere/opulence, 24–25, 29–30, 106, 113, 185n28; Böcklin and, 28, 187n7; film version, 112, 117; forest scenery in, 23–26, *24, 26,* 29–30, 114; Puck in, 27–28, *27*; revolving stage, vii, *24, 25*–26; success of, xiv, 24, 117, 140, 153; on US tour, 187n77
migration, xviii, 60, 101–3, 108, 117, 151, 173
Minna von Barhelm (Lessing), 24, 146
Miracle, The (Vollmoeller): atmosphere of, 97, 103–7; Berlin production, 94, 100–101; film version, 112, 125; London production, 50, 92, *94, 95*–100, *95–96,* 103–5, *105,* 107; Madonna figure in, 93–94, *94,* 104, *105*; masses in, 92, *94,* 96–97, *96*; New York production, viii, 92, *98,* 103–8, 144; pantomime in, 97–99, 124, 126; plot/text of, 93–94, 99–100, 104–5; scenography/costumes for, 94–97, *94–96, 98,* 103–7, *105,* 125; scope/significance of, 91–92, 109, 141, 143–45
Miss Julie (Strindberg), 45
mobility. See touring
modernism, x, 103, 159, 168
modernity: America and, 58, 102–3, 159; Berlin's, 10, 55; beyond to, 80; discontent with, 53; rejection of, 159–60, 162
modernization: architectural forms of, 69, 71; discourse of, 50–55, 67–68, 78, 80; historical experience of, xxii–xxiii, 1, 171–73; vs. pantomime,

126–27; Reinhardt's theater and, 29–30, 90, 148, 169–71; technological progress and, 59–60
Moissi, Alexander, 46–47, 141
Moltke, Helmuth, Graf, 60
Mommsen, Theodor, 72
Monahan, Michael, 106–7
Monroe, Marilyn, 185n13
monumentality, 1, 21, 65; Grosses Schauspielhaus/*Oedipus the King,* 69–71, *71,* 73–79, *77; The Miracle,* 95–97, *95–96,* 102, 106
Morgenstern, Christian, 11–12, 18
Moscow Art Theater, 88–89, 103, 108
Müller, Corinna, 119
Müller, Gisela, 52–53
Müller, Heiner, 176
Müller, William, 30, 39
Müller-Fürer, Theodor, 29
Munch, Edvard, 35–37, 40
Münchner Kammerspiele (Munich), 7
Münchner Künstlertheater (Munich), 90
municipal/state theaters, xvii, xxi, 82, 90, 158, 173
Münz, Rudolf, ix, xii
Muppet Show, 17
museums, 6, 64–65, 186n50
music halls (*Tingeltangel*), xx, 6–8, 20, 55
Musikfesthalle (Munich), 65
Mutscher, Hans, 95
mythical subjects/spaces: fairy world, 24–30, *26,* 114; Greek tragedies/mass theater and, 72–80, *74, 76–77, 79*; medieval/religious, 93–95, *94,* 99–100, 104, 106–7; national lineages, 60–62, *63,* 156; primeval world, 159; Thespis's wagon, 86

Napoleon I, Emperor, 61
nationalism: historical context, xvi–xvii, 150, 155–56, 167–68; theater/pageant forms, 60–62, 67–68
National Socialism: masses and, 81; Reinhart's interactions with, 129, 149, 173; seizure of power by, viii, xvi–xvii, 129; terror/destruction of, xx, 150, 152, 156–57, 175–76; *Thing-Spiel* of, 183n47
national theater, 67, 80–81

nation-state, xvi, xix, 60, 150
Naturalism, xxii–xxiii, 1–2, 5, 7, 11, 31–35, *34*, 45, 72
nature/natural world: vs. bourgeois life/metropolis, 5, 160, 174, *174*; evoked in Grosses Schauspielhaus, 69–71, *70*, 76; in Reinhardt's aesthetic, 23, 25–26, *26*, 113–14
Nelson, Rudolf, 10–11, 21
Neues Theater (Berlin): productions at, vii, xiv, 24, 140; Reinhardt's leadership, 22, 23, 137, 140, 146; space/location of, xiv, *xxvi*, 23, 68, 137. See also *Midsummer Night's Dream, A*
Neuweiler, Arnold, 80
New York: metropolis of, 102, 106–7, 174; *The Miracle* in, viii, 92, 98, 103–8, 144; other arts/theater in, 56, 58, 88, 108, 135; Reinhardt's 1923 tour, 102–9; Reinhardt's exile/burial, 149, 174–76, *174*; Reinhardt's unrealized plans in, xix–xx, *xxv*, 100–102, 108, 145
Nielsen, Asta, 120
Niessen, Carl, 36
Nietzsche, Friedrich, 5, 40, 63, 155
Notre Dame cathedral, 96

Oedipus the King (Sophocles/Hofmannsthal): actors selling lines in, 142–43; other productions of, 72, 92; Reinhardt's staging, 50, 68, 73–80, *74*, 76–77, *79*, 83, 85; text, 75, 77
Olympia Hall (London), 92, *95*, 95–96. See also *Miracle, The*
"On Actors" (Reinhardt), 171
one-acters, 16, 19, 45–47
Oresteia (Aeschylus), 78, 81

Pacher, Michael, 95
Pageant in German Rhymes (Hauptmann), 61–62, *62–63*
pageants (*Festspiele*), 60–64, *62–63*, 68, 97, 186n47
Pallenberg, Max, 99, 160
Palmer, John, 92, 97, 99
pantomime, 16, 56, 66, 92–93, 97–99, 101, 115, 124–27, 144. See also *Miracle, The*

Paquet, Alfons, 59, 65
parodies, 5, 11, 14–18
parvenu, 48, 82, 151–52, 155, 159–60, 162, 169–71
patrons/patron organizations, 10, 101–2, *134*, 136, 139, 158, 189n12
Perlmann, Michaela L., 45
Peymann, Claus, 137
Phaedra (Racine), 160–61
Pinthus, Kurt, 80–81
Piscator, Erwin, 81
Poelzig, Hans, 69–71, *70*
Poitier, Sidney, 185n13
political discourse, 7–9, 11, 16–19, 22
Prellwitz, Gertrud, 28
Projektions-AG Union (PAGU), 112–13, 116–17, 119–20
proletariat, xviii, 10, 118–19
Proverbs, 176
psychology/psychoanalysis, 45, 53–54, 72, 104–5
puppets, 62, *62*, 98–99, 158

Racine, Jean, 160–61
Rathenau, Walther, 139, 151, 192n10
Rauscher, Ulrich, 188n17
Regietheater, 29–30, 108–9
Regisseur, vii, xxiii, 16, 29–30, 49, 146
Reinhardt, Edmund, 138–39, 155
Reinhardt, Gottfried, 11, 151, 167, 175, 191n34
Reinhardt, Max: aesthetic of, 24–26, 36–39, 92, 114, 127–28, 141, 156, 171; anti-Semitic framing of, 152–58, *153*, 161–62, 166; biography/career, vii–viii, xv, xx, xxiv, 139, 151–52; bourgeois culture and, xix, 20–21, 41–44, 47–48, 50, 85, 139, 169–71, 173; on/in film, 111–13, 118, 120–23, *122–23*, 127; genius/legend/myth of, vii–viii, xxiii, 37, 39, 49, 101, 147, 167; literary portraits of, 157–62; metropolitan culture and, xix–xx, xxiv, *xxv*; on Naturalism/Brahm, xxii–xxiii; personal relationship with Jewishness, 149–50, 162, 165–66, 174–75; programmatic eclecticism of, 1–2, 14–16, 22, 50, 67–68, 72, 85, 108, 111; roles acted by, *12*, 38, 153–54, *153*, 162; on shape of masses, 72,

80–83; Stanislavski and, 88–89, 108–9; US exile/burial of, 108, 117, 149, 173–76, *174*; viewed as parvenu, 48, 82, 151–52, 155, 159–60, 162, 169–71. *See also individual productions/films/theaters*
Reinhardt's theatrical empire, 85, 129–30; advertising/public relations for, 146–47; corporate structure of, 145–46; Edmund's role in, 138–39; expansion as strategy, 90, 112–13, 140–41, 189n12; literary portrayal of, 157–60; modernization and, 148, 169–71; multiple use as strategy, 90, 141–45, 162; patrons/investors, 139, 145, 147; Reinhardt as brand, 145–47; tours and, 90, *91*, 143–45. *See also economics*
Reinhardt Theater (unrealized/New York), xix–xx, *xxv*, 101–2, 108, 145
Reiniger, Lotte, 4
religious processions, 93, 96–97, *96*, 100, 106–7
Residenztheater (Berlin), 33, 39
Reutter, Otto, 49
revolving stage, vii, 24, 25–26, 125
revue culture, 10, 21, 50, 55–58, 72, 81, 118, 177n29
Richard III (Shakespeare), 81–82
ritual, 50, 60–64
Rivière, Henri, 4
roman à clef, 5, 157, 160
Royal Prussian Theaters, xxi
Rudin, Alexander, 142

Salome (Wilde), 28, 140
salon culture: intimate/private theater and, 44–47; Kammerspiele and, 41–44, 47–48, 50, 55, 139, 141; Schall und Rauch and, 20–21, 43, 47
Salzburg Theater Festival, viii, 50
satire, 3, 5, 7, 9, 14–19, 22
scenography: *Ghosts*, 35–37; lighting's role in, 16, 74–77, 80–81, 96–97, 124, 127; Meiningen aesthetic, xxi–xxii, 36; *A Midsummer Night's Dream*, vii, 23–26, *24*, *26*, 29–30; *The Miracle*, 94–97, *94–96*, *98*, 103–7, 125; *Oedipus the King*, 73–76, *74*; outsourced, 135, 141; stage technology, vii, 24, 25–26, 96, 104, 114, 125. *See also* costumes
Schall und Rauch (Berlin): aesthetic experiments in, *13*, 14–16, 19, 22; Kleines Theater and, 2, 9, 19, 21–22; opening of, vii, 2, 11–14, *12–13*, 139; Reinhardt at, vii, 12, *12*, 14–16, 19–20, 22, 47, 139; Serenissimus and Kindermann at, 16–19, *17*, 22; space/location of, *xxvi*, 19–21, *20*, 39, 41, 43, 69. *See also* cabaret
Scheffler, Karl, 70
Schildkraut, Rudolf, 162–66, *164*
Schiller, Friedrich, ix
Schlenther, Paul, 192n3
Schlierseer Bauerntheater, 101
Schmitt, Eduard, 66–67
Schneider-Duncker, Rudolf, 10
Schnitzler, Arthur, 22, 45
Scholem, Gershom, 150
Schreyvogel, Joseph, 192n3
Schulz, Andreas, xviii
semiotics, ix–x, 36–37, 73, 121, 124, 144
sensuousness, 50, 56, 63, 114, 126, 164–65. *See also* atmosphere
Serenissimus and Kindermann (characters), 16–19, *17*, 22
"serious" theater/art, xii, xv, xvii, 6, 22, 78–79, 89, 118–19, 130–31
sexuality/eroticism, 5–6, 28, 93–94, 105, 115, 158–59, 161–62, 187n7
Sezessionsbühne (Berlin), 12
shadow theater, 4
Shakespeare, William, xxi–xxii, 24, 81–82, 141, 146, 169; *The Merchant of Venice*, 162–66, *163–64*. *See also Midsummer Night's Dream, A*
Sherlock Holmes, 82
Simmel, Georg, 51–54, 131–32, 182n32
Sister Beatrice (Maeterlinck), 93
Sitz im Leben, 19, 120
Sliwinski, Adolf, 136
Social Democratic Party, 68, 136
society vs. community, 51–54, 64, 78–79, 155–56, 173
sociology, 50–53
Solomon, King, 176
Sonnenthal, Adolf von, 101
Sophocles. *See Oedipus the King*

Sorma, Agnes, 38–39
Sprengel, Peter, 18, 60–61
Spring's Awakening (Wedekind), 181n60
Stadttheater (Magdeburg), 67
stage names, 149, 158
Stange, Heike, 135
Stanislavski, Konstantin S., 88–89, 103, 108–9
state theaters. *See* municipal/state theaters
Stephen Wise Free Synagogue, 174–75
Stern, Ernst, 24, 62, 94–95, 95–96, 103–4, *105*, 107, 112
Stern, Fritz, 172, 192n10
Stilpe (Bierbaum), 5–6
Strasberg, Lee, 88, 174
Strauss, Richard, 8–9
Strecker, Karl, xxi, 169
Streisand, Marianne, 43–44
Strindberg, August, 44–45, 179n52
Stümcke, Heinrich, 25, 38–39
Sturmhoefel, S., 67–68
Sumurûn (Freksa): film, 112–13, 125, 128; theater production, 92, 98, 101, 112, 125–26, 128
superficiality, 57, 82, 158–59, 162
Szondi, Peter, 45

tableaux vivants, 99
Theater am Schiffbauerdamm (Berlin). *See* Neues Theater
theater architecture/design: Buntes Theater, 8, *8*, 20; Grosses Schauspielhaus, 68–72, *70*; Kammerspiele, 39–44, *40–41*, *43*; Olympia Hall, 95, 95–96; Schall und Rauch, 20–21, *20*, 41, 43, 69; unrealized plans, xix–xx, *xxv*, 67–68, *68*
Theater des Westens (Berlin), 136–37
theater historiography. *See* historiography
theater intermediaries: agents, 15, 101–3, 133–36, *134*, 158; assistants/advisors, 143, 146; designers, 133, *134*; diversification of, 133–36, *134*, 138; impresarios, 92, 102–4; investors, 138–39, 145, 147; patrons/patron organizations, 10, 101–2, *134*, 136, 139, 158, 189n12; press, *134*, 136, 146–47, 157, 170; producers, 82, 92, 97–98, 102, 133, *134*; publishers, 133, *134*, 135–36; scenographic firms, 135, 141
theater journals/magazines, xxii, 7, 134, 136, 147, 173
"Theater of Five Thousand" (Zeh), 67, 68
theater subscriptions, 68, 136, 138, 147
Théâtre Libre (Paris), 180n31
thick description, xiv–xv, xxiv
Thomass, Barbara, 144
Threepenny Opera (Brecht/Weill), 179n1
ticket prices, 10, 41–42, 47. *See also* economics
Tiller Girls, 56–57, 80, 177n29
Tingeltangel, xx, 6–8, 20, 55
Toller, Ernst, 184n108
Tönnies, Ferdinand, 50–54, 64
Toulouse-Lautrec, Henri de, 4
touring: cabaret/cinema/circus, 9, 66, 89, 118–19; economic motives for, xxii, 87, 90, 103, 107–8, 127, 143–45; historical significance of, xix, xxi, 86–90, 108–9; Meiningen Ensemble, xxi–xxii, 33, 36, 87–89; Moscow Art Theater, 88–89, 103, 108; pantomime, 126–27, 144; Reinhardt's reasons for, 85–86, 89–90, *91*, 101–2, 108, 143–45; transatlantic, 88–89, 100–103, 107–8, 144; of virtuoso actors, xxi, 86–87, 89–90. *See also* London; New York
trade unions, 68–69, 136, 189n14
tragedy, 33, 72–80, *74*, *76–77*, *79*
Tree, Herbert, 92, 101
Trianon-Theater (Berlin), 9
Tucholsky, Kurt, 19

Überbrettl, 5, 9, 14, 21. *See also* cabaret
über-marionette, 98–99
Übermensch, 5
Urban, Joseph, xx, *xxv*, 108
urbanization, xvii–xix, 10, 20–21, 42
utopianism, xix–xx, *xxv*, 33, 54, 78–79, 100, 126, 165–66

Vallentin, Richard, 22
Vardac, A. Nicholas, 124–25
variety shows (*Variété*/vaudeville), xx, 4–8, 10–11, 19–21, 55, 118, 120, 124

Index

Venetian Night (Vollmoeller): film version, 112, 115–17, *115–16*, 121–23, *122–23*; theater production, 92, 115–16
Vogt, Uwe, 116
Volkov, Shulamit, 150, 152, 157
Volksbühne, 136
Volk/völkisch movement, 60, 64, 155–57, 173
Vollmoeller, Karl, 145. *See also Miracle, The*; *Venetian Night*

Wagner, Richard, 60, 155
Waldoff, Claire, 10–11, 19
Wandervogel movement, 5
Warner Bros., 117
Warstat, Matthias, 184n101
Weavers, The (Hauptmann), 16–18
Wedekind, Frank, 6–7, 28, 179n52, 181n60
Wegener, Paul, 77, 79
Weiglin, Paul, 70
Weill, Kurt, 179n1
Weimar Republic: anti-Semitism of, 149, 152–53; bourgeoisie and, 31; internationalism of, 172–73; vs. modernity, 55; proclamation of, xvi–xvii; ritualized pageantry under, 60–63, *62–63*; theater demands of, 81, 168; views of American South, 160–61
Wilamowitz-Moellendorf, Ulrich von, 72

Wilde, Oscar, 28, 140, 179n52
Wild West Show, 89
Wilhelm II, Kaiser, 16–18, 168
Wilhelminian society, 2, 5, 10, 19, 82, 149, 152, 172
Wilhelm Meister's Theatrical Calling (Goethe), 157–58
Winkler, Heinrich August, xvi
Wintergarten Variété (Berlin), 188n18
Winterstein, Eduard von, 24–25, 77, 141
Wolzogen, Ernst von, 5, 7–10, *8*, 19–21, 40
word city, 55–56, 146
working class, xviii, 10, 118–19
world expositions, 4, 58–60, 65
World War I, xvi, 68, 80–81, 100–102, 108, 145, 156, 172–73
World War II, 149–50, 175

Yiddish theater, 162–63

Zeh, August, 67, *68*
Zickel, Martin, 12, *12*
Ziegfeld Follies, 177n29
Ziegfeld Girls, 56
Zimmermann, Clemens, 186n60
Zirkus Busch (Berlin), 66, 100
Zirkus Schumann (Berlin), viii, *xxvi*, 68–69, 73, 92, 183n82. *See also* Grosses Schauspielhaus
Zirkus Schumann (Frankfurt), 67
Zweig, Arnold, 162, 164–65

Index

Venetian Night (Vollmoeller): film version, 112, 115–17, *115–16*, 121–23, *122–23*; theater production, 92, 115–16
Vogt, Uwe, 116
Volkov, Shulamit, 150, 152, 157
Volksbühne, 136
Volk/völkisch movement, 60, 64, 155–57, 173
Vollmoeller, Karl, 145. *See also* Miracle, The; Venetian Night

Wagner, Richard, 60, 155
Waldoff, Claire, 10–11, 19
Wandervogel movement, 5
Warner Bros., 117
Warstat, Matthias, 184n101
Weavers, The (Hauptmann), 16–18
Wedekind, Frank, 6–7, 28, 179n52, 181n60
Wegener, Paul, 77, 79
Weiglin, Paul, 70
Weill, Kurt, 179n1
Weimar Republic: anti-Semitism of, 149, 152–53; bourgeoisie and, 31; internationalism of, 172–73; vs. modernity, 55; proclamation of, xvi–xvii; ritualized pageantry under, 60–63, *62–63*; theater demands of, 81, 168; views of American South, 160–61
Wilamowitz-Moellendorf, Ulrich von, 72

Wilde, Oscar, 28, 140, 179n52
Wild West Show, 89
Wilhelm II, Kaiser, 16–18, 168
Wilhelminian society, 2, 5, 10, 19, 82, 149, 152, 172
Wilhelm Meister's Theatrical Calling (Goethe), 157–58
Winkler, Heinrich August, xvi
Wintergarten Variété (Berlin), 188n18
Winterstein, Eduard von, 24–25, 77, 141
Wolzogen, Ernst von, 5, 7–10, *8*, 19–21, 40
word city, 55–56, 146
working class, xviii, 10, 118–19
world expositions, 4, 58–60, 65
World War I, xvi, 68, 80–81, 100–102, 108, 145, 156, 172–73
World War II, 149–50, 175

Yiddish theater, 162–63

Zeh, August, 67, *68*
Zickel, Martin, 12, *12*
Ziegfeld Follies, 177n29
Ziegfeld Girls, 56
Zimmermann, Clemens, 186n60
Zirkus Busch (Berlin), *66*, 100
Zirkus Schumann (Berlin), viii, *xxvi*, 68–69, 73, 92, 183n82. *See also* Grosses Schauspielhaus
Zirkus Schumann (Frankfurt), 67
Zweig, Arnold, 162, 164–65